Software Essentials for Graphic Designers

Photoshop, Illustrator, InDesign, QuarkXPress,
Dreamweaver, Flash and Acrobat

Mark Gatter

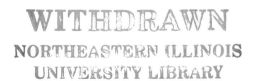
Yale University Press

Published in North America by
Yale University Press
P.O. Box 209040
New Haven
CT 06520-9040
U.S.A.
www.yalebooks.com

First published in 2006 by
Laurence King Publishing Ltd, London

Library of Congress Control Number:
2006928863

ISBN: 0-300-11800-7 12-12-06

Printed in Singapore

Design concept: Roger Fawcett-Tang
Design: Mark Gatter
Cover design: Frost Design, Sydney

Software Essentials for Graphic Designers

Contents

Introduction

For most graphic designers, there are four distinct areas in which a working knowledge is essential: page layout, vector drawing, image editing and website production. Some designers specialize in one particular area, but, for the greatest employability and to gain an overview of how everything fits together, it is best to know something about all four.

This is a daunting prospect for the beginner – consider the size of the manuals! – but the reality is that it does not have to be. The actual information required to accomplish everything needed for day-to-day use is only a fraction of the content of the manuals or the 'how to' books lining the shelves in local bookshops. This book focuses on the vital foundations needed for the main programs found in graphics studios worldwide. Also, as I have a strong background in commercial printing, I have included many pointers about sending work to a print shop, as this is, sadly, a misunderstood area.

For all software, learning and using keyboard shortcuts will speed up working time beyond belief. Most people approach shortcuts in the wrong way, trying to learn too many at once and, of course, they end up retaining and using on a regular basis only a handful of shortcuts like open, save, print. A friend once gave me the most useful advice about shortcuts: learn one a day, make sure you use it a few times and that way it will stick in your memory. Then, the next day, learn another, and so on. My own experience has taught me the wisdom of these words. As a result, when trying to generate variations of a logo in Illustrator, for example, I am able to work almost as quickly as I think – something I considered an unattainable dream when I first used the software.

By way of assisting in this process, I have included keyboard shortcuts for most operations immediately following their menu listing. Mac shortcut commands involve the use of the 'apple' key, which is known as the 'control' key on a PC, so I have used the words 'apple/control' to indicate a choice is to be made. The 'alt' key is (now) named as such on both platforms, so no variations are given.

I have often felt thankful that, as I have been working with the programs covered in this book for many years, I am no longer in the position of having to learn any of them from scratch. Early versions of these programs were comparatively simple, but now they have grown to awesome proportions and are regarded as the Godzillas of digital graphics. However, in teaching these programs to others, I have found that it is possible to convey the essentials of each one in a couple of days of (fairly) intensive work.

This book is a compilation of those courses. It will not teach you everything there is to know about any of the applications, but it will instruct you on the key issues that you need every day as a graphics professional. You will not find too much esoteric information here, but you will find the software essentials.

So, for example, if you need to learn Adobe InDesign, sit down at a computer with this book and work your way through everything in that chapter. There is a logical flow of information and methods that allows you to start using the program, regardless of the version, immediately. By the close of the chapter, you will have covered everything you need to know to accomplish at least 95% of what would be required of you as a professional.

This book has been written with a sincere wish to benefit others, and I hope it will be useful to you.

A brief overview:
How the various software packages fit together

Page layout
Page-layout software allows you to do precisely that: lay out a page. Whether you intend to produce a 400-page book, a magazine, a newsletter or a brochure, page-layout software is the assembly point for images, drawings and text. Therefore, it is also the file that will be sent to a printer either in native (QuarkXPress or InDesign) format or converted into a Portable Document Format (PDF), a brilliant (but not always straightforward) Adobe creation that bundles together everything as it looks in the page layout, either at high resolution to print using offset presses or at low resolution to email to a client for approval.

Early versions of page-layout software were not designed for drawing or image editing. However, things have changed. InDesign contains one drawing feature – the ability to apply a colour gradient to an outline (or stroke) – that is not even found in Adobe Illustrator (the industry-standard vector-drawing package). From v. 6.5 of QuarkXPress, basic image-editing functions are included.

Why has this happened? The problem seems to be that each new version of the software has to be bigger and better than the last to keep up with the competition. Also, assuming that you already have a program that delivers the full page-layout package, the most obvious areas for expansion are those covered by associated programs. Unfortunately, these new and exciting capabilities that go beyond the requirements of page layout itself may not be very good substitutes for the more detailed tools available in dedicated software. The logical development of this trend is towards all-singing, all-dancing mega-software with an associated learning curve that would make those of today seem comparatively gradual.

Nevertheless, the fundamental methods, those that are still needed every day in graphics production, have barely changed at all.

Vector drawing
A vector, to distinguish it from a bitmap, is a mathematical definition that connects two or more points. It is simply a path: it has no colour or thickness, merely a shape. No matter how much you zoom in on a page of vector shapes in outline mode, all you see are thin, black lines telling you where the shapes are. Fortunately, colour can be tagged to a vector

outline as a stroke or a fill, or both. Thus, if you switch the view of an Adobe Illustrator page from Outline (just the vector paths) to Preview (no vector paths, just the colours applied to them), everything changes: as you zoom in, shapes get bigger and outlines get thicker, but they still have clean, sharp edges that never become the pixelated 'fuzz' you see around a bitmap shape made up of pixels. This is because a vector is infinitely scaleable and can be enlarged to whatever degree is required with no loss of definition. Vectors are, therefore, ideal for text, logos, technical drawings and other illustrations requiring clearly defined edges.

Vector images can be exported from Illustrator as vectors or converted into bitmaps, depending on what they will be used for and how they need to look. For example, because they look so clean-cut, it is sometimes a good idea to bring vector logos into Adobe Photoshop and incorporate them, as a bitmap, into another image or background before importing the whole thing into the page layout. This has the effect of softening the vector edges and making them look less as if they have been cut out and pasted on.

Image editing

Images that are not vector based are made up of pixels and are known as bitmaps. Unlike vectors, bitmaps are resolution dependent – if you stretch them, the pixels just get bigger. The tools used in image-editing software are very different from those found in vector packages, but Adobe Photoshop (the standard program for image editing) is extremely well-equipped to allow the user to make almost any kind of adjustment, and each new version of the program offers more possibilities.

Rather than simply applying fill and stroke specifications to objects, most image editing relies on being able to select the pixels comprising the area that needs editing, while other pixels are left unselected and remain unchanged. Photoshop has several different tools to do this, some quite straightforward and others requiring some practice. The program also allows you to alter entire images, a single colour channel or a single layer. The choices are endless, and a successful understanding of the program includes knowing when to stop. Ask yourself, 'Is it convincing?' If it is, it is time to go to the next item on your list.

Images can be saved in a variety of formats and the choice should depend on the use to which the image will be put. If, for example, it is to be placed in a page layout destined for print, TIFF or EPS are the only suitable formats; however, if it is intended for a website, JPEG, GIF or possibly PNG formats are appropriate. Other formats exist, such as PSD, which is ideal for multi-layer archive copies as it offers the most flexibility for future editing.

Website production

Websites are based on related (but different) page-layout techniques and structures to those of QuarkXPress and InDesign. Dreamweaver, the industry favourite for website design and production, is similar to page-layout programs in that it is the assembly point for images and text. However, while text is still vectors and images are still (mostly) bitmaps, the rules governing how text appears and how the various elements are positioned in relation to each other depends on code.

Hyper Text Markup Language (HTML) has developed in leaps and bounds since 2000 and shows no signs of stopping. New ways of using background codes, not only HTML but also such others as Javascript, PHP and ASP, are constantly being discovered. However, it also seems to be a feature of website production that not all browsers support everything all the time. So, to build a successful website, you need to make clear choices regarding the audience you are targeting and the software and connection methods they are likely to use to view the site.

The design of a web page can support the presence of on-screen animations, sounds, movies and varying degrees of interactivity. Flash, sibling software to Dreamweaver, is used mainly for the creation of vector graphics, but these are graphics with a difference: instead of the static logos resulting from a conventional page layout, Flash adds a timeline and multiple layers that allow extremely sophisticated animated content. This can be set to run only when particular parameters have been met, such as from the moment the page loads in the browser or when triggered by viewer interaction.

Thus, while substantially different from page-layout programs, Dreamweaver's interface resembles that of a conventional page-layout application and requires many of the same skills for the creation of vector graphics and edited images for the web. It has, therefore, allowed website design a place alongside the more traditional graphics skills. Historically, this has not always been the case, and it is only since the advent of Dreamweaver that the tools of the techie have been placed firmly in the hands of the designer.

A word of advice

These programs are very adaptable in that the user can often select from several methods to achieve the same result. People, however, are less adaptable and there is a tendency in most of us to ignore the most efficient method in favour of another that we happen to have learned first. Before long, bad habits are developed. Unfortunately, many of these apparently similar methods have wide-ranging consequences in terms of how much they disrupt the creative workflow. The importance of this should not be underestimated – it is essential to make every effort to develop good habits or else the bad ones will hinder your productivity.

Along with the major applications, a host of other important, yet subsidiary, software can be found in contemporary graphics studios. These are likely to include utility software for managing font and image libraries, painting packages and 3-D graphics applications. All graphic designers require the applications featured in this book to ease the day-to-day workflow, but the need for additional software will only become apparent when a career direction has been made.

A word about colour

Many people are unaware that there are two kinds of colour systems associated with digital graphics: RGB and CMYK. As they are quite different, misunderstanding their abilities can lead to very unfortunate and unexpected results.

RGB stands for red, green and blue and is the colour system a computer uses to show everything on-screen. Each colour is made up of coloured light rather than pigments. Combine all three and the result is white; turn them all off and you get black. An equal percentage of all three produces a neutral grey. Mixing them at different strengths, it is possible to produce almost any colour.

CMYK stands for cyan, magenta, yellow and black, the components for the 4-colour-process offset printing method. They are also the colours of the different toners in colour laser printers and the different inks in inkjet printers (although some inkjet printers also use 'light' versions of one or more colour to create a less noticeable dot in lightly shaded areas). Incidentally, the letter 'K' is used to designate black because, for centuries, black was the only ink colour commonly available. When other ink colours were eventually developed, black remained the basic 'structural' colour for most print jobs as it was used for text, images and borders. As the position of these elements dictated where other colours needed to appear, black became known as the 'key' colour. Even today, it is still referred to as 'key' by the print industry.

While RGB can produce almost any colour, CMYK cannot. In fact, if the colour you want is bright, vibrant and saturated, it is a fairly safe bet that you want an RGB colour, and the closest CMYK comes to it seems a sorry substitute at first. However, as we do not complain about the miserable colour we see in printed material, perhaps it is possible to pick perfectly satisfactory CMYK colours. Or, is it the lack of comparison that prevents us from objecting? If we enjoy looking at a travel brochure, imagine how much better it would be if the colours on the page were the same as those of the actual objects, for example, the sky. Blue is the colour that suffers the most from being converted from RGB to CMYK and the results can be disastrous.

Some of the software discussed in this book guides designers in picking the right colours for the job, while other packages are not so helpful. The rule of thumb is to use only CMYK colours when designing for print. Do not specify anything in RGB. If the work is for a website, either RGB or CMYK can be used because all CMYK colours are contained within the RGB colour space. Note, though, that all colours should be specified as RGB or, for GIF images, 'indexed colour'.

And the CD...

This is not just a book. There is also a CD on which you will find the sample files mentioned in the chapters, tutorials in the form of mp3 movies and additional information and material. While the book covers multiple versions of each program, the movies on the CD are created using the most recent versions of the software available at the time of going to print. However, specific files were created using earlier versions wherever possible to enable as many readers as possible to open, use and benefit from them.

Acknowledgments

My heartfelt thanks for support and assistance in the creation of this book go to:

Peter Bone, a good friend with a terrible sense of direction.

James Newcombe at Nightingale Associates for some great shortcuts.

Richard Budd of Lionheart Graphics in Dorchester for his considerable help and advice.

Sarah Wright and Neal Bryant at Sussex University for their help with the Flash chapter.

Adam Hooper for the use of his computer and for several fine lunches.

Veloce Publishing, Dorchester, for allowing me to play around on their network.

Adam Ritchie for creating the CD sound bank.

Tony Simmons, mastermind of Strategy Internet in Sydney, and the only living Australian who thinks that the Ashes is a prize awarded at Wimbledon.

Kevin Quinn, TheMacMan (www.themacguy.co.uk), and wife, Julia, for all kinds of assistance but especially for their help during the creation of the CD.

Robin and Sue for putting up with me far too often.

My parents for putting up with me at all.

Melanie and Mike for their help and good humour.

Bean and Charlie for helping me not to take things too seriously.

My wonderful wife, Linda, for her unwavering encouragement and support.

Editor Catherine Hall for bravely going where few editors would willingly go: deep into the dark realms of Graphic Design.

Jo Lightfoot and her team at Laurence King Publishing for deciding that one book was not enough.

Chapter 1

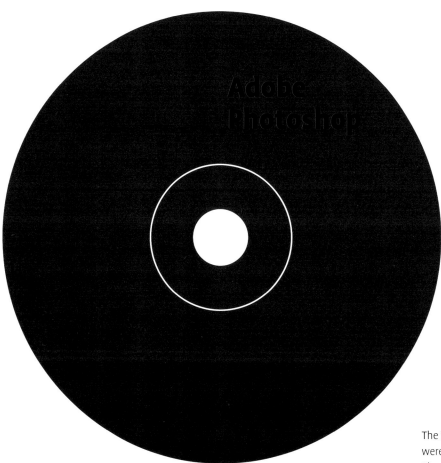

The images in this chapter were generated using Adobe Photoshop CS2.

The acknowledged industry-standard software for image editing, Adobe Photoshop repairs, adjusts, creates, combines and calibrates images, and also applies an almost endless array of special effects. It supports vector information in several forms, including editable text. The latest versions have been bundled with 'Image Ready', a semi-separate program that adapts images for inclusion on websites and that creates image maps, rollover buttons and GIF animations.

The fundamental building block of Photoshop's universe is the pixel, from which all bitmaps are constructed. Pixels are square, they each contain a single colour, there is no space between them, and they are usually (but not necessarily) very, very small.

Depending on the 'depth' of an image, each pixel is able to display one of a fixed number of colours. In a simple 1-bit image (which Photoshop somewhat confusingly refers to as a bitmap), each pixel can be one of two colours. The next level of complexity is an 8-bit image, a greyscale, which can contain 256 colours. An RGB image is typically formed of three colour channels, each of which is an 8-bit image, and each pixel can be any one of 16.7 million colours.

Photoshop is a source rather than a destination, as images saved here are usually heading for inclusion in page layouts or websites.

1   The Photoshop Environment

fig. 1 The Photoshop screen.

1.1 What Photoshop does

Photoshop does not use pages. It is a program in which you can open an existing image or create a new one. Images can be changed by selecting the parts that need changing or by altering the whole image. There is a mind-boggling array of tools with which a huge range of adjustments and special effects can be made.

It is possible to paint on images, to add text, to increase or decrease contrast, to merge more than one image together, to adjust light, shade and colour and to fix all kinds of damage (scratches, tears, stains). The more you use Photoshop, the more its magic is revealed.

Any part of an image can be made transparent to whatever degree necessary. You can build up an image using layers, which act as transparent overlays, onto which you can place other images and text and to which you can apply special-effect filters. Objects on layers can be moved, scaled and adjusted independently of things on any other layer in the same image. When the work is complete, it is possible to save both a multi-layer copy for future use and also to flatten it into a single layer, before saving it in a format suitable for print or Web.

1.2 The Photoshop screen

A set of menus runs along the top of the screen (**fig. 1**, previous page), beneath which sits the Options Bar, a horizontal area in which useful options connected with the selected tool appear. Elsewhere on the screen is the Toolbox, a floating window, but its default position is on the left side of the screen. The Options Bar and all floating windows can be turned on or off under the Window Menu. Any names on the list that are checked are currently open on screen; if you cannot see a window that is meant to be open, it is probably hidden under something else.

At the right end of the Options Bar is the docking well, a horizontal slot in which floating windows can be stored (with the exception of the Toolbox and Options Bar) by dragging them into the slot by their name tags and letting go. This means that they can be accessed without having to click on the Window Menu, and, as they close down after each use, they do not take up valuable screen space. However, while the official recommendation is to use this area as an organizational aid for the most commonly needed palettes, I do not work in this way. Some windows – Layers, for example – are so useful that I prefer to keep them open on-screen (almost) all the time. Others, such as the History window, will generally be used for a 'one-click' event, after which I am happy for it to close. For me, History is a useful addition to the docking well, while Layers is not.

In the lower-left corner of the screen is a percentage field, which adjusts depending on the degree of zoom being used. It is not accurate, because the size of something on-screen is based on the resolution at which the monitor is set. You can use the field as yet another zoom tool, by highlighting the number shown, entering something else and pressing the 'enter' key to update the view.

Some elements of Photoshop you will use again and again, while other things are required only rarely. This section covers all the really useful stuff as well as some important tips for everyday work.

1.3 Zoom and scroll

To begin, open one of the images on the CD by going to 'File > Open' and browsing to the image name. Either double-click on it or click once to select it and then click the 'open' button. If a warning window tells you that the embedded colour profile attached to the image you are opening differs from the profile you have set up for that 'working space' in Photoshop, do not worry about it now, but remember to read the Colour Management Settings (CMS) notes on p. 229.

Several images can be opened simultaneously in Photoshop, but only one can be active at any time. To make an image active, click on the info bar along its top. This bar contains the name of the image, a percentage indicating the viewing size and its current colour mode. On the image you just opened, hold down 'apple/control + spacebar' and click and drag with the mouse to draw a rectangle around the area you want to zoom in to. Release the button and that area will fill the screen.

There are three easy ways to zoom out:

1) Quite often you will zoom in to check something and then zoom straight back out again so your hands will already be in the right position for the following: hold down 'alt +spacebar' and click with the mouse to zoom out in increments.

2) Hold down 'apple/control' and tap the '-' (hyphen or minus) key. Each time you do so, you will zoom out an increment.

3) To zoom straight back out to see the entire image, choose 'apple/control + 0' (zero).

Scrolling the image is useful if you have zoomed-in so far that you no longer see the entire image on-screen. To do this, hold down the spacebar and drag with the mouse.

2   The Selection Tools

Most images that are worked on in Photoshop require either an overall or partial adjustment. To carry out a partial adjustment, areas can be isolated from the rest of the image by creating a 'selection'. The pixels contained within the selection are 'active', meaning that they can be adjusted, painted on, deleted or changed, while the rest of the image remains unaltered. Being able to make the right kind of selection is therefore extremely important.

A small arrow in the bottom-right corner of a tool button indicates the presence of a flyout menu. Hold the mouse down on the arrow to open the flyout menu. To use one of the tools shown, slide the cursor along the flyout to the required tool and release the mouse.

Open an image, and, as you go through this section, try drawing a few selections with each of the various tools, adding and subtracting areas until you feel confident. Also, try zooming in and out of the image, using the above methods so as not to develop bad habits.

2.1 The Marquee Selection tools

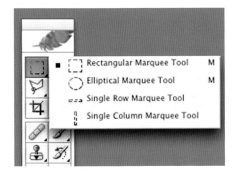

There are four tools on the Marquee Selection flyout, two of which – the Rectangular and Elliptical Marquee tools – are very useful and two of which – the Single Row and Single Column Marquee tools – I hardly ever use. The latter two select a single row or column of pixels across the image. Their main use is when a row or column of pixels appears in the wrong colour or shade, a problem that occurs when one of the image sensors on a scanner is beginning to fail. The affected pixels can then be selected and adjusted back into the correct range.

To create a rectangular selection, pick the Rectangular Marquee Tool and click and drag on the image to define a selection. When the mouse is released, the 'marching ants' – moving dotted lines – enclose the area.

Hold down the 'shift' key and a small '+' sign appears next to the cursor. Click and drag elsewhere in the image to add to the current selection. Additional areas do not need to be connected to the original selection. If you hold down the 'alt' key, a small '-' sign appears instead, indicating that the cursor can be used to click and drag to subtract from the selection. This function allows you to carve rectangular shapes out of the selection or even to cut holes in it. Watch the 'Marquee tools' movie tutorial on the CD.

Tip	Using 'shift' and 'alt' to add to and subtract from selections is common to all the Toolbox selection tools.

2.2 Deselecting a selection

If you have created a selection and then click on the image again but forget to hold down either the 'shift' or 'alt' keys, the existing selection will vanish. This is not the best way to 'deselect'; instead, go to 'Select > Deselect' ('apple/control + D').

To understand how selected areas function, click on the Brush Tool (fourth tool down on the right side of the Toolbox, see **fig. 1**, p. 12) and click and drag across the image and into the selected area. No matter how many times you try to paint outside a selected area, you will not succeed. However, as soon as the brush moves inside a selection, the tool becomes operational (**fig. 2**).

2.3 Undoing mistakes using History

As you did not want to paint on your image (yet), this is a good time to review the available options for undoing errors.

Many windows programs have a common 'undo-the-last-thing-I-did' keyboard shortcut and Photoshop is no exception. In Photoshop, it is an 'on/off' toggle, so repeating the command merely re-does what was just undone. This one-level undo is under 'Edit > Undo' and uses the keyboard shortcut 'apple/control + Z'. It is also possible to undo several consecutive operations, using 'apple/control + alt + Z'.

Alternatively, use the History window (**fig. 3**). As a default, this window retains the last 20 operations performed on an image. To go back even further, go to (Mac) 'Photoshop > Preferences > General' or (PC) 'Edit > Preferences > General' and re-set the window to record up to 99 operations. Note, however, that doing this uses a great deal of memory, so it is sensible to stick to 20 undos to begin with.

History is also set to 'linear' rather than 'non-linear'; in other words, it lists things in the order in which they happened. To return the image to a previous state, click on the history events one at a time, starting at the foot of the list, which is the location of the last thing you did. If, for example, you know that an error was made five states previously – the History window lists the type of event to help you figure this out – then click on the state immediately above the mistake. The image reverts and the subsequent states turn grey.

Continuing to work on the image at this point results in the grey states vanishing as if they belonged to a timeline that never happened. However, if you used the 'options' button to select 'non-linear', this will not be the case. Non-linear histories can be confusing and difficult to work with and I strongly suggest staying with 'linear'.

Aside from the ability to revert to a previous History state, it is also possible to take a snapshot of the image at any time by clicking on the small camera icon at the foot of the History window. Snapshots are stored at the top of the History window and remain there even if the state they show no longer exists. There is also an automatic snapshot of the image in its opening state.

2.4 The Lasso tools

Select the second button down on the left of the Toolbox to view the flyout that holds the Lasso, Polygonal and Magnetic tools.

Choose the Lasso Tool and click and drag on the image to create a shape. When the mouse is released, a selection of that shape appears. If you let go of the mouse before returning to your starting point, Photoshop completes the shape with a straight line. Hold down the

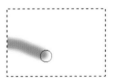

fig. 2 Only the pixels contained within a selection are active.

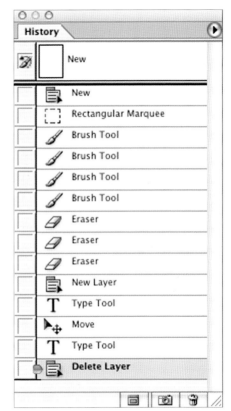

fig. 3 The History window.

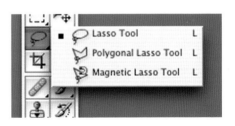

'shift' key and draw another shape. Now hold down the 'alt' key and subtract from the shape.

Next, try the Polygonal Lasso Tool. Click, move the cursor and click again, thus drawing a straight line segment. Repeat the process. Should you return to (or very close to) the starting point, the cursor displays the tool icon with a small circle next to it; if you click while it is showing, you will join up the ends of your selection, creating an enclosed shape.

There is a very useful technique that allows you to toggle between the Lasso and Polygonal tools without having to stop drawing the selection to retrieve the other tool. If, for example, you are working on a selection that requires freehand drawing around some shapes in the image, whereas other connected areas are made up of straight lines, the toggle will be particularly useful. Open the file 'lasso tools.jpg' on the CD and start dragging to create a selection with the Lasso Tool. Then:

1) Keep the mouse held down and press the 'alt' key
2) Keep the 'alt' key held down, release the mouse button and move the mouse.

You are now in Polygonal mode, but the 'alt' key must remain pressed down the whole time. Click to define a new anchor point and move the mouse again. Repeat this action several times and then return to freehand mode by:

1) Holding down the mouse button and releasing the 'alt' key
2) Keeping the mouse button held down and continuing to drag the cursor.

This also works in reverse; so if you start in Polygonal mode, use the 'alt' key to toggle into freehand mode.

Selections made with the Magnetic Tool normally require additional editing due to the difficulties involved in accurately controlling the movement of the mouse and also the subtle contrast differences between image areas, but the tool is still a valuable time-saver. Select the tool and, in the Control Bar, set a brush size, a tolerance and an anchor point frequency. Drag the tool along the edge of the object you wish to select. If the brush size is small and you drag reasonably accurately, the resulting selection will be quite accurate, too.

The tolerance setting determines how sensitive the tool is to the degree of contrast when it is deciding where to place the next anchor point. Enter a low number to enable the tool to differentiate between smaller degrees of contrast, leading to a more accurate result.

The anchor point frequency setting defines how often an anchor point is placed on a path. If you think a path needs an additional point, you can click to place one at any time. As before, when the cursor returns near to the starting point, it changes symbol and you can click to complete the selection shape.

Tip   **With both the Polygonal and Magnetic tools, it is possible to delete sections of the selection as you draw. Click the delete key and then redraw.**

2.5 The Magic Wand Tool

Extremely powerful and useful, this selection tool also uses a tolerance setting. It is used, for instance, on a product shot image, where an object has been placed on a table or against a background that should not be visible in the final image. The Magic Wand Tool can select the background, which can then be deleted it and perhaps replaced with a gradient. However, its tolerance setting is rather different from that of the Magnetic Lasso Tool. Here, the tolerance factor selects additional, adjacent pixels based on the colour of the pixel you first click on. The higher the tolerance, the more colours and shades will be selected. As before, 'shift' and 'alt' allow you to add to or subtract from selections.

The tolerance can be changed at any time during the selection process. It is advisable to begin with quite a high tolerance and then refine it to smaller and smaller numbers to avoid selecting similarly coloured areas that you do not wish to include. If too much is selected, use 'apple/control + Z' to undo. Then reduce the tolerance setting and try again. Watch the 'Magic Wand Tool' movie tutorial and practise using the file 'fossil beach.jpg' on the CD.

2.6 Grow and Similar

These are useful options when part way through making a tricky selection. 'Select > Grow' selects all adjacent pixels that come within the tolerance range, while 'Select > Similar' selects all pixels that fall within the tolerance anywhere in the image.

2.7 Saving and loading a selection

Complex selections should be saved regularly as they are being made, as should the image itself. After all, the History window will be no help if Photoshop crashes, but a saved selection will survive.

With a selection active in an image, open the Channels window ('Window > Channels', **fig. 4**), which shows the separate colour channels comprising the image. If it is a greyscale image, there is only one colour: black. If it is RGB, there are three: red, green and blue. In an RGB image, each channel appears as a greyscale image in this window, while in the actual image on-screen the channel displays in transparent colour and overlaps the other channels. However, if you click on one of the thumbnail images in the Channels window, only that channel appears in the image frame. And, unless you have told Photoshop to show channels in colour ('Photoshop > Preferences > Display & Cursors > Colour Channels in Colour'), channels show as a greyscale.

To save a selection as a channel, click on the 'save selection as channel' icon at the foot of the Channels window. To load it again, 'apple/control + click' on the channel thumbnail or select the channel and click on the 'load channel as selection' icon, also at the foot of the window. Selections can also be saved by going to 'Select > Save Selection', which opens the Save Selection window. If additional edits are then made to that selection, they can be incorporated into the saved selection by

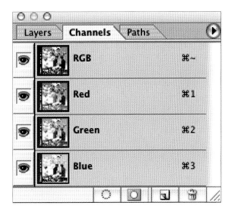

fig. 4 The Channels window.

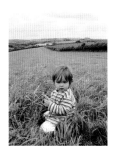

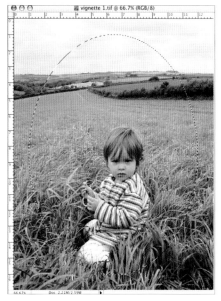

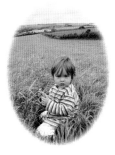

fig. 5 Feathering a selection
to create a vignette.

choosing 'Selection > Save Selection' once more. This time, if you choose to continue to work with the channel saved previously, rather than creating a new one, the window offers several choices, such as replacing the original selection, adding to it, subtracting from it, or intersecting with it. This is a great time-saver and well worth investigating. Watch the 'Saving Selections' movie tutorial on the CD.

2.8 Inversing a selection

Inversing a selection is another extremely useful procedure. Imagine that you have a photo in which the sky is a fairly smooth colour and needs no adjustment, but the rest of the image, which is much more detailed, needs to be lighter. To select the detailed areas without selecting any of the sky would be difficult, whereas selecting the sky alone would be much easier. Once the sky is selected, inverse the selection: instead of having all the sky and nothing else selected, none of the sky would be selected and everything else would be.

To try this, create a selection and then choose 'Select > Inverse' ('apple/control + shift + I' ['i', not 'L']).

2.9 Feathering a selection

A vignette (**fig. 5**), a particular photographic effect, was extremely popular in the late-nineteenth century. The process is very easy to carry out in Photoshop using an option called 'feather'.

Watch the 'Inversing and Feathering' movie tutorial and then open 'vignette.jpg' on the CD. From a point about 3cm in and down from the top-left corner, drag the Elliptical Marquee Tool to a similar position in the bottom-right corner. Release the mouse and an oval selection appears. Choose 'Select > Feather' and enter a value of 20 pixels. Ensure that white is the background colour by clicking on the small black and white icon just below and to the left of the colour chips at the foot of the Toolbox. Inverse the selection (see above), then hold the 'apple/control' key and click 'backspace'. The original oval remains, but all around it is filled white – with a soft, feathered edge. This is a vignette.

Any selection can be feathered, either by entering a value in the Control Bar, which will then apply itself to every other selection made until its value is physically put back to zero, or by choosing 'Select > Feather', which will only apply to the selection you have just drawn.

2.10 Modifying a selection

To expand or contract a selection by a specific number of pixels, go to 'Select > Modify'. A list of options appears, among which are 'expand' and 'contract'. Choose one, enter a pixel value and click 'OK'.

3   The Painting Tools

In most professional work, the task is not so often to paint as it is to repair. If you are fortunate, you may find someone wanting to pay you for being purely creative, but this is, alas, uncommon. Photoshop is primarily used in the workplace for making sure a photo displays properly, either in print or on the Web. Therefore, it is much more likely that you will be asked to work with light and shade, to fix incorrect colour casts and to repair damage. Image repair, however, can be very challenging and creative, so do not be disheartened.

Painting tools use a brush size and an opacity or strength, both of which can be chosen using the Control Bar. Click on the 'brush' icon near the left end of the bar to select a size and hardness (the harder the brush, the more clearly defined its stroke edges will be (**fig. 6**). The opacity setting is a percentage and is entered in the window to the right of the brush setting area. There will also be other options available, depending on the tool you are using.

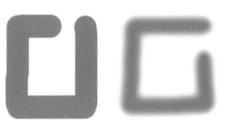

fig. 6 Showing the difference between a 'hard' and 'soft' edged brush.

3.1 Photoshop colour modes

There are four common colour modes for colour images in Photoshop as well as several others that are used less frequently. The main modes, in order of complexity, are: bitmap, greyscale, RGB and CMYK.

All images can be described as bitmaps – i.e., they are composed of pixels – but here the term is used specifically to refer to simple images made up of only two colours, the most basic of which are black and white. A common bitmap format is line art, for example, scans of pen-and-ink drawings and black-and-white diagrams, for which there is no requirement for shades of grey.

Greyscale images are also known as black-and-white images, but the terminology has become slightly confusing because a greyscale image in its simplest form can still hold up to 256 shades of grey, including black at one end of the spectrum and white at the other.

RGB stands for red, green and blue. This is the basic colour mode for TV and computer screens – and therefore websites – that use light rather than pigments to create colours. Light combines in ways that are almost completely opposite to the ways in which pigments combine. For example, if you combine red and green light, the result is yellow, whereas with pigments a dark brown is produced. The three RGB colours, at 100% strength, produce white, but to produce white with CMYK pigments, all four components are left out and the paper remains blank in that area.

While it is not a suitable colour mode for images that are being placed in page layouts destined for print, RGB is obviously the ideal mode for images on websites. It is also a very complete colour space, containing just about every colour it is possible to see. CMYK, on the other hand, is much more limited.

CMYK (cyan, magenta, yellow and black) colours are the components of the process-colour printing method, which is used to print most of the colour images we see every day. However, this colour space has some serious limitations of which every graphic designer needs to be aware.

For example, imagine receiving your first-ever painting set as a child. Filled with anticipation, you open the lid, only to find a miserable set of just four colours – one of which is black – from which you are expected to mix all the other colours you need. You might think to yourself, 'But where is the orange? And, what about purple and green?' A similar disappointment is experienced with CMYK colours. True, you can mix a range of oranges, but none of them will look particularly exciting when compared to the oranges you can create using RGB.

After a while, it becomes apparent that many of the colours you want cannot actually be mixed using the CMYK components. For some you can get close, but, in many other cases, the closest CMYK equivalent is far removed, and, if you make the wrong choice, the printed result could be seriously different from what you expected. A more in-depth discussion of this problem can be found in my book, *Getting It Right In Print* (Laurence King Publishing in the UK and Abrams in the USA, 2005).

3.2 The Clone Stamp and Heal tools

Used to repair images, the Clone Stamp Tool paints over unwanted areas or damage (such as scratches and spots) with undamaged parts of the same image. As it creates an exact copy, or clone, great care has to be taken. Noticeable repairs do not warrant the name 'repair', so to avoid these use a *soft* brush and redefine the source point *often*.

Closely related, but wonderfully different, the Heal Tool takes into account the colour and texture of the area you are trying to repair and adapts the information it takes from the source point accordingly.

If the area you are fixing contains detail, use the Clone Stamp Tool. If, however, the areas requiring repair are such things as scratches on a car – i.e., there may be slight colour, shade and textural differences, but basically it is a smooth area – use the Heal Tool.

Open image 'oh dear.tif' on the CD. There are various kinds of damage on the image: in the upper part, for example, there is a small tear and some spots. As these occur in a detailed area, they are best fixed with the Clone Stamp Tool. Select this tool and use the Control Bar to pick a soft-edged brush, 20 pixels wide, with an opacity level of 100%.

Tip   **All the painting tools use a brush-related cursor and the type of brush is chosen on the Control Bar.**

Click on the 'brush' icon to choose a size and hardness. In the case of the Clone Stamp Tool, it is always best to use a totally soft brush (a hardness of '0'), otherwise repairs are more easily visible. You can also define a brush size as a pixel radius. Make sure the radius is not too large or else you may clone unwanted material.

Start with an opacity of 100%, as this will cover up damage completely. Sometimes, a lower level is beneficial if, for example, you are blending together two different but adjacent areas (such as across the spine of a book in a double-page spread). Generally, however, a setting of 100% is the most useful.

Decide which part of the image can be used to repair the affected area and, holding down the 'alt' key, click on it to define the source point. Next, move the cursor to the damaged area and either click or click and drag. A cross appears over the source point, indicating the material that is being cloned (**fig. 7**), and moves in tandem with the cursor as you click and drag.

This is a key point: aside from watching the area being repaired, you also have to watch the source point. Whatever the source point crosses is repeated under the cursor. Also, if the source point moves across an area that has been repaired during the same click-and-drag operation, it will paint the original damage back in again.

Patience is essential in becoming adept with the Clone Stamp Tool. With a little skill, it is possible to fix entirely the most appalling damage in images that otherwise could never be used.

The Heal Tool is used in a similar way. However, as it is so good at adjusting the source material to the texture and colour of the area you are trying to fix, it needs far fewer source points. Another difference is that while the source point moves as you click and drag, if you start to repair a different area, the original source point will continue to be used until you redefine it.

To practise with this tool, select a brush (as for the Clone Stamp Tool, above) and 'alt + click' somewhere within the circle in the lower half of 'oh dear.tif' to define the source point. Then, move across to the damaged area and click and drag (**fig. 8**). As you do this, the brushstrokes are clearly visible and have a hard edge. As soon as the mouse is released, however, the adaptation to the colour and texture takes place, resulting in an invisible repair.

Remember, this is not the tool to use if there is any detail in the area you wish to fix as it will be unable to process the information properly and the end product will almost always be a fuzzy blob.

3.3 Creating custom colours

Regardless of the method of application, the accurate creation of a particular colour is a key skill.

At the foot of the Toolbox are two colour chips known as the 'foreground' and 'background' colours.

Click on either of them and the Colour Picker window appears (**fig. 9**). Select the basic colour area you want by clicking on the rainbow. Refine your choice by clicking on the exact shade desired in the large square on the left. The upper half of the small area to the left of the 'OK' button now changes to display the new colour, while the lower half continues to show the colour that was selected when this window was opened. In the large square, a small circle remains on the exact spot on which you clicked.

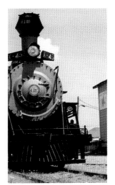
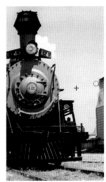

fig. 7 Removing unwanted areas with the Clone Stamp Tool.

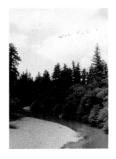
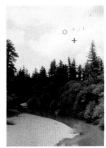

fig. 8 Removing damage with the Heal Tool.

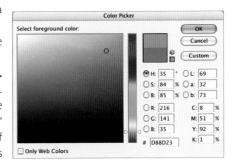

fig. 9 The Colour Picker window.

You can also enter colour specifications in the boxes in the lower-right quadrant of the Colour Picker window; if, for example, you know the CMYK percentages, enter each of them in turn. Regardless of how it might look on-screen, the colour should print accurately on an offset press.

When you click 'OK' in the Colour Picker window, the selected colour appears as the chip on which you clicked in the Toolbox. If you created a foreground colour, you can use it immediately with the Paintbrush and Pencil tools. Watch the 'Custom Colours' movie tutorial on the CD.

3.4 Saving and loading colours

It is possible to save a colour for future use at any time by using the Swatches window (**fig. 10**). First, the foreground colour chip must display the colour. If the background chip is showing it instead, simply click on the small, double-headed arrow just above and to the right of the chips to switch their position (the shortcut for this is 'X'). Open the Swatches window ('Window > Swatches'), click on the 'options' button and choose 'new swatch' from the list. In the resulting window is a small thumbnail of your colour, which you can name. When you click 'OK', it is immediately added to the colours in the Swatches window.

To load a colour shown in the Swatches window, move the cursor over it until it changes to an eyedropper. Click with the mouse and that colour displays as the foreground chip in the Toolbox.

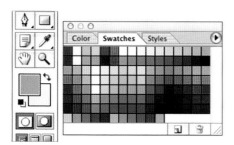

fig. 10 The Swatches window.

3.5 The Brush and Pencil tools

These are the basic painting tools and are found on the same flyout menu. They do much the same thing, but there is an important difference: even if you use a brush with a hardness setting of 100% with the Brush Tool, the resulting stroke will have a slightly soft edge. For a truly hard-edged (not anti-aliased) stroke, choose the Pencil Tool (**fig. 11**).

This can make pencil strokes seem rather ugly by comparison. However, if the image resolution is high enough –the minimum being 600dpi – pencil strokes appear completely smooth, because our eyes are incapable of detecting a pixelated edge at that level of detail.

Objects drawn with the Brush Tool are smooth enough to look clean even at 300dpi because they are anti-aliased, i.e., there is a softening of tone along their edges, so that the pixels' colour strength gradually fades out. This makes curves, especially, look smooth and unpixelated.

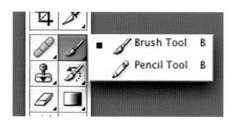

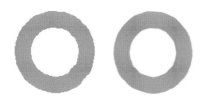

fig. 11 The difference between a pencil stroke (left) and a brush stroke (right).

Tip	The Brush and Pencil tools use the currently selected foreground colour.

3.6 Painting with gradients

The Gradient Tool, which does not rely on a brush-shaped cursor, creates smooth blends between colours. In its most basic form, a colour blend requires just two colours, but it is possible to create multi-colour gradients and even selectively apply transparency to them. Gradients can be saved to and subsequently loaded from the gradient library.

To create a gradient, choose a foreground and a background colour from which to produce a blend. Then, select the Gradient Tool.

The Control Bar changes to show useful options, including buttons for linear, radial and other kinds of gradient (**fig. 12**). Linear and radial tend to be the most useful gradients; the reflected gradient is next, then the diamond gradient, while the angle gradient is of almost no use at all.

A shaded bar indicates the loaded gradient. Click on this bar to open the Gradient Editor window (**fig. 13**), which holds the gradient library and the editing area.

The two most useful library items are 'foreground to background' and 'foreground to transparent'. The first uses the selected foreground and background colours as a basis for any edits, while the second is particularly useful for applying adjustment layers and creating masks (see pp 36–38). Photoshop indicates transparency by using a chequerboard pattern (see p. 33). All other library items load the colours shown on their swatches.

Near the foot of the window is a band of blended colour, which, if you have selected 'foreground to background' as the library item or have not used this window before, shows the current foreground colour at the left end and the current background colour on the right.

At both ends under the bar are paint pots. Click on the one on the left, and the colour chip fills with that colour. To change the colour, click on the chip to open the Colour Picker window and select another colour.

Click just under the shaded bar to produce a new paint pot filled with whatever colour currently shows at that point. This can of course be changed by following the method just described.

Transparency can be applied to the gradient by clicking just above the shaded bar. A different kind of paint pot appears, and the opacity field, beneath the bar, is activated. Click on the arrow button to show a slider, with which you can set a degree of opacity. Again, this is displayed in the shaded bar as a chequerboard area.

There are also small diamond shapes that appear between adjacent pots, above or below the line, when a pot is clicked on. These are the blend points for either transparency (above the bar) or colour (below it), and can be dragged to the left or right to emphasize the blend.

To save a custom gradient, name it in the 'custom' window and click the 'new' button. It is added to the gradient library. To load a library item as a blend, click on it and then on the 'OK' button.

Now, you are ready to paint something.

Gradients are extremely powerful painting tools that can add depth and sophistication to images. Whether you wish to paint on an image, a new layer, a blending mode or an adjustment layer, the more time you spend working with gradients, the more applications you will find.

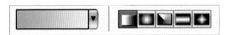

fig. 12 The gradient style buttons.

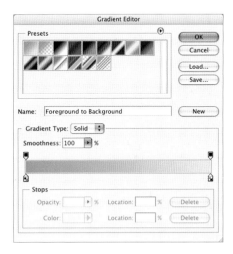

fig. 13 The Gradient Editor window.

3.7 The Paint Bucket Tool

Found on the same flyout as the Gradient Tool, the Paint Bucket Tool is not particularly useful. It is *very* useful to be able to fill a selected area or an entire layer with the background or foreground colour, but you should not use the Paint Bucket Tool for this task as it is tolerance-based and tends to fill only part of a selected area. Worse, it may leave out pixels here and there, which may not be noticed at the time. There is a much simpler method for filling layers and selections, which, once learned, is more effective.

To fill a selection with the background colour, hold down 'apple/control' and press 'backspace'. To fill with the foreground colour, hold down the 'alt' key and press 'backspace'. 'Edit > Fill' offers a wider choice but takes longer.

3.8 The Eraser Tool

Several different erasing tools figure on the flyout. To work with them, see 'Using Layers' on p. 32.

The eraser does what you would expect it to do, most of the time. Choose a brush and an opacity setting from the Control Bar, then click and drag on the part of the image you wish to erase, and – surprise – instead of erasing, it paints with the background colour.

The Eraser Tool *does* erase to transparency, but not on the 'background' layer, which has special properties that prevent it, initially, from supporting transparency. After all, it is the background layer and, therefore, there is nothing behind it. To erase part of an image requires you to be working on a regular layer, i.e. any other layer that has been added to the image.

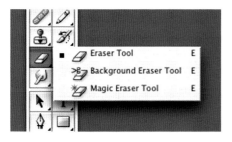

3.9 The Magic Eraser Tool

This eraser has a tolerance setting, removing everything that falls within the tolerance, either contiguous to where you click or across the entire image. I prefer to make a selection with the Magic Wand Tool and then delete it. That way, I can apply a feathered edge or modify the selection before actually erasing what it contains.

As with the Eraser Tool, erasure to transparency (rather than the background colour) cannot happen on the background layer.

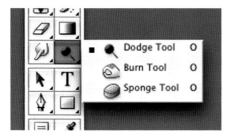

3.10 Dodge, Burn and Sponge tools

The Dodge Tool lightens pixels and the Burn Tool darkens pixels. Both techniques are applied with a brush and a degree of strength, called the exposure. Generally, the strength of most painting tools can be left at 100%, but the successful use of these two usually depends on applying their effects a little at a time. If they are even slightly overused, the results are clearly noticeable. In most instances, it is wise to avoid an initial setting higher than 10%. The Sponge Tool, also on this flyout, is used for desaturating image colour.

If you are trying to fix a gradual brightening or darkening of tone towards one edge of an image, rather than a localized hotspot problem, refer to 'Adjustment layers' on p. 36.

4   Image-Adjustment Tools

Almost all the important image-adjustment tools are found in the same place: 'Image > Adjustments >'. This area, however, also contains some potentially damaging tools and others that try to do your work for you – but without the benefit of knowing what kind of image you are working on and, therefore, without knowing what is or is not appropriate.

I recommend never using the 'brightness & contrast' adjustment as it destroys highlight and shadow data. Also, for two very good reasons, it is advisable to avoid any adjustments preceded by 'auto'. First, you will never learn how to do the adjustment yourself in a way that takes into account the tone and colour range of the image on which you are working. Second, it is very unlikely to do as good a job as you would.

| Tip | With all the image-adjustment windows, holding down the 'alt' key toggles the 'cancel' button into being a 'reset' button instead. This allows much more freedom for experimentation without having to continuously close windows to avoid applying the settings. |

4.1 Levels

I almost always begin adjusting images in the Levels window. One of the most important windows in Photoshop, it enables you to accurately calibrate images for print or any other purpose.

Go to 'Image > Adjustments > Levels' ('apple/control + L'). The black pile, or histogram, is a relative representation of the tone contained in the image. The three arrows beneath it are, from the left, the black point, the 50% mid point and the white point. Gaps in the black pile, either inside or at its ends, are tonal areas not represented in the image.

In most cases, images look their best when the tone extends across the entire range. This is not always true, however, and can only be decided on a project-by-project basis. For example, you may be working on a night scene and the majority of the image is in heavy shadows, or on a picture taken on a foggy day, in which case there are unlikely to be any hard shadows at all. Auto adjustments do not appreciate this kind of difference and will not take them into account.

If the histogram does not extend to either or both ends, the tone in the image stops short of either or both ends of the spectrum (from black to white). If this happens, the arrows can be moved in, towards the ends of the histogram, to extend the tonal range and improve the image.

Open image 'riverboat.jpg' on the CD and then open the Levels window. The histogram will look like this (**fig. 14**).

To make an initial adjustment, move the black arrow to the right, to point A, and the white arrow to the left, to point B. Look at the image again. To see how far it has come, rather than choosing 'undo' ('apple/control + Z'), use the History window. When making adjustments, it is sensible to return to the History window every so often to check how much things have improved since you began work. By doing this, it will reinforce your confidence in your abilities.

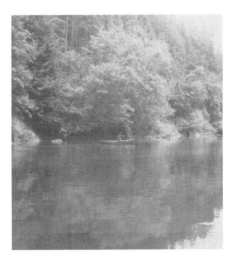

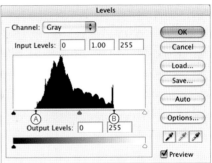

fig. 14 The original image and the Levels window before adjustment.

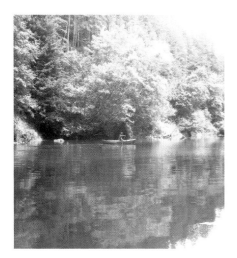

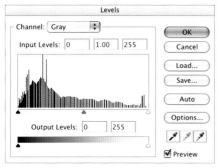

Fig. 15 The riverboat image and the Levels window after adjustment.

Click on 'OK' and open the Levels window again. The histogram should look like **fig. 15**, with gaps appearing throughout, each representing shades that do not exist in the image. This is perfectly reasonable; after all, the entire tone span from black to white in an 8-bit greyscale image is achieved with only 256 shades, and you had less than this number to begin with. What has happened is that existing shades have been redistributed evenly over the full span. No additional shades of grey have been created in so doing: there is the same number now as there was at the start. Fortunately, not very many shades of grey are needed to display a convincing image – 75 or so should be plenty.

Never make an adjustment with the centre slider until the black and white points have been taken care of. Once these points have been set satisfactorily, try adjusting the mid-tones to improve the image further.

Rather than moving the slider very slowly to the left or right, give it a good heave. Take it past the point, and obviously so, at which you would want to leave it. Then move it back gradually. A much better and faster adjustment is made this way.

If the image is to appear on a website, then, as far as tone levels are concerned and so long as it looks good on screen, your adjustment work may now be finished. However, if it is intended for a page layout destined for commercial offset printing, there is more to do.

During the printing process images gain contrast, and this must be compensated for beforehand. Having set the black and white points so that the full spread of tone is achieved, it is necessary now to squash the pixel pile to create a very small and controlled gap at either end. As the image goes through the printing process, it picks up only enough contrast to make the tone spread to fill the entire range, but without having the fine highlights and deep shadows fall off the edge. If this were to happen, the brightest areas would burn out completely and the darkest parts would fill in to black. While this is only a slight difference in terms of percentages, it makes a huge difference in terms of how the image looks.

There are long and involved ways of doing this and there are shorter and faster methods that are not quite as good. For the long and involved method, which allows you to fine tune the visual content of the image, see *Getting It Right In Print*. The shorter, alternative method is explained here and will still ensure that the highlights and shadows are placed exactly where they need to be.

Below the histogram in the Levels window is a shaded bar, with an adjustment arrow at both ends, and two numerical adjustment windows. These are the tools for setting the 'output levels'.

As mentioned, the full range of an 8-bit greyscale image holds up to 256 levels of grey, with black at one end and white at the other. It is important to remember that it is irrelevant whether you are adjusting a greyscale or a colour image – what you are dealing with here are degrees of light and shade in the image and the colour itself is unimportant.

Entering a number in one of the numerical windows pushes that end of the pile in from the edge of the range by the amount you key in. If 256 levels represent 100% of the range, then 1% equals 2.56 levels. So, if the values in the numerical windows are adjusted by approximately (decimal points cannot be entered) 2.56 for each percentage of adjustment, both ends of the pile can be squashed by a very specific amount.

There are rules of thumb about how much this should be done, and you may be able to talk to your printer to find out what figures they recommend, based on the equipment in their outfit.

If you are printing computer to plate (CTP) on good-quality coated paper, you should make an adjustment of 3% at either end (7 or 8 levels). If you are using CTP but printing on uncoated paper, make an adjustment of 6% at either end. If you are working with a film-based shop, use 5% for coated-paper jobs and 8% for uncoated.

For newsprint, the figures need to be higher, but just how much higher depends very much on the quality of the paper involved, as coarser stock encourages the ink dots to spread more. Unfortunately, there is a wide range of paper available under the broad heading of 'newsprint'. In this situation, and for Web offset printing (printing on a continuous roll of paper rather than on sheets, which is called sheet-fed printing) and screen printing, ask the printer to determine the best adjustment levels.

When you have made the appropriate adjustment, click 'OK'. To view the result, open the Levels window again and there will be a slight gap at either end of the histogram.

Small pixel 'tails' at one or both ends of a histogram can confuse the above method, as you have to decide whether or not to include them in your calculations. A very thin line extending out from the right end of the pixel pile represents just a few pixels of the very lightest shades of grey in the image. These are the subtlest highlights.

To decide whether or not to keep them, look at the lightest areas in the image (do not forget to zoom in if it helps). Click on the white-point arrow at the right end of the tail and drag it to the left end. The detail in the light area vanishes (if it did not, you were not looking at the lightest area but somewhere else entirely) and you know now what the result will be if you cut the tail off. There is no right or wrong. It is entirely up to you. If you want to hold on to those details, the tail has to stay, but be aware that the lighter mid-tones of the image will have less contrast.

The same decision needs to be taken for any tail at the left end of the histogram. It is advisable to cut it off at this end, as leaving it in can be more dangerous to the image as a whole, because it results in less contrast between the darker mid-tones and can create grey, grainy shadow areas that would look better if they were stronger and more clearly defined. Try cutting it off with the black point arrow. Then try leaving it in. Does cutting it off lose very much? The answer, generally, is no. We are much more likely to notice a loss of detail in the highlights than we are in the shadows.

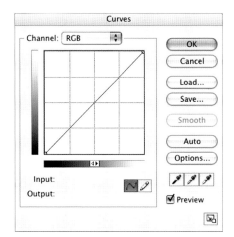

fig. 16 The Curves window.

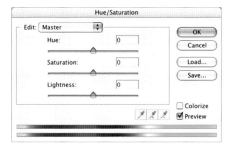

fig. 17 The Hue/Saturation window.

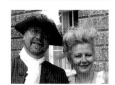

fig. 18 Before (right) and after (below) using the Hue/Saturation window.

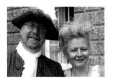

The more work of this kind you do, the better at it you will become. Follow the above method reasonably closely and there should not be any horrible results. Remember, the printed result is the yardstick for how well you are doing, and what you learn from a finished job is vital for improving your method and building your confidence.

4.2 Curves

Whereas the Levels window sets the overall spread of tone in an image, the Curves window (**fig. 16**) adds contrast. It is opened by going to 'Image > Adjustments > Curves' ('apple/control + M').

A diagonal line runs across the square grid in the window. Grabbing this and pulling, towards either the top-left or bottom-right corner, is exactly the same as making a mid-slider adjustment using levels.

Click on the line to add anchor points; to delete an anchor point, click on it and drag it away from the line.

To add contrast, place an anchor point in the centre of the line. Grab the line halfway between the centre and one of the two ends and pull to create a very slight 'S' bend. The image either loses or gains contrast, depending on which way the line is pulled. Be careful: you hardly need to pull on the line to produce a strong result.

Do not assume that the same movement will always have the same effect as some image modes need to be pulled in different directions. Keep looking at the image to see what is happening. Also, do not pull the line so far that the curve 'flatlines' along the top or bottom edges of the frame, because it would cause those shades to be completely burned-out to white or burned-in to black.

4.3 Hue, Saturation and Lightness

Open 'red faces.jpg' on the CD. The colour in this image is reasonably well balanced, but the faces are too red (**fig. 18, above**). This is a fairly common problem and is easily fixed with this highly useful tool.

An alpha channel has been added to this image, which can be seen by choosing 'Window > Channel'. The Channels window stores the saved selection of faces in the image. Load the channel as a selection (either select the 'load channel as selection' icon at the foot of the window or 'apple/control + click' on the channel thumbnail image), and then feather the selection by 10 pixels to soften the selection edge, so the adjustment will blend smoothly into the rest of the image.

Choose 'red' as the colour you wish to adjust from the 'edit' list at the top of the Hue/Saturation window ('Image > Adjustments > Hue / Saturation' (**fig. 17**), and drag the slider slightly to the right to make the shades of red more orange. Rather than substituting orange for red faces, it is possible to reduce the saturation, the strength of the pigment. Drag the saturation slider slightly to the left and the faces begin to look quite natural (**fig. 18, below**).

4.4 Shadows and Highlights

Only available in CS versions of Photoshop, these functions are very useful when working with excessive contrast. In CS1, CMYK images cannot be adjusted with this tool; in CS2, they can.

Open the file 'shadow and highlight.jpg' on the CD. For an image with excessive contrast (**fig. 20**, **above**), the histogram in the Levels window shows a pile at both ends and nothing much in the middle. Shadows and Highlights allow you to lighten the shadows and darken the highlights separately, thus pushing more of the image information towards the central area of the histogram and creating a more balanced result.

Go to 'Image > Adjustments > Shadow/Highlight' to open the window (**fig. 19**). As a default, the shadows setting opens at 50%, which may be much more than the image requires. Drag the slider back to zero to see the image as it appears on-screen and then use both sliders to lighten shadows or darken highlights. For more options, click on the 'show more options' box in the lower-left corner.

4.5 Variations

If you are unsure which way the colour in an image should be adjusted, go to 'Image > Adjustments > Variations'. Here, you can compare, simultaneously, a number of thumbnail versions of the image, each with a different colour cast added (**fig. 21**). Because all the options can be seen at the same time, it is much easier to decide what adjustment is needed.

Colours have opposites; for instance, the opposite of (CMYK) magenta is (RGB) green. So, if the image is too magenta, adding some green could fix the problem.

The rosette of seven images shows variations in both the RGB and CMYK systems. Click on any image and it moves into the three 'current pick' positions: one at the top, next to the original; one in the centre of the rosette; and one on the right of the central position, where you can make lighter or darker choices. Under the options, in the top-right corner, you can adjust shadows, mid-tones (the default and usually most useful option), highlights and the overall colour saturation. There is also a slider to increase or decrease the coarseness of the variations shown. As you make adjustments, a revised thumbnail of the image appears next to the original at the top, allowing you to compare the result. When finished, click 'OK' to apply the changes and return to the Photoshop screen. Practise using the files 'variations 1.jpg', 'variations 2.jpg' and 'variations 3.jpg' on the CD.

| Tip | Every time you open Variations, click on the original image in the top-left corner to reset the colour levels. Otherwise, Photoshop automatically applies the same settings that were last used. |

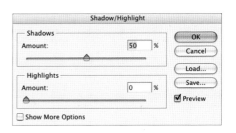

fig. 19 The Shadow/Highlight window.

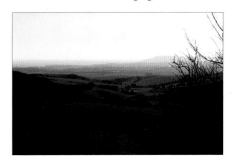

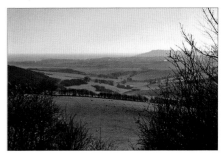

fig. 20 Before (above) and after (below) a Shadows and Highlights adjustment.

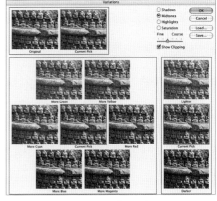

fig. 21 The Variations window.

5   Using Layers

Layers permit a great deal of flexibility when building up a complex image. Think of a layer as a clear sheet of film placed over the existing image onto which other images, or parts of images, can be placed. The whole layer can be repositioned independently of any other layer. A layer's opacity can be set anywhere between 0 and 100%, its colour can be changed, parts of it can be erased or added to – and all these options are possible without disturbing anything else above or beneath it.

Every image starts as a single layer. In Photoshop this default layer has special properties and is called 'background' in the Layers window. All other layers are numbered in the order of their creation.

The background layer behaves in slightly different ways from other layers. For example, transparency cannot be applied to it nor can another layer be dragged beneath it. Also, the eraser does not rub out; instead it paints using the colour currently shown by the 'background' colour chip. Sometimes, this is helpful, and sometimes not. Should you want to make the background layer behave like any other layer, double-click on it and, in the window that opens, click 'OK'. Watch the 'Layers and Gradients' movie and practise using the file 'old buckle.tif' on the CD.

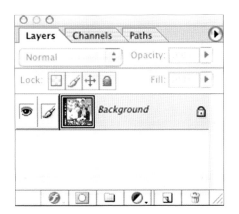

fig. 22 The Layers window.

5.1 The Layers window

Access the Layers window through 'Window > Layers' (**fig. 22**). As with other floating windows, it has an 'options' button and several icons along its foot. There is also an 'opacity' window for applying transparency and a 'blending mode' window to allow the colours on one layer to work interactively with other layers beneath it. Watch the 'Changing Colours' movie and practise using 'geranium.tif' on the CD.

There are six icons along the bottom of the Layers window in versions up to CS1. These are, from the right: 'trash' (used for discarding layers), 'new layer', 'new adjustment layer', 'new layer set', 'new layer mask' and 'layer styles'. In CS2, a 'link' icon was added on the left. Layers in previous versions are linked by clicking in the small window to the right of the 'eye' icon for each layer that needs to be linked to the active (shaded) layer. To link multiple layers in CS2, select them by 'shift-clicking' on them and then click on the 'link' icon. Layers are unlinked in the same way.

To add a new layer, either click on the 'new layer' icon or choose 'new layer' from the 'options' button. To copy a layer, either drag it onto the 'new layer' icon (being careful not to drop it into the trash by mistake) or choose 'duplicate layer' from the 'options' list.

5.2 Working with multiple layers

Each layer appears in the window as part of a stack, with the lowest layer at the bottom. Automatically numbered as it is created, a layer can be more appropriately named by double-clicking on its name.

If there are a number of layers in an image, they can be dragged to different positions within the stack. Click and drag on the layer, then release the cursor on the dividing line between any two other layers. The order of the stack determines which objects in the image overlay others.

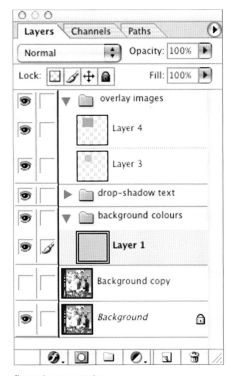

fig. 23 The Layers window in a multiple-layer file.

In a complex image, layers can be placed into 'layer sets' (**fig. 23**), which act like file folders and can make an otherwise cumbersome stack easier to work on.

To merge a layer into the layer beneath it, select the uppermost of the pair and press 'apple/control + E'. This is the 'merge down' command, which is also found under the 'options' button.

When all work on an image is finished, a very important choice has to be made. If you are likely to need to work again on the individual layers, save the image in PSD (Photoshop document) format, which preserves multiple layers. However, if you need the image for print or Web, it should be flattened (i.e., all the layers are merged down into a single layer) and then saved (under a different name) in TIFF, EPS, JPEG or GIF format. To flatten all the layers in an image, click on the 'options' button and choose 'flatten' from the list. Once flattened, an image cannot be unflattened unless that option is still available in the History window.

5.3 Applying transparency

Any degree of opacity can be applied to any layer (except the background layer) by selecting it and then clicking and dragging on the 'opacity' slider near the top of the Layers window.

A chequerboard pattern indicates areas of transparency on an image (**fig. 24**). The pattern is merely a visual guide and does not print.

To make a layer invisible, click on the 'eye' icon in the left-hand column (this is an on/off toggle).

5.4 Importing images, layers and selections

A complete image or part of an image can be imported into other images. To import an entire image, open it and place it so that you can see at least part of both the source and destination images on-screen. Make sure that the image to be imported is the active image – by clicking on its name bar – before you begin.

Select the Move Tool (top right in the Toolbox) and click and drag from the source image across to the destination image. As you do this, the border of the destination image darkens and a small '+' appears next to the cursor as the source image is dragged onto it. Release the mouse button.

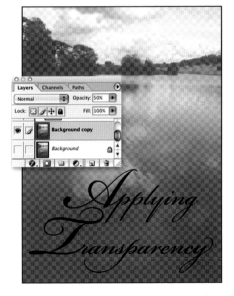

fig. 24 Applying transparency to a layer.

Tip   **Drag the image all the way onto the pixels of the destination image itself; it will not be imported if you let go part of the way there.**

This process automatically creates a new layer in the destination image. Individual layers are imported in much the same way: drag the layer from the Layers window and drop it onto the target image.

There are two ways to import a partial image. The first is to select the area you wish to import. Then, using the Move Tool, click and drag from within the selected area and onto the destination image. As before, a new layer is created. The second option is to select the area and go to

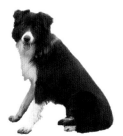

fig. 25 Transforming an imported object.

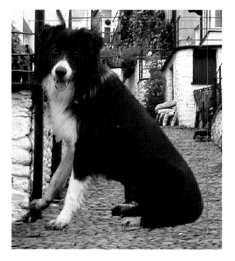

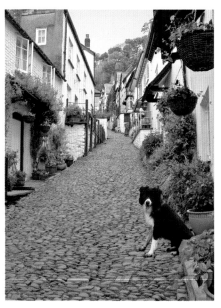

'Edit > Copy' ('apple/control + C'). Then, click on the blue name bar on the top of the destination image to activate it and choose 'Edit > Paste' ('apple/control + V'). Again, a new layer is created.

5.5 Transforming layer objects

Once an object, layer or image has been imported, some adjustment is usually required to move it into the correct place and to make it the right size. Fortunately, objects on an individual layer are very easy to resize, distort, flip and rotate, independently of any other part of the image.

The Free Transform Tool resizes an entire layer or an object on a layer. First, decide what you are resizing. To resize an entire layer, select that layer by clicking on it in the Layers window (it becomes highlighted in blue). Should you wish to resize an object that is the only thing on an otherwise transparent layer, 'apple/control + click' on the thumbnail image of that layer in the Layers window to create a selection around the object. To resize an object that is on an opaque layer or a layer on which there are other objects, select the object using one or more of the selection tools (see p. 16).

When you have the right area selected, go to 'Edit > Free Transform' ('apple/control + T'). A frame, similar to that seen when using the Crop Tool, surrounds either the imported layer or the selection, depending on what is being transformed (**fig. 25**). If the imported layer is larger than the destination image, the frame may not be completely visible and you should 'zoom out' ('apple/ control' + '-') until most or all of the corner handles are visible.

To keep a scaling transformation proportional, hold down the 'shift' key while you click and drag one of the corner handles towards the centre. The selected object shrinks. When it is the desired size, press 'enter' to apply the transformation.

The framed object can be moved during the transformation process by clicking and dragging within the frame, but do not click and drag on a handle or the central star. Dragging on a handle only resizes or rotates an object, while the central star is the point of rotation.

To rotate, click and drag to re-position the star as needed and then place the cursor just outside the frame near one of the corner handles. It turns into a small, curved two-headed arrow. As long as this icon is showing, you can drag to rotate the object. Again, press 'enter' to apply the transformation and the frame vanishes.

Several other transformation tools are found in a flyout under 'Edit > Transform'. These include Distort, which allows you to move the corners of the transformation frame independently; for example, you can correct foreshortening problems in images of tall buildings. Perspective is another, which makes one corner handle mirror the movements of its opposite. Practise using 'charlie.psd' and 'transform2.jpg' on the CD.

| Tip | **To clear a transformation frame without applying it, press the 'escape' key. This also clears cropping frames.** |

5.6 Text layers

Click on an image with the Text Tool to add text. A new layer is automatically created and appears in the Layers window with a large 'T' as its thumbnail image, indicating that text on that layer is still editable (**fig. 26**).

Editable text layers are unique in that they can be saved with an image in a multi-layer format (TIFF), which can then be imported into a page layout. As long as it is printed – as proofs or to film or plate – by a PostScript printer, the text retains its vector format and appears as clear and sharp as text produced within the page-layout program itself. Of course, the image beneath this text remains resolution dependent, i.e. it is made up of pixels at a fixed resolution (**fig. 27**).

Even though 300dpi is suitable for images destined for offset printing, text – especially small text – has a fuzzy edge if it is generated at the same resolution. Keeping text as infinitely scaleable vector information, therefore, is key to how well it displays.

The above does not apply to images placed in websites because websites do not support multi-layer formats except in the case of 'rollover' buttons, in which a single image contains several different states, each of which is a separate layer (see p. 48). Generally, small text on websites should not be generated as part of an image because restricting text to a screen resolution of 72dpi has an even worse effect on it than rasterizing it to 300dpi for offset printing.

To merge text with an image, select the text layer and choose 'Layer > Rasterize > Type'. Rasterizing is a process that breaks vector information into pixels. It is also used in commercial printing, where it changes an image made up of 'dots per inch' (pixels) into a grid of round dots known as a 'line screen'.

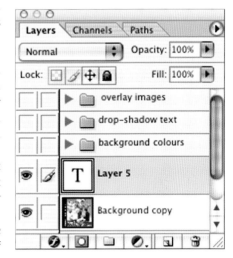

fig. 26 The Text Tool, top, and a text layer holding editable text.

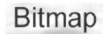

fig. 27 Left, bitmap text; right, vector text.

fig. 28 The Control Bar text tools.

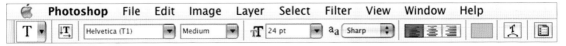

When a text layer is rasterized, the 'T' in the thumbnail vanishes, indicating that the text is now a graphic shape, and not text. Before rasterizing text, you can click and drag across it with the Text Tool to highlight all or some of it. While the text is highlighted, various options in the Control Bar (**fig. 28**) can be used to change such formatting attributes as font, size and colour. The 'character' and 'paragraph' windows can also be accessed to edit leading, horizontal and vertical scale, kerning and tracking, and more. See p. 92 in the InDesign chapter for details on text formatting. You can also use the 'create warped text' button (**fig. 29**), which distorts text using various wave shapes.

5.7 Layer styles

Before or after rasterizing text, layer styles can be applied. Previously, adding an effect such as a drop shadow meant following several rather tedious steps. Now, (almost) all you have to do is select 'drop shadow'

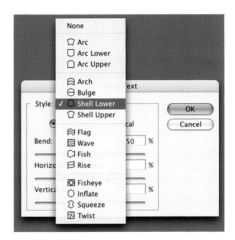

fig. 29 The Warp Text window.

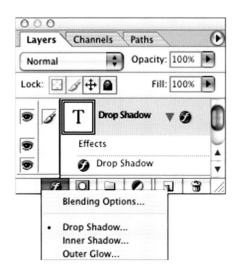

fig. 30 Adding layer styles.

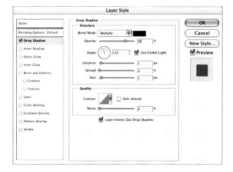

fig. 31 The Layer Style
window and the result.

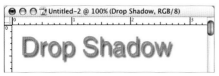

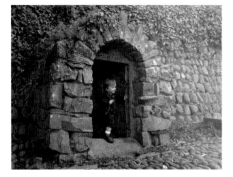

fig. 32 A problem image,
over-exposed to the right.

from the list under the 'layer styles' button at the foot of the Layers window (**fig. 30**).

When this is done, the object(s) on the selected layer immediately show the current drop shadow parameters and the Layer Style window opens (**fig. 31**). On the left of this window is a list showing the other available layer styles.

Click on the name of a style to apply it to the image. At the same time, the editing window for that particular style opens. Change any of the settings to produce variations on the effect. The check box next to the name allows you to turn the settings on or off.

In the case of the drop shadow, the blending mode determines some of the viewing characteristics. 'Multiply', the default, increases the saturation of the colours involved. Other variables change the opacity, spread and size of the shadow. Moving the arm in the circle changes the direction from which the shadow is created. Keep the 'preview' area checked to see live updates in the image.

On the layer to which the styles are applied, a small arrow appears next to a 'style' icon. If this arrow is clicked on, the sub-layers can be toggled in and out of view, although they cannot be selected individually in the same way as a full layer. Each style listed has its own 'eye' icon to turn the style on or off.

To edit an applied style again, either double-click on the sub-layer or reselect the effect from the 'styles' list at the foot of the Layers window.

5.8 Adjustment layers

Adjustment layers affect all the layers below them in the stack and can be used, for example, to add a levels adjustment. However, unlike the levels adjustment discussed on p. 28, a layer adjustment keeps the adjustment separate from the image. So, instead of changing the pixels themselves, the adjustment acts as a filter through which the pixels are seen. This filter can be changed or removed to reveal the unchanged image beneath.

Adjustment layers are most valuable when you need to adjust only part of an image. Open image 'small red.jpg' on the CD (**fig. 32**). It is lighter down the right side, but this gradually fades until the image appears at full strength towards the centre. A levels adjustment layer can bring the lighter area back up to full strength and then the adjustment layer mask can remove it from the areas where it is not needed.

As adjustments cannot be applied to 'background' layers, make a duplicate of it and select it.

Click on the 'adjustment layer' icon and choose 'curves' from the list. A new layer appears in the Layers window, showing the 'adjustment' thumbnail on the left and a white mask thumbnail on the right, and the Curves window opens. Adjust the diagonal line to the shape shown in **fig. 33**. Complex adjustments can be done in stages.

The half of the image that was OK to begin with now looks horrible – do not worry. For the moment, the main thing is that the right-hand side of the image now looks slightly darker than it needs to, rather than lighter. I usually overdo the adjustment rather than trying to get the exact setting, as it is easy to edit the effect later using the opacity slider in the Layers window.

Click 'OK' and the Curves window closes.

The colour chips in the Toolbox revert to black and white because the next stage is to colour the mask. At the moment, the mask is white, meaning that the adjustment is visible in full across the entire image. However, by painting on the mask with black or a shade of grey, degrees of transparency are applied to the curves effect selectively, thus allowing the unchanged image beneath to show through. This is a very important point to understand and it will mean that masks will be easy to work with in the future.

With black and white as the default colours in the Toolbox (black should be the foreground colour), choose the Brush Tool with a 20-pixel brush size. Click and drag the brush on the right side of the image, thereby covering up, or masking, the adjustment effect and seeing the original image density reappear. Simultaneously, the thumbnail image of the mask updates to show the painted area.

Undo that operation (through the History window or by choosing 'apple/control + Z') and the mask reverts to being completely white.

Next, choose the Gradient Tool. Make sure that 'foreground to background' is selected as the gradient type (click on the shaded bar in the Control Bar and select the top-left library item) and that the 'linear' gradient style button is selected (on the far left of the set in the 'options' bar). Hold down the 'shift' key and click and drag across the central third of the image from left to right, and let go. The 'shift' key constrains the angle of the gradient brushstroke to being horizontal.

Immediately, the left side of the image undergoes a substantial improvement as the levels effect is removed. However, the gradient (visible in the layer thumbnail) fades towards the right, allowing the adjustment to increase, resulting in the right side of the image still looking darker than it should.

To fix this, slide the opacity level for the adjustment layer down to 90% to weaken the effect of the adjustment (**fig. 34**).

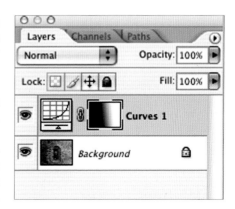

fig. 33 Using a curves adjustment to fix the over-exposure.

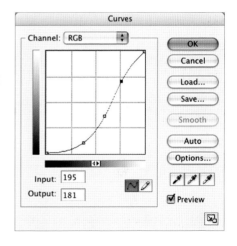

| Tip | The colours used to paint the gradient were both 100% opaque, so the gradient can be re-painted as many times as needed to refine the effect. |

Watch the 'Adjustment Layers' movie and practise using the file 'temple.jpg' and 'small red.jpg' on the CD.

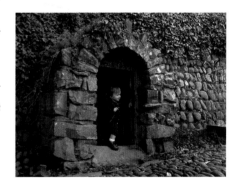

fig. 34 The adjusted image.

6	Using Masks

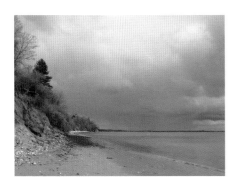

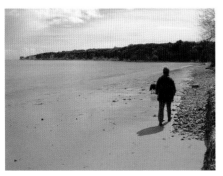

fig. 35 Two separate images...

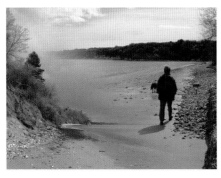

fig. 36 ...become one
composite image.

6.1 Layer masks

As we saw in the adjustment layers section (see p. 36), a mask can turn a simple curves adjustment into something much more complex and subtle. Masks, specifically layer masks, can also be used to blend two images together. To achieve this, it is first necessary to get both images in the same frame but on different layers. Choose the images carefully – the result will be more effective if you have a good idea of what you want to accomplish beforehand.

Watch the movie 'Layer Masks' on the CD and then open the images called 'Swanage-1.jpg' and 'Swanage-2.jpg' (**fig. 35**). These photographs were taken within minutes of each other on a beach, one looking left and the other looking right. As a result, most of the image detail in Swanage-1 is in the lower-left of the shot, whereas most of the detail on Swanage-2 is in the upper right. Helpfully, both images are exactly the same size.

Import Swanage-1 into the canvas area of Swanage-2 (see p. 33). Pull it with the Move Tool until it fits into the frame. If you do not feel it snap into position, choose 'View > Snap' and try again.

When both images occupy the same area (but on different layers), make sure that the upper, imported layer is active and then click on the 'layer mask' icon at the foot of the Layers window.

A second thumbnail appears to the right of the image thumbnail in that layer, just as in the example in the section on adjustment layers. The difference here, though, is that you can work on the image or the mask. Click on the image and the colour chips at the foot of the Toolbox can be specified as a colour. In this mode, you can work on the image. Click on the mask thumbnail and the chips revert to greyscale. Painting in the image area now only affects the mask. It is obviously very important to keep track of which one is active.

Click on the mask and select the Gradient Tool. Select a 'foreground to background' gradient with a 'linear' style.

Click just above and to the right of the image's centre and draw a line 4–5cm long towards the lower-left corner and let go.

The two images now appear, blending into each other (**fig. 36**).

From the thumbnail image of the mask, you can see that as the shades of grey become progressively darker, more of the image beneath shows through. This is because shades of grey represent the degrees of transparency that the mask has applied to the image sharing its layer.

As the gradient colours are opaque, you can click and drag as many times as you want – each time repaints the mask. Keep on painting, and you should be able to refine your mask quite quickly to produce the exact image blend required. If you click on the gradient swatch in the Control Bar, you can select 'foreground to transparent' (rather than 'foreground to background'), meaning that each stroke on the mask adds to the previous strokes. This method is definitely more difficult, but allows a much more complex mask shape to be built up.

Of course, you can also paint directly on the mask with any other painting tool and with any shade of grey. If you 'alt + click' on its thumbnail, the mask appears as the visible image, allowing you to paint on it in more detail.

6.2 Quick masks

Applied as a channel rather than as a layer, quick masks are (mostly) used to produce a special effect as a gradient.

To add a quick mask to an image, open image 'St Catherine's Chapel.jpg' on the CD, and then click on the 'quick mask' icon near the foot of the Toolbox.

Open the Channels window. A new channel, called 'quick mask', has been added below the other channels. It is the active channel, so painting on the image at this point will mean painting on the mask.

As with an active layer mask, the colour chips at the foot of the Toolbox revert to black and white whenever the quick mask channel is selected as the active channel.

With black as the foreground colour and with the quick mask channel active, click and drag horizontally from right to left across the central third of the image to paint a 'foreground to background' gradient (**fig. 37**).

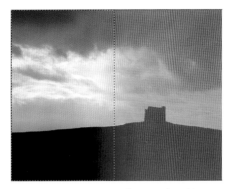

fig. 37 Quick mask icons (top) and a resulting selection.

Wherever the gradient painted a shade of grey, the image shows a transparent red colour. This is the mask and the shades of red represent degrees of protection against the application of a special-effect filter.

To load the mask, 'apple/control + click' on the mask channel. A selection appears. Photoshop has in fact recognized the gradient involved, but selections can only display what looks like an on or off appearance.

Now that the mask is loaded as a selection, click on the composite channel at the top of the channel stack to return to the image view. Also click on the 'eye' next to the quick mask channel to switch off the red appearance. Apply a special-effect filter, such as 'Filter > Pixelate > Crystallize', with a setting of 10.

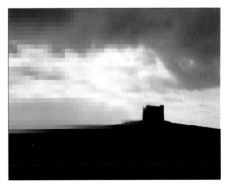

fig. 38 A filter applied to the above selection.

The effect will be applied as a gradient, only visible on one side of the image and fading towards the central area (**fig. 38**).

Watch the 'Quick Masks' movie and practise using the file 'path.jpg' on the CD.

6.3 Paths and clipping paths

When an image is imported into a page layout, clipping paths prevent any part of the image that falls outside their boundary from displaying.

Clipping paths are vectors and can, therefore, cut right across pixels. They are not anti-aliased, so there is no softening of tone around their edges. As a result, the images inside them can sometimes look as if they have been cut out and pasted into a page layout. So, they must be used with care. Also, whenever you import a clipping-path image, make sure that it prints – sometimes they can cause printing problems.

To create a clipping path, a path must be drawn or a selection made.

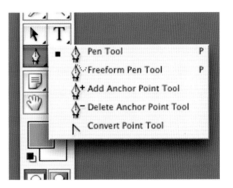

fig. 39 The Pen Tool is used to draw a path.

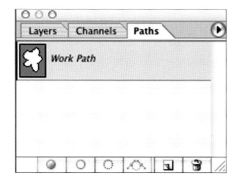

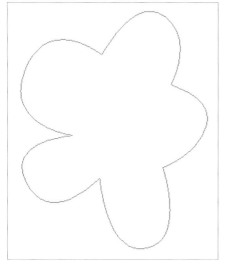

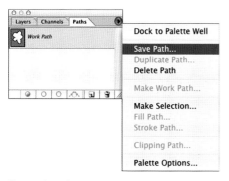

fig. 40 The Paths window
and a vector path drawn
with the Pen Tool.

fig. 41 Path window options.

1) Drawing a path

To draw a path, use the Pen Tool (**fig. 39**), which works in much the same way in Photoshop as in Illustrator (see p. 58). Identical keyboard shortcuts are also available: the 'apple/control' key toggles the cursor to the Direct Selection Tool, while the 'alt' key toggles it to the Convert Point Tool.

First, open the Paths window ('Window > Show Paths') and draw on the image with the Pen Tool (**fig. 40**). As you draw, a work path layer, with a thumbnail image of the path, appears in the Paths window.

In general, you can draw closed or open paths. Click in the grey area below the work path layer and the path vanishes from the image; click on the work path layer and it reappears. To add to the path(s) shown, simply select the Pen Tool and continue drawing.

Once drawn, paths can be saved (work paths are not saved with the image, but saved paths are), filled and stroked. To view these choices and more, click on the 'options' button. While you can choose the tool used to apply the stroke, Photoshop automatically uses the last brush size and shape associated with that tool, so select these elements beforehand. Only closed paths can act as clipping paths.

Having drawn a closed path, choose 'save path' from the 'options' list (**fig. 41**). Click on the 'options' list again and select 'clipping path'. Another window opens, which, if you have saved several paths, allows you to select one of them as the clipping path. You can also pick a 'device flatness' setting, which determines how many straight lines are used by the printer to approximate the curves in the path.

Save the image and import it into a page-layout program to see the result. If any background shows through, you should re-edit the path and repeat the process.

2) To create a path from a selection

Once a selection is made, you can choose either the 'make work path from selection' icon at the foot of the Paths window or click on the 'options' button and select 'make work path' from the list. The difference between the two methods is that using the 'options' button lets you enter a tolerance setting, whereas the icon option applies the last tolerance setting used. This is important because a tolerance setting of 0.5 results in a path that tries to follow the shape of each individual pixel in the original selection. It could, therefore, contain so many anchor points that it becomes too complex to print. A setting of 1, on the other hand, allows the resulting path to 'average' the shape designated by the selection. It will be smoother and have fewer anchor points, which solves potential printing problems. However, as it is slightly less accurate, it may need a little additional editing using the Pen tools. Of the two methods, I almost always use the 'options' button, and apply a tolerance setting of 1.

Save the path and generate the clipping path, following the instructions given in the previous method.

7   More Techniques

7.1 Resolution and image size

The number of pixels in a linear inch of an image's width (and also its height) is known as the image resolution. This has come to be referred to as 'dpi' within the graphics and printing industries, rather inaccurately considering that these 'dots' are actually square and have no space between them.

Consider this: if someone asks you to supply an image, saying 'I need it at 150dpi', have you been told what is needed? If instead you are told that the image is required at 15 x 20cm, would you know what to send? Certainly, if you had both sets of information, you would have a very clear idea of the size *and* resolution of the required image. Otherwise, you are only armed with half the information you need.

Controlling both the physical size and the resolution of an image is of utmost importance. To do this effectively, you must first know the appropriate resolution for different kinds of use.

For websites, the resolution has to be 72dpi; for digital printing and desktop (office) printers (including inkjet) it needs to be 150dpi; and for commercial offset printing it should be 300dpi.

Tip   **Some digital printers insist on 300dpi images. If you encounter this, you should consider sending the printer a page layout containing four copies of an image – three at 300dpi and one at 150dpi – all at the same size and ask them to print it. Then, ask the printer to tell you which one was the 150dpi version.**

The physical size of an image depends on the specific requirements of the job. However, if you take a 72dpi, 15-x-20cm image and turn it into a 300dpi, 15-x-20cm image, all you are doing is spreading the original information over a larger number of pixels. The result is that a lot of important detail will appear to be missing.

Some readers may have noticed that, while talking about resolution, I suddenly mentioned size, which up until that point seemed to be a separate issue. It is not. The physical size of an image and the resolution *together* control how big the image is and how much detail it contains.

To see how Photoshop deals with image size, open image 'image test.tif' on the CD and then choose 'Image > Image Size' (**fig. 42**).

The top half of the Image Size window shows the width and height of the current image, either as a percentage (not useful) or in pixels (very useful).

The lower half of the window shows the image's width and height in units, such as centimetres, and the resolution. Make sure the units for the resolution are dots (pixels) per inch and not dots per centimetre.

Below this area are two very important check boxes: 'constrain proportions' and 'resample image'. Keeping only the 'constrain proportions' box checked means that the width, height *and* resolution of the image are linked to each other. Then, whichever of the three is

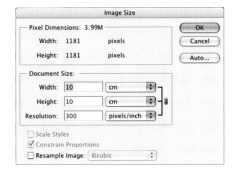

fig. 42 The Image Size window.

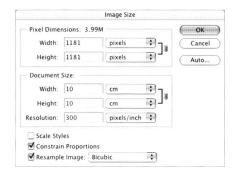

fig. 43 Using the Image
Size window to change
image resolution.

changed, the other two automatically adjust to maintain not only the proportions but also the file size. In this scenario, the number of pixels in the image (shown in the top half of the window) becomes locked and cannot be changed.

If the 'resample image' box is also checked, only the width and height are linked (**fig. 43**). This prevents the image from becoming distorted, but allows you to change the resolution and therefore the file size.

> **Tip**   **File size refers to the size of the file and not to the physical area covered by the image.**

If, for example, someone requests an image at 300dpi and at 15-x-20cm, the first thing to do is open the Image Size window to see what the settings actually are. If the size is correct, but the resolution is only 150dpi, would it be good enough? After all, it sounds as if the image is already halfway to the size being requested.

However, if the 'resample image' box was deselected and the resolution changed from 150 to 300dpi, the width and height would also change. In this case, to a 7.5 x 10 cm image, which is actually only a quarter of the requested size.

So, although it is tempting to reselect the 'resample image' box and change the width and height to 300dpi, so doing will spread the available detail (only a quarter of what is needed) over the entire image. The quality would suffer accordingly. To try this for yourself, open 'image test2.tif' on the CD.

Most of the time, images can be enlarged to 120% of their original size without anyone noticing. And, if you sharpen the result just a little, it crisps things up even more. Go beyond this percentage, however, and you risk seriously degrading the quality of the picture.

Incidentally, it is *never* a good idea to place an image in a page layout and then stretch it to a larger size. If you do this, the pixels get larger and become visible, while the image becomes correspondingly less visible: if we see the dots, we stop seeing the image. Instead, take back the image into Photoshop and try to deal with it there.

7.2 Canvas size

To change the size of an image by adding a new, blank area along one or more edges, go to 'Image > Canvas Size' (**fig. 44**).

In the window, the current image is represented by the central square in the grid. You can reposition it by clicking in another square. If it remains in the centre, any size increase is added equally on all sides; if it is positioned to the left, any new width is added on the right; if it is on the bottom row, new height is added at the top.

Enter new dimensions in the 'width' and 'height' windows, reposition the image and click 'OK'. New areas are filled with the current background colour automatically, unless the 'background' designation of the default layer has been changed, in which case, new areas are

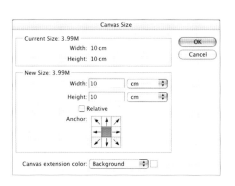

fig. 44 The Canvas Size
window.

transparent. If the new dimensions represent a decrease in the image's original size, you will be reminded that the operation involves clipping the image.

| Tip | This is a useful technique for adding a buffer zone to one side of an image, around which text will wrap on a website. The Dreamweaver alternative, 'H-space', adds space on both sides of the image to create a slightly indented appearance (see p. 159). |

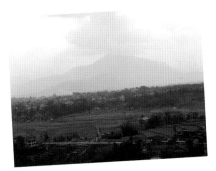

7.3 Cropping and straightening images

fig. 45 The Crop Tool icon (left) and a crooked image.

Images are often crooked as a result of the way they have been scanned or because the photographer held the camera at an angle. They can be straightened, as well as cropped, using the Crop Tool (**fig. 45**).

Click and drag to draw a frame within the image, as shown.

The cropping frame can be rotated. First, drag one of the frame's corner handles and place it on top of what would be, if it were not crooked, either a horizontal or vertical element in the image. If neither exists, line up the handle with something that you can use as a guide.

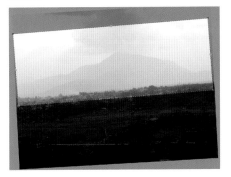

Hold the cursor just outside the frame at the opposite corner. When it turns into a double-headed, curved arrow, click and drag to rotate the frame, lining up its edge with the guide elements within the image (in this case, the true horizon).

Drag out the sides of the frame as far as possible to retain as much of the original image as you can. To complete the cropping action, press 'enter'. The image is straightened and cropped at the same time (**fig. 46**). Watch 'Straightening Images' movie and practise using the file 'Lake.jpg' on the CD.

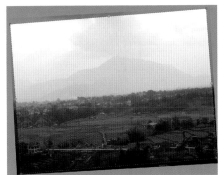

| Tip | If you create a cropping frame, but decide against using it, it can be cleared by pressing the 'escape' key. This also applies to transformation frames. |

7.4 Useful special effects:
Gaussian Blur, Unsharp Mask and Noise

There are a huge number of special effects available in Photoshop, and to go through all the options would require a book in itself. While this is a fascinating part of the software that is well worth exploring, it is also an area in which you are less likely to be paid for your time. It is unfortunate, but the fact is that most Photoshop work is concerned with the less, rather than the more, esoteric image adjustments. However, while that is generally true, there are some filter effects that are likely to be extremely useful to you on a daily basis.

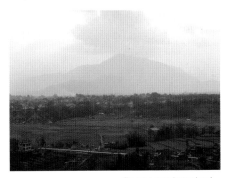

fig. 46 A straightened and cropped image.

Gaussian Blur
Useful because it is editable, Gaussian Blur blurs a selection to whatever degree is required. It is particularly useful when the background in a

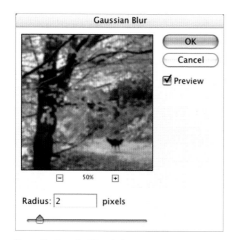

fig. 47 The Gaussian Blur window.

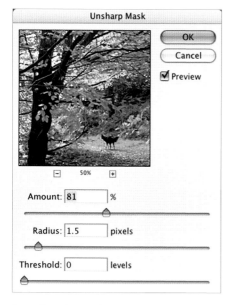

fig. 48 The Unsharp Mask window.

portrait shot needs to be softened to focus attention on the subject. Open image 'busy.tif' on the CD. A selection of the background has already been made and saved as an alpha channel.

Load the alpha channel as a selection. Go to 'Filter > Blur > Gaussian Blur' and try different slider settings to see the various effects (**fig. 47**).

Useful applications of Gaussian Blur include making a selection around the figures in a portrait shot in which there is also a very 'busy' (i.e. detailed) background, such as foliage. Using this tool the background can be blurred, meaning that the eye is less likely to stray there and the visual focus of the image is improved.

Unsharp Mask
Probably the most useful of the sharpening filters, Unsharp Mask is also editable and is found under 'Filter > Sharpen > Unsharp Mask'.

Sharpening cannot create detail that did not exist; instead, it boosts the contrast on either side of edges found within the image. Although it is an illusion, it can be very effective as long as the image is not very blurred to begin with.

Before adjusting the settings, check the 'preview' window so the changes are visible as they are made.

Of the three sliders in the window, 'threshold' determines the range of colours affected by the filter. A setting of 0 affects the entire image and that is where I usually place the slider. 'Radius' specifies how far from an edge the sharpening effect will spread, while 'strength' adjusts the degree of contrast applied. I usually set the radius somewhere between 1 and 2 pixels – beyond that the effect becomes too easily visible. The strength setting is up to you. But, remember that however the image appears on-screen, it will be more defined in print: if *you* can see the boosted edges, so will everyone else (**fig. 48**).

| Tip | It is almost always worth adding a little sharpening to images that have been scanned, which while not actually blurred tend to be slightly 'soft' in appearance. |

Noise
Whenever you paint a selected area with a gradient, you should add Noise to it to prevent any banding appearance in the subsequent print. To do this, choose 'Filter > Noise > Add Noise'. The image begins to look sandblasted if too much noise is applied, so the key is to add just enough to jiggle around the pixels to prevent banding, but not enough to detect anything. On a 300dpi image, a setting of '3' works beautifully (**fig. 49**, opposite).

7.5 Actions

Actions record of a series of operations that can then be applied to other images. To create an action, open the Actions window ('Window > Actions'), click on the 'options' button and choose 'new action' from the list. Give your action a name and location, and click 'record'. From that point, everything you do to the current image will be recorded. When you are done, click on the 'options' button again and choose 'stop recording'. The action is then saved. To apply the action to another image, select it in the 'actions' list and click on the 'play' button (a triangle pointing to the right) at the foot of the Actions window.

Tip   **Some actions, if they use prior history states or other layers, may not be applicable to the image to which they are being applied. For best results, keep it simple!**

7.6 Image types and their uses

Some image formats are good for print, while others are only suited to websites. The following list covers the main varieties.

Suitable for print (commercial offset printing): TIFF and EPS files in CMYK, greyscale or bitmap format.

Suitable for printing on in-house, desktop systems: TIFF and JPEG files in RGB, greyscale or bitmap format.

Suitable for websites: JPEG files in RGB format (even if they need to look like greyscales) and GIF files, which have a special format called 'indexed colour'.

To convert an RGB image to CMYK, greyscale or indexed colour, go to 'Image > Mode' and select from the list. This may cause considerable colour changes.

7.7 Saving files

To save a file, choose 'File > Save As', allocate it a name and a location and then select a format from the list. Work can continue on the file and saving can be updated using 'File > Save' ('apple/control + S').

Should a warning appear, indicating that Photoshop can only save the file as a copy, it probably means that something is being done incorrectly, such as trying to save an image that has additional alpha channels as a JPEG file. If this happens, go back and work out what the problem is before proceeding.

Multi-layer files can be saved in 'Photoshop document' format (PSD) or, in later versions, as a TIFF.

Tip   **I find it very useful to be able to know at a glance whether the filename I am looking at represents a multi-layer 'archive' image, a single-layer 'print' image, or something that I have optimized for the Web (see p. 46 for optimization information) without having to open it. Therefore, I always save multi-layered files with a .PSD extension, single-layer printable files with .TIFF (with no LZW compression), and Web-suitable material with either .JPEG, .PNG or .GIF extensions.**

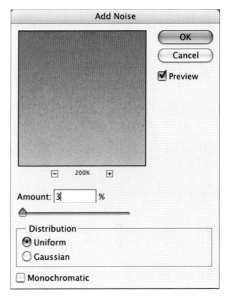

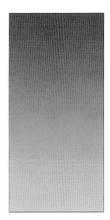

fig. 49 Adding Noise to a gradient.

8   Web Tools

fig. 50 The Image Ready
icon on the Toolbox.

Photoshop comes bundled with a second program called Image Ready,
which is used to do several useful things for website images. To open
Image Ready from within Photoshop, click on the icon at the foot of the
Toolbox (**fig. 50**).

8.1 Optimizing images

Optimizing allows images to retain almost all their quality while losing
much of their file size, meaning that they load faster in a browser
window and the viewer is less likely to get bored and go elsewhere. It can
be carried out in Photoshop *or* Image Ready. The process is identical.

In Photoshop, choose 'File > Save for Web'. At the top of the window,
choose either the '2-up' or '4-up' tab to display the original image plus
one or the original image plus three. Different settings can be applied to
each copy and the one that has the highest image quality, the smallest
file size and compares the closest to the original can be saved as the
optimized image (**fig. 51**).

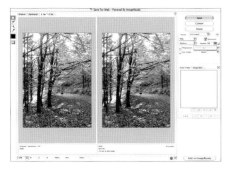

fig. 51 Optimizing an
image for use on the Web.

Tip   **The regular zoom and scroll controls work on all images
opened in the Optimization window.**

The image on the left is the original. At its foot is information about
its size and download speed. The file size information is misleading, as it
actually states the size the image would be if it were saved as an
uncompressed TIFF, regardless of its current format.

Click on the image on the right. In the top right of the window,
choose JPEG as the image type and enter a quality setting of 60.

The immediate recalculation at the foot of the image shows a
substantial reduction in file size (even if it was a JPEG to begin with),
while showing almost no visible change in quality. Continue to adjust
the settings until a balance has been achieved between the quality and
the file size needed. Then, click on 'save', name the new file and return to
the Photoshop window. When closing the original file, do not update the
image or you may overwrite the original with the optimized version.

To optimize in Image Ready, choose 'Window > Optimize' and click
on either the '2-up' or '4-up' tabs at the top of the image frame. Then,
proceed as detailed above.

fig. 52 The Slice and Slice
Selection tools.

8.2 Slicing images

A large image can be sliced into sections to make it easier to load on a
website. Each slice becomes a separate image and can be optimized
accordingly. The HTML code generated by the slicing operation tells
Dreamweaver and the browser how to display all the slices as a seamless,
single image.

First, create a new folder called 'slices' within a defined Dreamweaver
site (see p. 152). Open the image 'Taj Mahal.jpg' on the CD in Photoshop
and resize it as needed for your website. Then, click on the bottom-right
icon in the Toolbox to open Image Ready.

The image opens on-screen. Choose the Slice Tool in the Toolbox and click and drag on the image. These movements divide the image into smaller areas (**fig. 53**). Now select the Slice Selection Tool. Click on each slice in turn and optimize it using the Optimize window (see above). When finished, choose 'File > Save Optimized As' and browse to the 'slices' folder created earlier.

The file name, which can be changed, shows an HTML extension. Ensure that 'HTML and Images (*.html)' is set as the 'save as type'. Leave 'settings' on default and select 'all slices' as the 'slices' setting. Click 'save'.

The images, and HTML code governing their placement, are saved to the specified location. The images are placed in a sub-folder that Image Ready creates automatically.

To place the file in an HTML page, first open it as an HTML document in Dreamweaver.

Copy ('Edit > Copy') the HTML code from the beginning of the slice object to the end, i.e. from '<!— ImageReady Slices' to '<!— End ImageReady Slices —>'.

Open the page on which you wish to place the file in 'split' view (half design view, half code view). Click on the page to define the entry point for the sliced image and copy the slice code into the code section (not onto the page). Then, click on the page.

The table that holds the images should appear, but the images themselves may not. If not, click on one of the 'broken image link' icons in the table. The name of the missing slice will appear in the 'SRC' area in the Properties window. Drag the pointer at the right of the 'SRC' area and drop it on the correct image name in the Files Panel. Repeat for the other images.

Tip   **If you did not understand some of the above, read the Dreamweaver chapter (p. 142).**

8.3 Creating an animated GIF

Each frame of an animated GIF needs to be created from one or a combination of separate layers in Photoshop. They are then linked together in Image Ready.

On the CD, open 'duck.psd' in Image Ready (**fig. 54**). Also, open the Layers window ('Window > Layers') and the Animation window ('Window > Animation').

In the Animation window, click on the 'new frame' icon 11 times to create 11 new frames (**fig. 55**).

In the Layers window, turn on (i.e. ensure that the 'eye' icon is visible) layers A and B, as these will appear in all the frames. Then, turn on layer 1. Click on the second frame and turn on layer 2. Click on the third frame and turn on layer 3, and so on (**fig. 56**, overleaf).

Beneath each frame in the Animation window is a time setting that determines the duration of that frame's appearance in the browser window. You can select the time from the list or input your own. When all

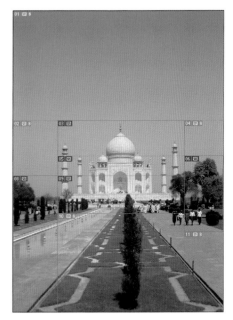

fig. 53 A sliced image.

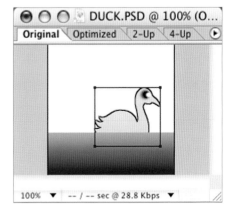

fig. 54 Creating an animated GIF image.

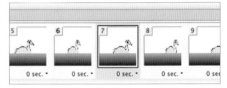

fig. 55 Create as many new frames as the animation will require.

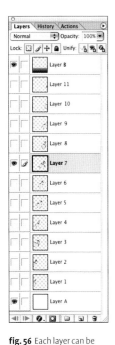

fig. 56 Each layer can be turned on or off individually, thus controlling the content of the selected frame.

the frames have been designated, use the playback controls to preview the animation.

Tip	When you preview the result, it runs directly from your hard drive, so no on-line bandwidth limitations are involved. It may, therefore, run much faster than it will on a website. Choosing a suitable frame duration (based on 12 frames a second) is, therefore, a good idea.

You can optimize animations in the same way as images (see p. 46). However, instead of choosing JPEG format, select GIF. This enables you to reduce the number of colours to decrease the file size even further.

When ready, choose 'File > Save Optimized As' and browse to a location. Animated GIFs are easier to deal with than sliced images because there is no need to save the HTML code. GIF animations can be placed in Web pages in just the same way as JPEG images.

8.4 Creating a 'rollover' button

On the CD is an image called 'rollover.psd', which contains three layers: one represents an 'up' state, i.e. how the button looks when there is no interaction; another an 'over' state, which will activate when the cursor 'rolls over' it; and the third, a 'down' state, activated if the button is clicked on. Open this in Image Ready.

In the Image Document window, click the '2-up' tab and optimize the image, in GIF format (see p. 46, **fig. 57**). Then, open the Web Content, Slice and Layers windows.

The Web Content window contains a single copy of the button image. By visually turning the 'up' layer on, and the others off, you can set this image to show the 'up' state of the inactive button. Then, click on the 'options' button in the Web Content window and choose 'new rollover state' from the list.

In the 'slices' area of the Web Content window, a sub-heading of 'rollover states' appears, beneath which is another copy of the image, called 'over'. Once again, use the Layers window to set this to display the 'over' state of the button.

Create another rollover state in the same way, for the 'down' state of the button. The windows should now look as shown in **fig. 58**.

You can preview the result in Image Ready, in the Image Document window, by first clicking on the Preview Document Tool in the Toolbox. When you do this, the button image reverts to its 'up' state, but toggles through the other states as you roll over or click on it.

A link can be specified in the URL field in the Slice window, but first the 'preview' mode has to be stopped. To do this, click on one of the fields in the Slice window. This prompts the appearance of a warning window where, if you click 'OK', preview mode will be switched off. Then, enter the URL information (which must also contain the 'http://' if it is to be a link to an external URL) in the Slice window.

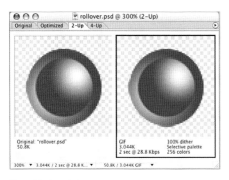

fig. 57 The '2-up' tab.

Choose 'File > Save Optimized As' and enter a filename and location, which should be the same folder as the one in which you plan to save the other HTML documents for your site. Choose 'HTML and Images (*.html)' as the 'Save as type', so that the correct HTML code is saved as well as the images themselves. Click 'save'.

To place the button in another HTML document, open the button's HTML file in Dreamweaver. In 'code' view, you will see two sections of code governing the rollover event and the link information, one in the 'head' and one in the 'body' section of the document. The 'real' script is contained, in both cases, between two greyed-out lines of code that are not needed.

Copy the script in the 'head' section, from '<script type="text/javascript">' to '</script>' at the end, and paste it into your new document directly beneath the '<meta http...' line in the 'head' section. Then, in the 'body' section, copy from the '<a href="http://...' at the beginning to the '</a>' at the end, and paste it into the 'body' section of the new document at the location in which you want the button to appear.

There is another line that needs to be copied from the original document. At the beginning of the 'body' tag, you will see that there is a whole line of code, ending with 'onload="preloadImages();">'. This is necessary for the different button images to be available when the cursor moves over the image or clicks on it. Copy that whole line and paste it over the existing '<body>' tag in the new document to replace it.

If you wish to use the button in a document located in a different folder, you will see in the Files Panel in Dreamweaver that the action of saving the button also created a separate sub-folder named 'images', in which the three rollover images are stored. This folder, and its contents, will also need to be copied to the new location in order to maintain the links between the button images and the HTML code.

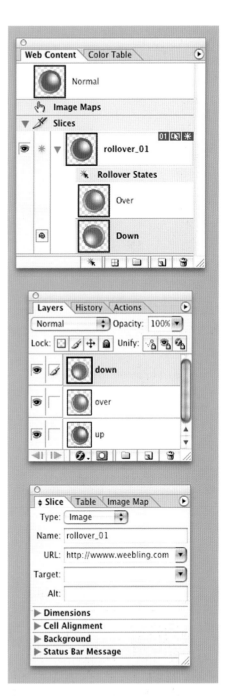

fig. 58 The Web Content, Layers and Slice windows as they should appear at the end of the rollover button creation process.

Chapter 2

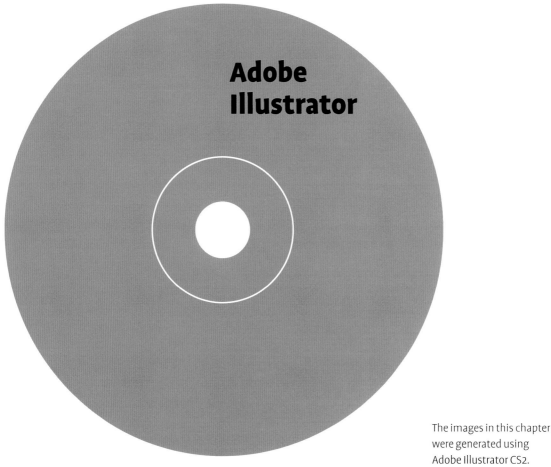

The images in this chapter were generated using Adobe Illustrator CS2.

Illustrator is recognized worldwide as the professional tool of choice for the creation of vector-based art. It began life as a fairly basic vector-drawing program, an area in which it continues to excel, although a great many bells and whistles have been added.

Drawn objects can be warped, twisted, rotated, sheared, trimmed and distorted, and other graphics can be brushed or sprayed onto them. Transparency can be applied to anything on the artboard and attributes copied from one object to another. Text can be added in several formats and customized in terms of colour and shape. Images can be imported and incorporated into Illustrator layouts. Illustrator drawings can be converted from vector to bitmap and then developed further using many of the same effects and filters found in Adobe Photoshop.

Vector shapes are easy to manipulate and colour, so they are the perfect format for such projects as logo design development. But, because Illustrator is also an extremely creative package, it is often the software of choice for the design of book covers, posters and trade show displays, as well as for more 'traditional' applications, such as technical drawings (see the files 'ad.ai', 'ad2.ai', 'technical drawing.ai' and 'book design.ai' on the CD).

Once an Illustrator creation is complete, it can be exported in a variety of formats, suitable for websites, page layouts for print or for further work in such applications as Adobe Photoshop.

1   The Illustrator Environment

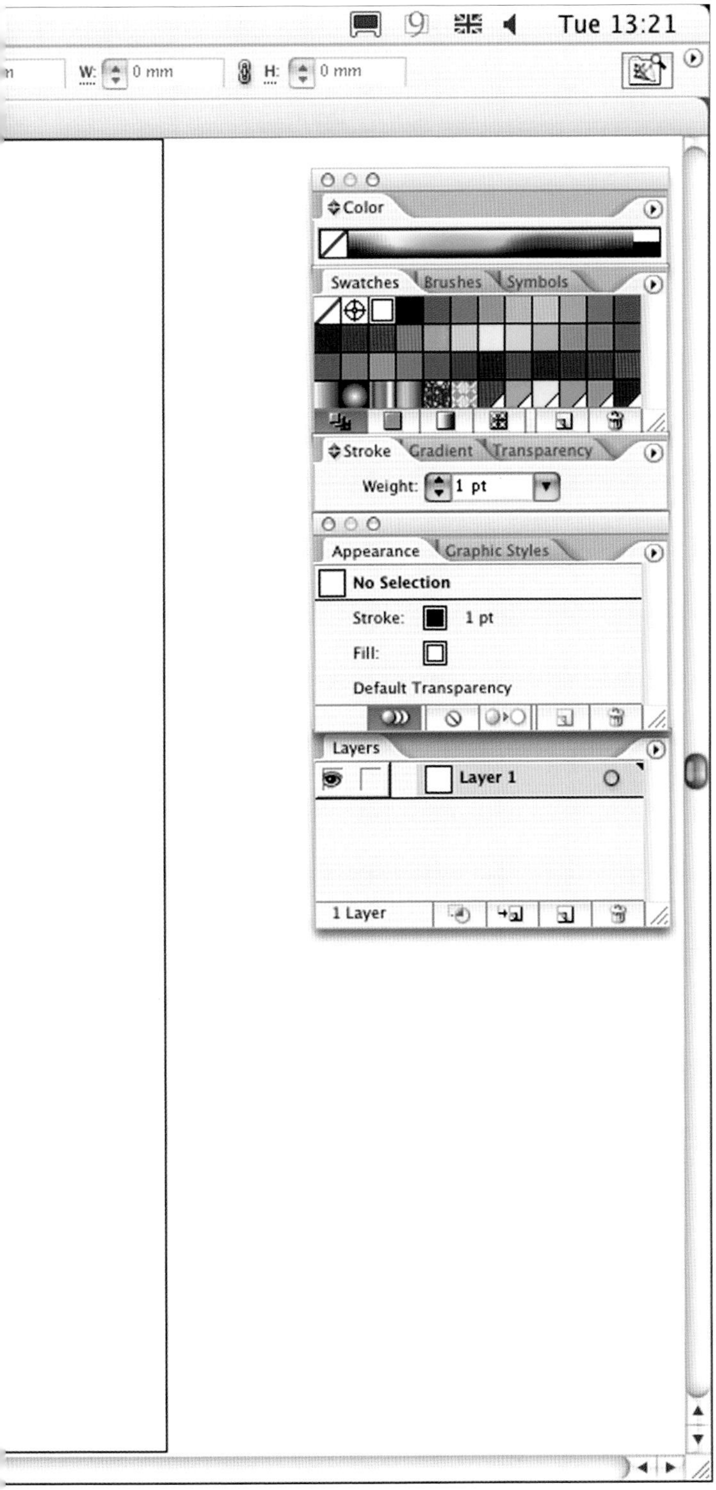

fig. 1 The Illustrator screen.

1.1 The Illustrator screen

Very similar in appearance to the screens of InDesign and Photoshop, the Illustrator screen (**fig. 1**, previous page) also has the usual menus across the top and a vertical Toolbox on the left side of the screen. The Toolbox and any floating windows can be repositioned by dragging on the bar at their top.

Directly below the menus in CS+ versions is the Control Bar, which displays useful information and options associated with the selected tool or object.

In the lower left of the screen, a percentage field appears whenever a document is open. Here, you can adjust the screen view by choosing a setting from the drop-down list or by highlighting the current percentage and entering a new one.

Scroll bars are positioned beneath and to the right of the document area, but are not usually required due to the advantages of other scrolling techniques (see p. 55).

Above and to the left of an open document are the rulers, which can be toggled in and out of view using 'View > Show [or Hide] Rulers' ('apple/control + R'). Their units of measurement can be changed through the Preferences window, which is opened by choosing (Mac) 'Illustrator > Preferences > Units &...' or (PC) 'Edit > Preferences > Units & ...' (the precise wording varies according to the version being run).

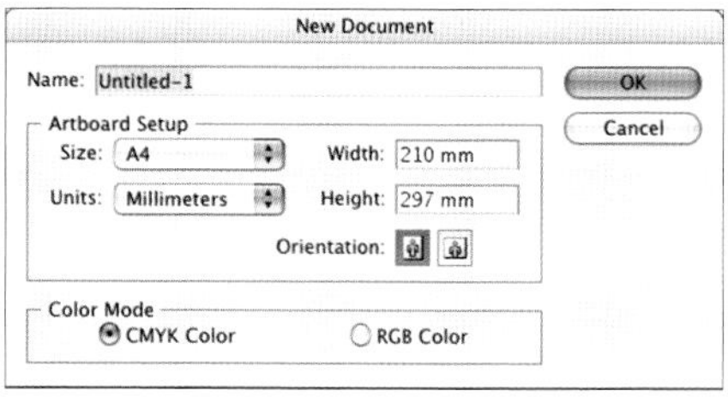

1.2 Setting up a new artboard

Choose 'File > New' ('apple/control + N') and the New Document window appears (**fig. 2**).

This document is not described as a page, but rather as an artboard. Choose a size from the drop-down menu or enter specific width and height measurements. Click on either the 'portrait' or 'landscape' icons to select the artboard orientation. Also, choose a unit of measurement for the page, which will then apply to the rulers normally visible above and to the left of the working area.

Very importantly, select either CMYK (cyan, magenta, yellow and black) or RGB (red, green and blue) from the list. This does not prevent you from creating a custom colour in another mode, but it helps to steer the document towards being suitable for either print or Web. If you are producing graphics for a website, pick RGB because all on-screen colours are combinations of red, green and blue light.

CMYK, on the other hand, are the names of the inks used in 4-colour-process offset printing (i.e. colour printing). As the range of colours produced with CMYK falls far short of those that can be created with RGB, it can be very detrimental to the final result if the wrong one is chosen by mistake. If the document is destined for print, always choose CMYK.

When ready, click 'OK', and the artboard appears.

There may be a dotted line on the inside edges of three or four sides of the artboard. This is an indicator of page tiling – the area that will actually fit the default printer. On a large artboard, there may be several rectangles

fig. 2 The New Document window.

formed by these lines, showing how the printer would tile the entire image, i.e. break it up into printable areas when printing it out at 100%.

If Illustrator is being used to create elements for page layouts, such as logos, then page tiling is not necessary and it can be turned off under 'View > Hide Page Tiling'.

1.3 Zoom and scroll

fig. 3 The Rectangle Tool.

Select the Rectangle Tool **(fig. 3)** and click and drag on the artboard to create a shape. The shape drawing tools are covered in more detail on p. 62, but first it is important to be able to navigate the Illustrator environment.

For a closer view of the rectangle, zoom in by holding down 'apple/control + spacebar', and the cursor changes into a magnifying icon. Click and drag –do not just click – to draw a bounding box around the area to magnify. Release the mouse button and the screen view will zoom to that exact area. If you only click, the screen magnifies in increments and not necessarily to the exact area you want. Illustrator is capable of zooming in to an incredibly high magnification, meaning that it is possible to be extremely accurate when the need arises.

To zoom out, hold down 'apple/control' and press the hyphen key, although in this case it helps to think of it as the minus key. To zoom out to a full-page view, press 'apple/control + zero', using the number keys that run along the top of the keyboard.

To scroll the view of the artboard, hold down the spacebar and click and drag on the screen. This command works regardless of the selected tool, except when working with the Text Tool, in which case, a lot of space will suddenly appear in the active text.

Once the above methods have been learned, it will never again be necessary to stop working to go and click on the Magnifying Tool or the grabber hand. Nor will it be necessary to have the Navigator window cluttering up the screen.

1.4 The zero point

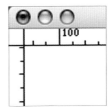

fig. 4 The zero point.

The zero point for both rulers can be re-positioned by clicking and dragging on the small box in the top-left corner where the two rulers meet **(fig. 4)**. Wherever it is released on the working area becomes the new zero point for both the horizontal and vertical rulers. The zero point is very useful for measuring accurately from one point to another.

1.5 Scroll bars

Positioned opposite the rulers, scroll bars are below and to the right of the working area. If you have difficulty using the spacebar scrolling technique described earlier, click and drag on the sliders (or, for a much larger movement, click to the side of one of the sliders) to scroll the view of the window.

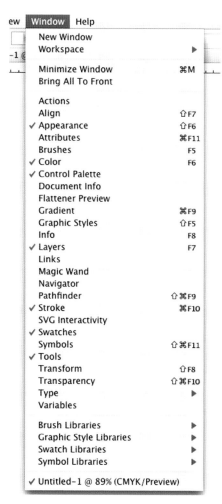

The Windows list.

fig. 6 Shared characteristics of most Windows include 'options', 'new' and 'trash'.

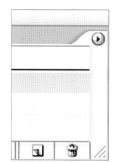

fig. 7 A tool flyout as a separate window.

1.6 Guides

Simple guides can be dragged onto the artboard from the rulers. When placed, they can be locked, released, hidden and cleared using options under 'View > Guides'. They do not have a snap feature, which is a kind of magnetic attraction enabling objects to be easily aligned with them. This is, however, a feature of smart guides, which are activated by clicking on 'View > Smart Guides' ('apple/control + U').

Smart guides are temporary, only displaying when a possible alignment occurs between two objects while one of the objects is being drawn or moved. To see their effect, activate them and then draw two rectangles on the artboard. When an edge of the second rectangle is close to becoming aligned with an edge of the first, a smart guide appears along those edges and exerts a snap, allowing the two objects to be aligned with each other.

1.7 Windows

As in Photoshop and InDesign, many of the ways in which objects can be manipulated are found in the various floating palettes or windows, which are listed under the Window Menu (**fig. 5**). If there is a check next to any item on the list, it is already visible on-screen.

Windows share certain features (**fig. 6**): they have an 'options' button, a small triangle in a circle, on the same level as the window's name; they can be switched off by clicking on (Mac) the red dot and (PC) the small 'x' at the top of the window; and they can be minimized to take up less screen space, by clicking on (Mac) the green dot and (PC) the small '-' icon. Additionally, they usually have a 'trashcan' icon at the foot of the box, for deleting content, and a 'new' icon that looks like a page with its lower-left corner turned up. Clicking on the 'new' icon invariably begins the creation of a new example of the objects with which that window is concerned.

Many windows share a frame with other windows, which can be viewed by clicking on the name tabs at the top. The options visible under the 'options' button change to reflect the active window within the frame.

To close a window, click on the button on the left in the bar across its top. To minimize it, click on the central button.

1.8 Flyout tool menus

Some of the tools in the Toolbox have a small arrow in their lower-left corner. This indicates a flyout menu, holding additional tools with related properties. To see the flyout, click and hold the cursor on the tool button. Slide the cursor along to the tool you need and release the mouse button. Alternatively, slide to the end and release the button on the small vertical bar. This allows the entire flyout to be visible on-screen as a separate window (**fig. 7**), from which any of the tools can then be selected. Close tool windows by clicking on the button in the top bar.

2   The Toolbox, Part I

2.1 The Selection tools

The top two tools in the Toolbox, Selection and Direct Selection, have almost exactly the same function in Illustrator and InDesign. There are, however, some subtle differences – for example, the third tool, Group Selection, only exists in Illustrator.

The Selection Tool

To select an object, click on it using the top-left tool in the Toolbox, the black arrow. This is the Selection Tool, which resizes and moves objects. When the outline or visible fill of an object is clicked on, a selection frame appears, with handles at the corners and in the centre of each side. Click and drag on these to resize the shape. If the 'shift' key is held down while clicking and dragging on a corner handle, the resizing is constrained to being proportional. To move the shape, click and drag on its centre point, its outline or its fill (if it has one).

Tip	An unfilled shape cannot be selected by clicking in the fill area, as there is nothing there.

Objects can also be selected by clicking and dragging with this tool to draw a 'bounding box' around them. The box only needs to touch an object to select it, it does not need to enclose the whole thing. When the mouse button is released, all the touched objects are selected. This method of selection ensures that objects are not accidentally moved.

Hold the cursor just outside a handle on a selection frame and it changes to a 'rotate' (a curved, double-headed arrow) icon. When this is visible, click and drag to rotate the object.

To select additional objects or to deselect them, hold down the 'shift' key and click on the objects.

Hold down the 'alt' key and click and drag on an object to create a duplicate. If the 'shift' key is held down as the duplicate is dragged away, its movement can be constrained to being vertical or horizontal.

If an image is imported ('File > Place'), dragging on the handles with the Selection Tool resizes it (in InDesign, only the frame holding the image is affected by this action). Illustrator does not assign an imported image a holding frame, it merely places the image on the screen. It is not possible, therefore, to give such an object a wider stroke setting, for example.

The Direct Selection Tool

In the top right of the Toolbox is the Direct Selection Tool, a white-filled arrow that is used for reshaping objects. When this tool is used to select something, only the anchor points along the object outline appear. Click and drag on these to reshape the object. Clicking on the fill of an object selects all the corner handles, in which case dragging on any one of the handles repositions the whole shape. Using the bounding-box method, however, allows certain anchor points to be selected and not others. Additional points can then be selected by holding down the 'shift' key and either clicking directly on them or dragging to enclose them. Hold down the 'shift' key and click on a selected anchor point to deselect it.

Anchor points can be added to (or deleted from) object outlines and their curve-handling characteristics can also be changed using the Pen Tool (see below).

Imported images cannot be reshaped with this tool.

The Group Selection Tool
This shares a flyout menu with the Direct Selection Tool. It is used to select just one object that is part of a group (see p. 73). Otherwise, all the member objects of a group would move and be resized together.

2.2 The Magic Wand Tool

A tolerance-based tool, the Magic Wand's action is connected to an adjustable setting. A higher setting means that when an object is clicked on, any other object(s) that falls within the tolerance values is also selected. Lower settings allow only objects sharing very similar characteristics to be selected.

To change the tolerance values, double-click on the tool button and a small window appears on-screen (or, you can go to 'Window > Magic Wand'). The window displays checkboxes for certain object characteristics. If only 'fill colour' is visible, click on the 'options' button and choose one or more of the 'show' options. You are then able to change their tolerance values.

2.3 The Lasso tools

In earlier versions of Illustrator, there were two Lasso tools: the Direct Selection Lasso and the Lasso. The Lasso Tool, which selected entire objects, has been discontinued, while the Direct Selection Lasso, renamed the Lasso Tool, remains. It allows you to create a freehand bounding box and thus select a more complex group of anchor points, as sometimes it is not possible to select the points you want by dragging to create a simple rectangular shape.

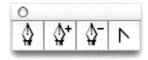

2.4 The Pen tools

One of the most important sets of tools in Illustrator, the pen group takes some getting used to. The best methods for using the pens are not self-explanatory, so please read this section carefully.

The Pen Tool is a Bézier tool, meaning that it can be used to draw straight or curved vector line segments. (A line segment is any section of a line between two anchor points. Anchor points are the elements that hold a line in a particular shape.)

Straight line segments require anchor points at every place the line turns in a different direction. Curved lines need anchor points for the same reason, but these points will also have Bézier handles attached to them. Bézier handles are visible when an anchor point is being clicked and dragged and when it is selected. They shape the curve of the path by exerting a kind of magnetic attraction (**fig. 8**).

Once a path is drawn, the tools on the pen flyout can be used to add or delete anchor points. They can also change the anchor points' shape-altering characteristics, either by moving the Bézier handles or by converting the anchor points, for example, by creating a sharp corner at a point where the line had previously been a smooth curve.

Rather than having the disruption of having to stop drawing to go and select one of the other tools, it is easy to set up a toggle that allows keyboard shortcuts to be used to access the other tools (see 'Setting up a Pen Tool toggle', below) while remaining in pen mode.

To create straight line path segments, click on the page, move the cursor to a new position and click again. Each click creates a new anchor point, which is connected to the previous point by a straight line segment. Repeat the action as needed. To stop drawing, click on a different tool.

To create curved line path segments, click and drag the cursor, then move it to a new position and click and drag again. Each click creates an anchor point, and each drag pulls a Bézier handle away from it, which influences the shape of the connected line segments.

It is a very common mistake to think that the handle is the line and to click and drag on it. But, this will not produce the desired line shape. The key to success is to click and drag and move to a clear place on the screen before clicking and dragging again.

The handles that appear along the path of the dragging motion act as tangents to the resulting curve. The length of the handle reflects its strength in influencing the curve; while the angle of the handle shows the direction of its influence on that end of the line segment.

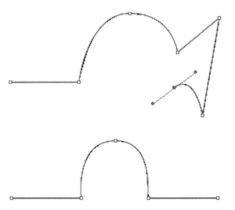

fig. 8 Drawing with the Pen Tool.

Setting up a Pen Tool toggle

To set up the toggle between the Direct Selection and the Pen tools, click on the Direct Selection Tool in the Toolbox and then click on the Pen Tool to select it. That is all there is to it. Now, even though the Pen Tool is actually selected, when the 'apple/control' key is held down, the cursor toggles back to the Direct Selection Tool, thus making it easy to edit a shape while drawing it.

Bézier handles, anchor points and line segments can be moved using the Direct Selection Tool. Try clicking and dragging on all three to see what happens. To select more than one anchor point, click and drag a bounding box around them, or, click on one point to select it and then 'shift-click' on others. When selected, anchor points appear filled, whereas unselected points appear empty.

Adding anchor points

Hover over an existing line segment with the Pen Tool and a small '+' sign appears beside the cursor. While it is visible, click on the line to add a new anchor point.

Deleting anchor points
Move the cursor over an existing anchor point and a small '-' appears. Click on the point to delete it.

Converting anchor points
Hold down the 'alt' key to toggle the Pen Tool into the Convert Point Tool, which converts a smooth curve into a corner, or vice versa, by clicking on an anchor point. Or, you can click and drag on an anchor point, thus creating a new set of Bézier handles, which can be moved independently of each other, either while still using the Convert Point Tool or with the Direct Selection Tool.

To add to an existing line
Select the Pen Tool and bring the cursor close to one of the line's ends. A small diagonal slash appears next to the cursor. While this is visible, click on the end of the line and continue to draw. It is not necessary to have the line selected to do this. A previously unenclosed, or open, path can be closed in this way, see below.

To join two ends
To close a path and thereby create an enclosed shape, connect to one end (as above), and then bring the cursor near to the other end. A small circle appears beside it, indicating the 'click zone', i.e. click while the circle is visible to join the two points and thus close the shape.

This is an example of POINT type|

fig. 9 'Point' type results from clicking on the artboard and typing.

To join two separate paths
The Pen Tool can be used to connect two separate paths. First, follow the instructions for 'To add to an existing line' and then for 'To join two ends'.

Simplifying a path
Too many anchor points, in an extreme case, can prevent a path from printing. If this happens, go to 'Object > Path > Simplify' to remove some of them. This command opens a window with a slider on which you should specify how close the result should be to the original. Unfortunately, path simplification methods, whether automatic or manual, are likely to change the original shape to some degree.

To go over this section, watch the three 'Pen Tool' movies in the Illustrator section on the CD, and open the 'Pen Tool.ai' and 'anchor points.ai' files to practise.

2.5 The Type tools

There are three ways to enter text in Illustrator – as point, area or path type – and each one has a horizontal and a vertical option. All three can be created with the Type Tool, but other tools on the flyout are required to create vertical type.

1) Click anywhere on the artboard with the Type Tool to enter text at a point, and begin typing. This is useful for small amounts of text (**fig. 9**).

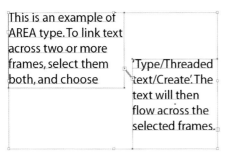

This is an example of AREA type. To link text across two or more frames, select them both, and choose 'Type/Threaded text/Create'. The text will then flow across the selected frames.

fig. 10 Linking 'area' type frames.

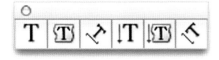

2) Click and drag with the Type Tool to create a frame for area text. Area text boxes can be linked, allowing text to reflow between them if the size of the frame is changed. This is a useful option for longer amounts of text (**fig. 10**). To do this, draw a second frame with the Type Tool. To link the first block of area type to the second, select both blocks and go to 'Type > Blocks > Link'.

A text wrap, when type is made to flow around something, works only with area type (**fig. 11**). Place the type behind the object around which you want it to wrap, then select the object and the text frame and choose (non-CS versions) 'Type > Wrap > Make' or (CS versions) 'Object > Text Wrap > Make'. If you are using a non-CS version to wrap text around a placed image, draw a rectangle of roughly the same size and shape as the image and apply the text wrap to it instead (as text wraps cannot be applied to the images themselves).

3) With the Type Tool, click on the outer shape of an object or on a path. Text flows along a path in the same direction as the path was drawn, so be careful to draw from left to right (**fig. 12**).

When a path is clicked on with the Type Tool, it vanishes. To make it appear, select it with the Direct Selection Tool and give it a width and a colour. Type can be moved along a path by clicking and dragging with the Selection Tool on the 'I-beam' point at the path's start.

In the above methods, text can be edited using any conventional word-processing methods. Cut, copy and paste are under the Edit Menu, while font and size are under the Type Menu and can be applied by either clicking and dragging with the Type Tool to select an area or by selecting text with the Selection Tool. Alternatively, in versions from CS onwards, the Control Bar, which runs across the screen just under the menus, can be used. Watch the 'Type tools' movie on the CD for a tutorial on these three methods.

The Character and Paragraph windows, under 'Window > Type', show most of the useful options: size, font, leading, kerning controls, tracking controls, horizontal and vertical scale, baseline shift, alignment and indents, among others (**fig. 13**). Additionally, CS2 allows you to create paragraph and character styles in the same way as in InDesign (see p.92).

There are further helpful type utilities under the Edit Menu (in pre-CS versions, see the Type Menu), including a spell checker and 'Find > Replace'.

Editable type can be filled and stroked with solid colours and patterns, but to fill it with a gradient requires saving the gradient as a style first (see p. 66).

Type can be broken apart to edit the shape of letters, or to apply gradient fills that are not styles, by going to 'Object > Expand'. This changes the type from editable text to a graphic of the same shape. Alternatively, choose 'Type > Create Outlines' ('apple/control + shift + O').

Practise using the file 'knockout type.ai' on the CD.

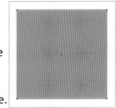

A text wrap (PIC), when type is made to flow around something, works only with area type. Place the type behind the object around which you want it to wrap, then select the object and the text frame and choose (non-CS versions) 'Type/Wrap/Make' or (CS versions) 'Object/Text Wrap/Make'.

fig. 11 Using a text wrap.

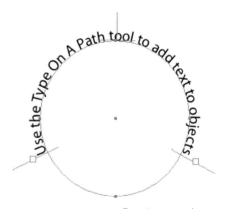

fig. 12 Type on a path.

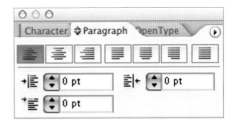

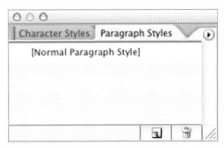

fig. 13 The Paragraph and Paragraph Styles windows.

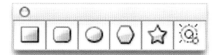

2.6 The Shape tools

Shapes drawn with any of these tools can be edited using the Direct Selection and Pen tools.

The Rectangle Tool

This is one of the most useful tools in Illustrator. To draw a rectangle, select the tool and then click and drag on the page. To draw a shape with specific dimensions, select the tool and click on the page without dragging. In the window that opens on-screen, enter a width and height and click 'OK'. A rectangle of that size appears on the artboard.

This method of setting preferences works with all the tools on this flyout menu, and, for each of them, the measurements and settings entered will remain active until they are changed, so multiple objects of the same shape and size can be created.

To constrain the shape to a square, hold down the 'shift' key as it is drawn.

Holding down the spacebar allows you to move the rectangle (or any other shape) as it is being drawn, a very useful technique that allows objects to be positioned very accurately without the need for lots of measuring.

Rounded rectangles

Click and drag to draw the shape. While the mouse button is held down, use the up and down arrows on the keyboard to increase or decrease how rounded the corners are. Clicking on the right and left arrows produces maximum and minimum rounding to the corners. Alternatively, click on the Rounded Rectangle Tool and then on the page to specify a size and corner radius value.

The Ellipse Tool

Click and drag to create an ellipse; if the 'shift' key is held down simultaneously, the shape formed is a circle.

The Polygon Tool

This tool draws symmetrical shapes with a specified number of sides. To change the number of sides, choose the tool and click on the page to open the Preferences window. Key in the number of sides and/or the dimensions and click 'OK'. While being drawn, the object can be rotated with the cursor. Hold down the 'shift' key while drawing, to draw the shape from the centre.

The Star Tool

Select this tool and click on the page to define the centre point. Enter the number of points for the star and/or the inner and outer radius values. Or, while clicking and dragging, hold down the 'alt' key until the inner radius points are at the desired size, then immediately switch to the 'apple/control' key to hold them at that point while continuing to drag the outer radius. The tool remembers the settings used from the last time the 'apple/control' key was used.

The Flare Tool

A strange and interesting tool, this draws an extremely complex object and, because the results can be fairly spectacular, it is easily overused.

Click and drag to set the scale of the flare and then click elsewhere to define the end point. Double-click on the tool (or select it and click on the artboard) to display the options window for, among other things, size, brightness and complexity. The permutations are endless, yet the effect is instantly recognizable.

Watch the 'Shape tools' movie on the CD for a tutorial.

2.7 Other drawing tools

The Line Segment Tool

Next to the Shape Tool in the Toolbox, the Line Segment Tool is used to draw straight lines. To use it, click and drag on the artboard: the initial click begins the line, which ends wherever the mouse button is released. To constrain the line to horizontal, vertical or 45°, hold down the 'shift' key while dragging.

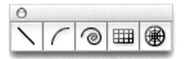

It is a tool that is often used to draw precise objects, so it is very useful to work with it in conjunction with the Transform window, with which you can create a line of an exact length, precisely positioned on the artboard.

Other tools on this flyout menu are more esoteric and so therefore are used less often.

The Paintbrush and Pencil tools

Effectively, these are identical, in that they are both freehand tools to which such effects as brushstrokes can be applied (see 'Colouring objects' on p. 65). To use either tool, click and draw on the artboard. When the mouse is released, a slightly smoothed version of the drawn path appears.

Double-click on their buttons in the Toolbox to open a preferences window (**fig. 14**). The 'fidelity' slider edits the accuracy of the resulting path compared to the one actually drawn: the higher the value, the smoother the path and the fewer anchor points it has. The 'smoothness' slider acts in a similar way. A mouse is a very inaccurate drawing tool (try signing your name with one!) so there are unlikely to be major differences regardless of how the sliders are set.

If the paths drawn with the Paintbrush Tool are not required to appear as filled shapes, de-select the 'fill new brush strokes' box.

Whenever the Paintbrush Tool is selected, one of the brushes in the brush library becomes active. To see the library, go to 'Window > Brushes' ('F5'). While a line – any line, not just those drawn with the Paintbrush Tool – is selected, one of the brushes can be applied by clicking on it in the window.

To change the parameters of a brushstroke, double-click on its button in the window.

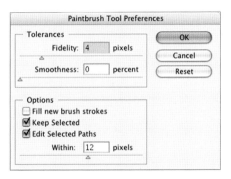

There are four different types of brushes in the library: calligraphic, scatter, art and pattern. Calligraphic brushes are shaped like the nib of a pen and influence the resulting line in the same way. Scatter brushes

fig. 14 Customizing the Paintbrush Tool.

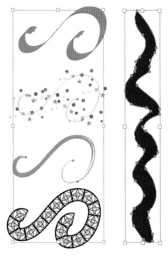

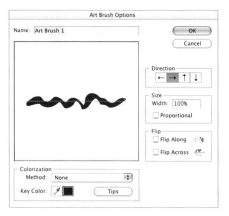

fig. 15 The four types of brush: calligraphic, scatter, art and pattern.

fig.16 Creating a new brush shape.

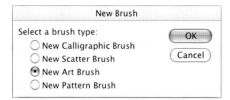

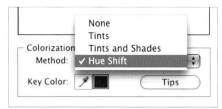

fig. 17 The Art Brush Options window.

scatter a graphic around the area of the drawn line. Art brushes draw a shape along the drawn line; while pattern brushes generate a pattern along the line (**fig. 15**).

Custom brush shapes can be created and saved in one of the library categories. For example, to save a drawn shape as an art brush, select it (**fig. 16**), click on the 'options' button in the brushes window and choose 'new brush'. Select 'new art brush' from the list, click 'OK' and the Art Brush Options window opens. This window can be re-opened at any time to adjust its settings by double-clicking on the brush icon that is added to the library each time a new brush shape is created. In the lower left of this window is the 'colorization' area. Click on the 'method' arrow and choose 'hue shift' from the list (**fig. 17**). Then, having drawn the line and selected this brush, it can be coloured using the stroke settings (see p. 65). Click 'OK', and the new brush is immediately added to the library.

Practise using the file 'creating new brushes.ai' on the CD.

Tip   A brushstroke, once used, immediately assigns itself as the new default stroke setting and applies itself to all subsequently drawn lines. To remove this (annoying) effect, the default can be cleared from an object by deleting it in the Appearance window ('Window > Appearance' or 'shift + F6'). The attributes of the selected object appear as a list (fig. 18). To clear the brushstroke, click on the stroke layer to highlight it and then on the 'trash' icon at the bottom right of the window.

Tip   In a complex drawing, it can be very difficult to select the correct object. To make it easier, toggle into 'Outline' mode – 'View > Outline' ('apple/control + Y') – in which only the vector paths (i.e. the object outlines) appear, as thin black lines. Fill or stroke colours are not visible. Objects can be selected, moved, and so on, in the usual ways. Toggle back to 'Preview' mode – 'View > Preview' ('apple/control + Y') – so the fill and stroke colours show. Watch the 'Outline and Preview' movie tutorial and practise using the 'Outline and Preview.ai' file on the CD.

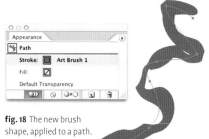

fig. 18 The new brush shape, applied to a path.

3   Working with Colour

Colours can be added to an object once it is drawn. Shapes and lines can be coloured in two basic ways: on the stroke (the outline) or the fill. As well as solid fills and strokes, blends (gradients) between two or more colours can be applied. To apply a gradient to text, see 'Creating and applying Graphic Styles', p. 66.

| Tip | Gradients can only be applied as fills in Illustrator, whereas in InDesign, they can also be used on strokes (and editable text). |

3.1 Solid fills

Near the foot of the Toolbox are two overlapping icons (**fig. 19**). One is a square, the other a frame. The square shows fill characteristics, while the frame shows the stroke setting. The Colour and Swatches windows ('Window > Colour', 'Window > Swatches') display the same icons.

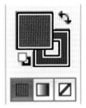

fig. 19 The 'fill' (foreground) and 'stroke' (background) icons.

Clicking on one of the icons moves it in front of the other icon in *all* the windows in which they are visible. Depending on which icon is to the fore, whatever colour is chosen becomes the fill or stroke setting for the next object(s) drawn or for any shapes that were selected at the time.

3.2 Colouring objects

Adding colour can be done in either the Swatches or Colour windows.

To use the Swatches window, select the object(s) and go to 'Window > Swatches' (**fig. 20**), which contains swatches for gradient, pattern and solid fills. To apply a solid colour as a fill, click on the 'fill' icon at the top of the window (or in the Toolbox) and click on the desired swatch. To colour a stroke, first click on the 'stroke' icon in either location.

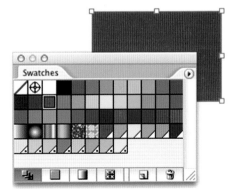

fig. 20 Colouring objects using the Swatches window.

Now select an object and go to 'Window > Colour' (**fig. 21**). Again, select either the 'fill' or 'stroke' icon and colour the object using one of three methods: moving the sliders in the window, changing the percentage values or by clicking in the rainbow bar at the foot of the window. To have no colour, click in the box with the red diagonal slash. To apply black or white, click on the relevant colour chip at the right-hand end of the rainbow bar.

To change the width of a stroke, select the object, go to 'Window > Stroke' and enter a width. 'Points' – a 72nd of an inch – are the units commonly used for strokes and type sizes. Image borders and ruled lines are often given a stroke value of 1pt and $\frac{1}{2}$ pt, respectively, but, of course, the decision is yours.

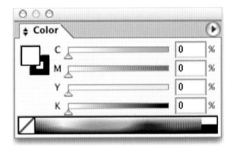

fig. 21 The Colour window.

3.3 Creating a new swatch

Any colour created using the Colour window can be added to the existing swatches library by clicking on the 'options' button in the Swatches window and then choosing 'new swatch' at the top of the list. The colour showing in the currently selected 'fill' or 'stroke' icon (whichever is overlapping the other) appears in the window. Gradients can be introduced to the swatches library in the same way.

3.4 Editing a swatch

Double-click on a swatch to produce a window in which you can edit the values shown. Unlike in InDesign, Illustrator does not update objects to which an edited colour swatch has already been applied, unless that object is selected at the time.

3.5 Gradient fills

Blends between two or more colours can be created in the Gradients window, and the technique is very similar in Photoshop, InDesign and Illustrator. Results can be saved as swatches or styles.

Ensure that the 'fill' icon overlaps the 'stroke' icon in the Toolbox, as gradients cannot be applied as strokes. To fill an object with a gradient, select it and go to 'Window > Gradient' (**fig. 22**).

Next, click on the bar at the foot of the Gradient window. If this is the first gradient to have been applied in the document, the bar displays as a linear gradient in greyscale colour, with white on the left and black on the right. Simultaneously, the object is filled with the same blend.

Click on the white paint pot, just under the bar at the left. Then, click on the 'options' button in the Colour window and select CMYK from the list. Adjust the sliders, and the colour at that end of the gradient updates. Alternatively, click in the rainbow bar to choose a colour. Repeat this using the black paint pot. More colours can be added by clicking beneath the gradient bar. New paint pots appear, displaying the current gradient colour, but this is changed by using the Colour window while the pot is selected.

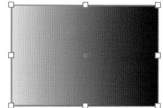
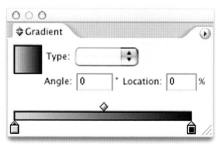

fig. 22 The Gradient window.

Tip	If you try to colour a paint pot by clicking on a colour in the Swatches window, the entire object will become filled with that colour. To only affect that paint pot, hold down the 'alt' key and then click on the swatch. The Swatches window can also be used to apply a previously saved gradient swatch.

Each time a gradient is edited, the selected object updates to display the edited settings.

'Linear' or 'radial' gradients can be picked at the top of the Gradient window. In the case of linear gradients, an angle for the display can be chosen.

Once a shape is filled with a gradient, it can be repainted using the Gradient Tool in the Toolbox (**fig. 23**). Select the shape, click on the tool and click and drag on the page. The gradient is repainted over the area between the start and end points of the dragging movement.

fig. 23 The Gradient Tool.

3.6 Creating and applying Graphic Styles

Gradients, and other appearances, can be saved as Graphic Styles (known simply as 'Styles' in pre-CS versions). Then, a gradient can be applied to such objects as editable text, which otherwise have to be converted into a non-text format. To do this, fill a drawn shape with a gradient, as already described, and drag it into the Graphic Styles window, thus adding it as a new style library item. To apply it to type, highlight the text and click on the style. It can be applied to any selected object in the same way.

3.7 Applying transparency

For a designer, the ability to apply transparency to objects is, quite simply, a wonderful thing.

Go to 'Window > Transparency' ('shift + F10'), select an object and click and drag the opacity slider to a percentage value (**fig. 24**). Transparency can be applied to anything that can be placed on an Illustrator artboard, even imported bitmaps.

The 'knockout group' option in the Transparency window (click on 'show options' if it is not visible) allows a group of objects, all of which have some degree of transparency applied to them, to act as transparent to adjacent objects while not displaying all the various overlaps created between themselves.

In a graphic made up of several partially transparent objects, some appear to be more covered up than others that are nearer to the top of the hierarchy. Choose a blending mode (see the drop-down list in the top-left corner of the Transparency window), such as 'soft light', to make them appear as if they overlap to the same degree. This changes the object characteristics, especially the way in which they overlay other objects, and enables them to blend with each other in terms of their transparency.

Using the Appearance window, the transparency of just the fill or just the stroke of an object can be altered.

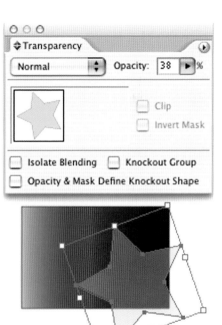

fig. 24 Applying transparency to objects.

4

The Toolbox, Part II

Tip   **For all these tools, select an object and double-click on the tool button to open a dialogue window that allows you to change the tool's current settings.**

4.1 The Rotate Tool

Select an object and then click on this tool. A 'rotation point,' around which the object rotates, appears at the centre of the selected object. To reposition this point, click anywhere on the screen or drag the point with the cursor. Now, click and drag anywhere on the screen. The further away the dragging motion is from the point of rotation, the more controlled the rotation.

If you hold down the 'shift' key, an object is constrained to 45° movements. To create and rotate a copy around the same point, press and hold down the 'alt' key after beginning to drag the original.

4.2 The Reflect Tool

On the same flyout as the Rotate Tool, this tool is used to create a mirror image of the original object by either flipping the original shape or by creating a duplicate.

There are two ways to use this tool:

1) To create a vertical or horizontal reflection of an object, first select the object and then double-click on the tool button. Enter the desired settings and check the 'preview' button to see what the results would be.

2) To create a reflected copy of an object, select the object, double-click on the tool button, click 'copy' and then click 'OK'. Next, click on two points to define the line across which the object's copy is to be reflected.

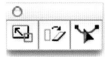

4.3 The Scale Tool

This works in almost the same way as the Scale Tool in InDesign (see p. 105). Select an object, then the Scale Tool. A 'point of scale' icon appears in the object's centre. As with the Rotate Tool, either drag it to a new position or click to reposition it; usually it is most useful to place it on a corner of the object to be scaled. Imagine a diagonal line drawn from that corner and out of the opposite corner. Place the cursor somewhere on that line, beyond the object, and click and drag. To keep the operation proportional, hold down the 'shift' key while dragging.

4.4 The Free Transform Tool

Given that most of this tool's features (such as rotation and resize) are possible with other tools, the Free Transform Tool is not very useful. However, it can make perspective adjustments.

Select a shape, such as a rectangle, and then choose the Free Transform Tool. Click and drag on a corner handle and, while dragging, hold down 'apple/control + alt + shift'.

4.5 The Warp Tool flyout

The Warp Tool flyout holds several tools for reshaping objects. These are sometimes, but by no means always, useful, so only a brief description of them follows. For all these tools, assume that there is already a selected object on the artboard.

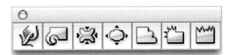

Also, in much the same category as the Warp tools is the Twist Tool, which is actually on the Rotate Tool flyout, but which is much closer to the Warp tools in terms of operation, so is discussed here.

Twist
With this tool an object's shape can be changed by clicking and dragging on it, distorting it into a symmetrical spiral (the tool was dropped in CS2).

Warp
Warp is an adjustable tool (double-click on it to see the Properties window), which distorts an object by making the cursor act as if were a magnet. The size of the brush assigned to the cursor is changed by holding down the 'alt' key and clicking and dragging. To constrain the shape to circular, also hold down the 'shift' key. Brush sizes are changed in this way for all similar tools that use a brush.

Twirl
Another adjustable tool, Twirl pulls objects into spirals. The size of the resulting spiral is determined by the size of the brush assigned to the cursor.

Pucker
Acting as a magnet on the outline(s) of an object, the adjustable Pucker Tool shrinks areas. By carefully moving the cursor around it is possible to snag an outline at several different points.

Bloat
This tool bloats outlines until, eventually, they match the circumference of the brush size assigned to the cursor. This can be done inside or outside an object.

Scallop
Random, smooth and arc-shaped details are added to the outline of an object with this tool.

Crystallize
With this tool, random spiked details appear on the outline of an object.

Wrinkle
Both random arc- and spike-shaped details are applied to the outline of an object with the Wrinkle Tool.

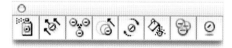

4.6 The Symbol Sprayer Tool

Objects in the Symbols window Library are used by the Symbol tools. To create new symbols, draw something – it can be one object or multiple objects – shade it (even with gradients) and then select it. Click the 'options' button in the Symbols window and choose 'new symbol' from the list. Name the symbol and click 'OK' to add it to the library.

The tools on the flyout allow the following operations on sprayed symbol objects: spray, move, scrunch (pull towards the cursor), resize (to increase size, click and drag; to decrease, 'alt-click' and drag), spin, stain (a solid fill colour must be chosen first), screen (apply transparency) and style (combine the original appearance with the chosen style). The closer the symbols are to the cursor, the more they are affected.

4.7 The Mesh Tool

Draw a shape, fill it with a solid colour and click inside it with the Mesh Tool. A grid of interlocking lines is created with each click of the mouse button. At the intersections of these lines are editing points, which can be selected using the Direct Selection Tool in exactly the same ways as anchor points along paths. When selected, the area around them can be coloured using the Swatches or Colour windows. Each editing point has Bézier handles, which can be adjusted, and the points themselves can be dragged to new positions; these movements influence the shading of any added colour (**fig. 25**). Click within the areas enclosed by the interlocking lines, and that sector of the shape can be dragged to a new position. On the CD, watch the 'Mesh Tool' movie for a tutorial and open the 'Mesh Tool.ai' file to practise.

Using the Pen Tool, anchor points – which will be square and not round – can be added or deleted along the mesh lines.

While this is a useful tool, a better mesh is produced by drawing the object and then going to 'Object > Create Gradient Mesh'.

A mesh can even be applied to an object filled with a gradient: select the object, choose 'Object > Expand' and check 'gradient mesh'. The resulting mesh will be based on the original gradient.

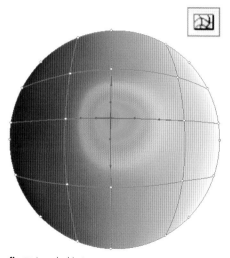

fig. 25 A mesh object showing the mesh grid.

Tip	Mesh objects cannot be created from compound paths, text objects or linked EPS files. If a mesh is applied to an imported image, the image vanishes. A mesh object cannot be converted back to a path object.

4.8 The Blend Tool

Draw three different shapes and fill each with a different colour. Experiment with the following methods:

1) Select all three objects and choose 'Object > Blend > Make'. Using the menu commands in this way creates a blend between objects according to the order in which they were drawn. Depending upon the settings, a smooth or multi-step blend is created, combining both the shape and the colour (**fig. 26**).

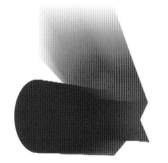

fig. 26 A blend object.

2) Undo the above operation using 'apple/control + Z'. Click on the Blend Tool in the Toolbox, then click on each object in turn. This time, the blend follows the order in which the objects were clicked on.

3) Again, undo the operation. Select all three objects with the Selection Tool and choose the Blend Tool. (It is not actually necessary to select the objects first, but doing so makes the anchor points visible.) Click on an anchor point on the left side of object one, then a point on the right side of object two, and, finally, one on the left side of object three. The resulting blend also causes the transformation to twist (**fig. 27**).

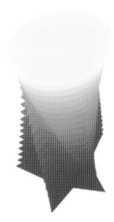

fig. 27 A twisted blend object.

While a blend group is selected, the nature of the blend can be adjusted by double-clicking on the Blend Tool. Aside from a smooth blend, there are blends of 'specified steps' and 'specified distance'. There are also two orientation choices. Use the 'preview' button to see the effect as you change the settings.

To break apart a blend group, go to 'Object > Blend > Blend Options' and click 'expand'. This results in a simple group of objects. The hierarchy of the overlap between the objects can be reversed in the same window, using 'reverse front to back'.

Practise using the 'blends.ai' file on the CD.

4.9 The Eyedropper/Paint Bucket tools

In pre-CS versions, the Eyedropper Tool picked up the attributes of an object and the Paint Bucket Tool transferred them to other objects. In CS+ versions, the Paint Bucket has gone. Instead, select the object(s) to be changed and click on the source object with the Eyedropper. If you select multiple objects and then click on one of them with the Eyedropper Tool, all take on the attributes of the object on which you click. Double-click on the Eyedropper to view an editable list of the attributes it can pick up.

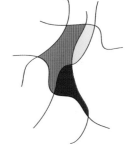

4.10 The Live Paint Bucket and Live Paint Selection tools (CS2 only)

Draw a series of interlocking lines, select them, and click on them with the Live Paint Bucket Tool to create a Paint Bucket group. Then, click in the spaces to fill them with the current fill colour.

Stroke or fill elements in a Live Paint group can be re-coloured using the Live Paint Selection Tool: click to select line segments and fill areas, and then click on a colour swatch (**fig. 28**).

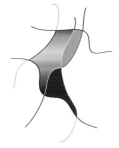

fig. 28 A paint bucket group, coloured with (above) the Live Paint Bucket and (below) the Live Paint Selection tools.

4.11 The Scissors and Knife tools

An object can be cut into sections using the Knife Tool. Select an object, then the Knife Tool. Beginning outside the object's outline, draw a line through the object and out the other side (you can see the path as you drag). The result is two separate objects. To cut in a straight line, hold down the 'alt' key before you begin cutting.

The Scissors Tool allows you to cut a path into sections by clicking with the mouse.

5   Working with Images

Most common image formats (including TIFF and JPEG) can be opened or placed in Illustrator. If you choose 'File > Open', Illustrator creates a new document to hold the image; if you choose 'File > Place', it imports the image into the current document. Either way, images can be resized and rotated using the Selection Tool and adjusted in many ways with filters and effects. It is also possible to pick up colours from bitmap images using the Eyedropper Tool.

Images cannot be reshaped with the Direct Selection Tool, which can only move them around. To create a shaped bitmap, see 'Masks' on p. 74.

Tip	**Many filters and effects (see p. 74) only work if the document has been created in RGB rather than CMYK mode, regardless of the colour mode of the image. If most of the filters appear greyed-out (i.e. unavailable), choose 'File > Document Colour Mode' to change the document to RGB. Filters cannot be applied to 'linked' images, only to those that have been embedded in the document. So, don't forget to uncheck the 'link' box in the Place window when importing the image.**

6   More Techniques

6.1 Arranging and grouping objects

Each successive shape or line that is drawn appears on top of previously drawn objects, creating a hierarchy. To bring an object to the front, choose 'Object > Arrange > Bring to Front' ('apple/control + shift +]'). In the same location is the 'Send to Back' command. Two others also appear here: 'Bring Forward' and 'Send Backward', which relate to the entire hierarchy of objects on the artboard, so choosing one of these may not achieve the desired result if the objects concerned are too far apart within the hierarchy. However, 'Bring to Front' and 'Send to Back' always work, and it is only necessary to understand these two to create the required hierarchy.

When more than one object is selected, they can be grouped using 'Object > Group' ('apple/control + G'). As a group, they can be moved and resized together without losing their relative positions to one another. To ungroup, choose 'Object > Ungroup' ('apple/control + shift + G').

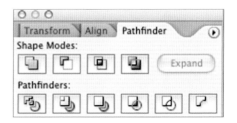

fig. 29 The Pathfinder window.

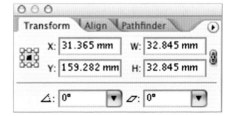

fig. 30 Using the Pathfinder window to merge objects.

6.2 The Pathfinder window

It is easy to create a single, complex shape from several simple shapes by using the Pathfinder window (**fig. 29**), which also offers many other shape-interaction options.

Draw two or more shapes and position them to overlap. Select them and choose 'merge' from the Pathfinder window: all overlapping sections of the outlines vanish, leaving a single outline (**fig. 30**). This is different from the 'add' option, which leaves the original shapes intact, as can be seen by toggling into 'outline' mode ('apple/control + Y').

On the CD, watch the 'Pathfinder' movie for a tutorial and open the 'Pathfinder.ai' file to practise.

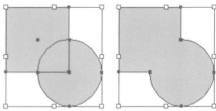

fig. 31 The Transform window.

6.3 Repeating an action

The 'transform again' command ('apple/control + D') repeats the previous action and can be applied to the original object or a duplicate. For example, draw a long, narrow rectangle, copy it and then paste it using 'paste in front' ('apple/control + F'). Rotate the copy manually or by a specific increment using the rotation controls in the Transform window (**fig. 31**).

'Paste in front' again, then use the 'transform again' command to rotate it. Each time you use the command, the object is rotated an additional increment. By repeatedly using the 'paste in front' command, followed by as many 'transform again' commands as are required to drop the copy into the next position, it is possible to create an entire circle of rotated shapes.

Unfortunately, Illustrator does not remember a specific point of rotation, so it always defaults to the centre of the object. However, if the object is grouped with another that has no outline or fill characteristics, a centre of rotation can be created that lies between them, around which the pair of objects then rotates. This, together with the Transparency window, allows the creation of some beautiful objects (**fig. 32**).

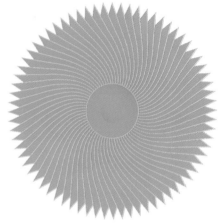

fig. 32 Two objects created using rotate and repeat actions.

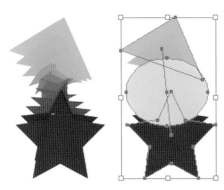

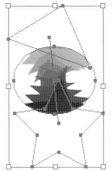

fig. 33 Using mask objects.

6.4 Filters and effects

While the lists under each of these look remarkably similar, they are in fact quite different.

Filters change the structure of objects to which they are applied and can only be applied to imported bitmap images. They can only revert to their original appearance if the command is still available in the 'undo' list.

Effects change the appearance of objects, not the structure itself. This means that the command can be removed at any time in the Appearance window (see tip on p. 64). Effects can be applied to imported bitmap images and to vector art. Some of the more useful effects are: 'Stylize > Add Arrowheads' (for drawn lines), 'Stylize > Drop Shadow' and 'Blur > Gaussian Blur'. All of these are editable.

6.5 Masks

Any shape can be used to create a clipping mask, which defines the visibility of the object(s) beneath it.

Draw a variety of shapes and fill them with different colours. Then, draw a smaller shape on top of them. Select them all and go to 'Object > Clipping Mask > Make'. The top object becomes a window through which only those parts of the other objects that are within its boundaries can be seen (**fig. 33**). This method can be applied to imported bitmaps, allowing them to be defined within a specific shape.

Practise using the file 'using masks.ai' on the CD.

6.6 Layers

It is usually possible to manage all the objects on an Illustrator artboard using 'Object > Arrange > Send to Back' or 'Bring to Front', but it may prove practical to separate objects into layers in a more complex drawing.

Go to 'Window > Layers' (**fig. 34**). Each document has a default background layer. To create a new layer, either click on the 'new layer' icon at the foot of the window, or click on the 'options' button and choose 'new layer' from the top of the list. Each layer is colour-coded and, whenever an object on a layer is selected, the selection frame displays in that colour. Also, a small square of the same colour appears on the right of the layer; it can be dragged onto another layer, thereby moving the object. As in Photoshop, to turn a layer off visually, click on the 'eye' icon on the left.

More than one layer can be selected (using either 'shift-click' or 'apple/control + click') and merged using 'merge selected' under the 'options' button.

Layers can be flattened, i.e. merged into a single layer, through the 'options' list. However, generally, it is not necessary to do this because whatever objects are visible on the page when it is saved in EPS format, or exported as a TIFF or JPEG, are also included in the resulting image.

Layers can be dragged to new hierarchical positions in the Layers window, thus changing the relative front to back order of the objects on the artboard.

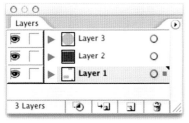

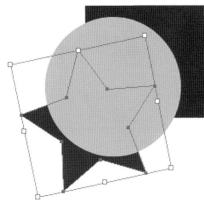

fig. 34 The Layers window and layered objects.

7   Saving Illustrator Files

Illustrator documents should be saved in native Adobe Illustrator format, which allows them to be re-opened and edited further. If the objects created in an Illustrator document are intended for inclusion in a page layout, it is best either to save the results as an EPS file or to export them in TIFF (or, possibly, JPEG) format. Illustrator objects can be copied and pasted into an InDesign page layout. However, this means that these objects have not been saved as separate image files, and are embedded rather than being linked, which may be a disadvantage later on.

If an Encapsulated PostScript (EPS) file (a proprietary Adobe format) is made up of purely vector information, its main advantage over other formats is that it is infinitely scaleable. Free from the constraints of a pre-determined resolution, an EPS file can be used at whatever size is needed. But, vector-edged objects sometimes look like they have been cut out and pasted on, so an EPS format may not always be the best option. EPS files can be imported into almost any page-layout format, whereas some software cannot import native Illustrator format. If imported successfully, both EPS and Illustrator formats have transparent backgrounds, very useful attributes for objects that have any shape other than rectangular (page shape), as it allows them to be placed over existing colour backgrounds.

TIFF and JPEG are bitmap formats. Therefore, they have a fixed resolution that cannot be scaled up very much without bringing serious consequences. The golden rule is: to whatever degree you can see the pixels, you stop seeing the image.

Both TIFF and JPEG formats are normally opaque rectangular (or square) objects, and this can make them unsuitable for placing on an existing background colour. However, since v.7 of Photoshop, TIFF files can be saved with a transparent background (see options under the Help Menu).

TIFF is (ideally) an uncompressed format, whereas JPEG is not only compressed but also looses some of the data. There *are* compression utilities for TIFFs (notably LZW), but very occasionally this leads to a corrupted file or unexpected results when printing.

For images that are quick and easy to work with during the design process, use low-resolution RGB TIFF versions of Illustrator objects, to be replaced with high-resolution CMYK TIFF files prior to sending the work to the printer (see p. 104 in the InDesign chapter). Alternatively, use EPS files, which tend to have small file sizes and are, therefore, quick to work with even at the design stage. It is recommended, however, that you try printing an EPS file on a PostScript printer (which translates PostScript information into a visible image) as soon as you place it in a page layout. If it prints for you, it will print for someone else. Unfortunately, the converse is also true, and waiting until the last minute to run a proof laser print may result in a missed deadline.

Chapter 3

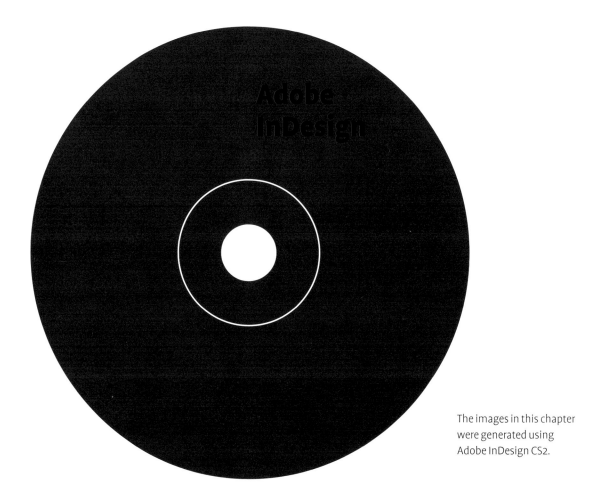

The images in this chapter were generated using Adobe InDesign CS2.

InDesign, Adobe's primary page-layout program, is an incredibly versatile and capable piece of software. In the US it has already picked up a healthy share of the page-layout software market, and, while things seem to be evolving slower in Europe, there is no doubt that it is quickly gaining popularity.

InDesign offers some drawing capabilities that cannot be found even in Illustrator, let alone other page-layout programs; for example, it is possible to add a gradient to an outline. It is also easy to create and apply a gradient to text as a fill, which, in Illustrator, first requires the user to save the gradient as a style. Furthermore, transparency, to an exact percentage, can be applied to any object placed on a page. These properties have clear benefits for graphic designers.

Even though InDesign's drawing abilities are better than most software, it is first and foremost a page-layout program. If you want to edit images, you need Photoshop; to draw creatively, Illustrator is required; to produce web pages, Dreamweaver is essential. But, when you have finished drawing and photo editing, InDesign is an extremely sophisticated assembly point for the images and text, whether for books, magazines, CD/DVD covers, newsletters or anything else that requires a printable page.

Aside from offering options not found in other software, InDesign has the distinct advantage of having been created by the same people who gave us Acrobat, and thus the ease with which it can produce PDF documents is second to none. This is particularly relevant given the current trend in commercial printing to request PDF documents rather than work in native file formats.

1   The InDesign Environment

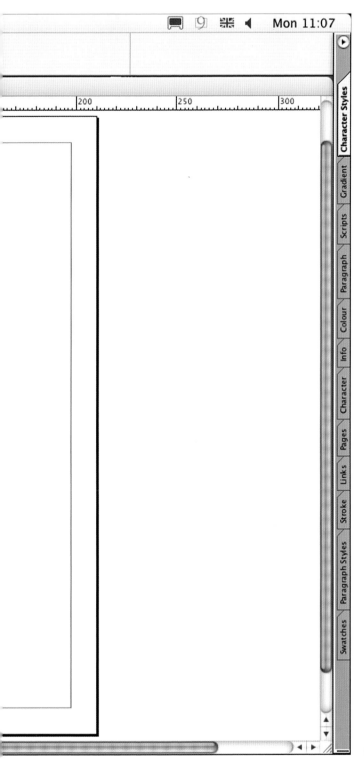

fig. 1 The InDesign screen.

1.1 The InDesign screen

As this program was intended to compete with the industry-standard software existing at the time of its creation, namely QuarkXPress, InDesign is visually quite similar to Quark (**fig. 1**, previous page). Many of the floating windows are almost identical to Quark's in appearance and purpose, and many of the on-screen features are found in all main graphics software. For example, along the top of the screen are the menus, beginning with 'File' on the left and ending with 'Help' on the right. There is a floating Toolbox, which can be grabbed by the shaded bar at its top and dragged to another position, and at the junction of the horizontal and vertical rulers (in the document window) is a repositionable 'zero point'. See the 'Zero Point' movie on the CD.

Below the menus are the rulers – one along the top of the screen and one down the left side – which can be toggled on and off using the View Menu ('View > Show [or Hide] Rulers') ('apple/control + R'). The ruler units can be chosen in the Preferences window, which is opened by choosing (Mac) 'InDesign > Preferences > Units and Increments' or (PC) 'Edit > Preferences > Units and Increments'.

Regardless of which tool is active, temporary guides can be pulled from the rulers and onto the page to act as alignment aids. They can be repositioned with either of the selection tools. To delete them, click on them with either selection tool and press the backspace key.

In the lower-left corner is a percentage window, into which a value for the degree of zoom can be typed, or it can be selected from the drop-down list. Immediately to the right is a window showing the current page number. Clicking on the arrow at the right of this window opens a list along which you can scroll to the document or master page you require. Master pages are discussed in more detail on p. 101.

At the foot of the screen on the right are the scroll bars. In CS versions, the floating window tabs are positioned down the right edge of the screen, outside the scroll bar area.

1.2 Creating a new document

Choose 'File > New' ('apple/control + N') and the New Document window opens (**fig. 2**).

At the top is the 'document preset' area, where you can select a saved set-up (only available in CS+ versions).

The number of pages in the document can be specified here, but it is also easy to add or delete pages later.

To create a facing-page document, check the 'facing pages' box, thereby making the default master page and the layout of the document based on two-page spreads, just as if it were a book or magazine. Exceptions to this layout are the first and last pages, which in a regular publication are stand-alone left- and right-hand pages, respectively.

Unlike Quark, in which all master-page elements can be edited on the document pages, InDesign only allows them to be edited on the master pages themselves or via specific instructions from within the

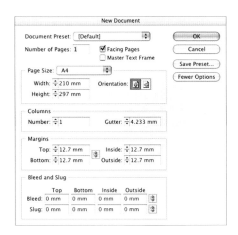

fig. 2 The New Document window.

document. For this reason, I usually leave the 'master text frame' box unchecked (see p. 101).

The page size is chosen either from the list or by entering a width and height for a custom size. Orientation can also be specified.

To create guides to divide the page area, which is designated by the margins, into equal columns, go to the 'columns' section. A gutter is the space between columns.

Margins are guides placed within the page area at a set distance from the edges, and can be specified in this window. If you are working on a facing-pages document, the margins read as 'top, bottom, inside and outside', the last two referring to the binding and outside edges of a multi-page document. Otherwise, they read as 'top, bottom, left and right', as there is no binding edge on a single-page document.

The 'bleed' and 'slug' specifications only feature in CS versions of InDesign and are accessed by clicking on the 'more options' button on the right.

If the document's pages contain images or other elements that need to bleed off the page (i.e. the trim to the final page size will cut into the images so that they run right to the edge), a 3mm additional image dimension should be allowed on that edge of the page. Printers do not actually need that much extra, but it is the convention. Also, printing machines are certainly capable of much better registration accuracy than 3mm, but subsequent operations – folding, collating, binding and trimming – may be less precise. Entering a value of 3mm in each of the bleed windows produces an additional set of guides that distance away from the page edges, against which bleed elements should be positioned. PDF documents created in InDesign can be instructed to include the additional bleed dimension specified.

The slug creates additional space on one or more sides of the page (usually only at the foot) into which information can be placed that needs to be communicated to the printer.

To save the settings so that they can be used again, click on the 'save preset' button (only available in CS+ versions).

Finally, click 'OK' and the first document page appears.

1.3 Zoom and scroll techniques

This section will seem somewhat repetitive for those readers who are also investigating Photoshop and Illustrator, as the keyboard shortcuts are very similar in all three. Of course, this is deliberate: Adobe want us to feel completely at home, regardless of which member of the CS suite we happen to be using. In the future, perhaps, all the programs comprising this formidable set will be merged into one huge graphics application. Should this happen, many of us would feel little inclination to spend our working hours elsewhere.

To zoom in, hold down 'apple/control + spacebar' with one hand, and click and drag with the mouse to indicate the area to zoom to. Release the mouse button and that area becomes the new view.

An alternative method is to press 'apple/control' and the '+' key. This zooms in, in increments, up to an astounding (but rarely useful) 4000% view. If an object is selected when you do this, it becomes the central element in each successive view.

To zoom out, press 'apple/control' and either the '-' key to zoom back out in increments, or the zero key to go straight back out to a full-page view.

To scroll the page, hold down the spacebar and click and drag with the mouse. This will not work when the Text Tool is selected; in that case hold down the 'alt' key instead of the spacebar. Be aware of this at all times, because holding down the spacebar while actively working in text has fairly obvious results, whereas holding down the 'alt' key and dragging with either of the selection tools selected creates a copy of that object.

The only alternatives to the above scrolling methods are to click on the grabber hand icon in the Toolbox or to use the scroll bars at the foot and to the right of the screen, both of which should be considered as time-wasting last resorts.

1.4 InDesign CS vs previous versions

The leap from InDesign v.2 to CS1 introduced some very useful changes to the basic screen.

The Control Bar

This is similar to the Measurements window in Quark and the Control Bar in PageMaker. It is positioned beneath the menus across the top of the screen, and the options displayed in it change to reflect the object or tool currently selected. For instance, if you are working with text, it is a useful place to add italic or bold highlights to text already formatted with a paragraph style (see p. 93). Also, if you are creating text or picture frames, you can resize them here or move them to exact X and Y co-ordinates.

Docking windows

Down the right side of the screen is an area in which the floating windows can be docked in pull-out frames. The windows' name tabs remain visible and they can be opened by clicking on them. Alternatively, drag the name tab out of the docking area and onto the screen, where it behaves exactly like the floating windows in InDesign v.2.

Most of the windows listed under the Window Menu can be dragged, by their name tabs, into any part of the docking area.

Users of CS1 will find that the text wrap function is now listed with other text-related windows under the 'Window > Type and Tables > Text Wrap'. Those using CS2 will find that it has been returned to the v.2 position, in the Window Menu.

1.5 Basic working methods

It will be useful to look at these common working methods before going further, as they are needed almost all the time.

Selecting objects

As in Illustrator and QuarkXPress, objects can be selected in two ways using the Selection Tool. First, you can click and drag to create a bounding box around them (**fig. 3**). Any object touched by this box becomes selected when the mouse button is released. Second, you can 'shift-click' on objects to select and deselect them. This method works with anything on the page.

If an object is selected and dragged on quickly, only the outline of the frame, or shape, is visible as it is moved around. If you click and hold on the object for a couple of seconds, a 'live' preview of the actual object, complete with its contents, becomes visible as you drag it. If a text wrap is involved, everything updates as it is moved. This can be very useful because it takes the guesswork out of the result. For more information, see 'The Selection tools' on p. 85.

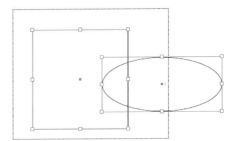

fig. 3 Selecting multiple objects.

Grouping and locking items

When several items need to be moved together while retaining their relative position to each other, it is advisable to group them. To do this, select all the objects involved and choose 'Object > Group' ('apple/control + G'). As a group, they all move together when dragged. To ungroup, select them and choose 'Object > Ungroup' ('apple/control + shift + G').

Items can also be locked into position to protect them from being moved. To do this, select them and go to 'Object > Lock Position' ('apple/control + L'). They are unlocked by selecting them again and choosing 'Object > Unlock Position' ('apple/control + alt + L')

Arranging objects

Each object drawn or placed on a page appears in front of all other objects. To place an object behind or in front of everything else, select it and choose either 'Object > Arrange > Bring to Front' ('apple/ control + shift +]') or 'Object > Arrange > Send to Back' ('apple/control + shift + ['). The other commands, 'bring forward' and 'send backward', move the selection through one layer of the existing hierarchy.

For examples of arranging, grouping and locking, see the 'Arrange, Group and Lock' movie on the CD.

Using Quark shortcuts

When converting from QuarkXPress to InDesign, you may wish to continue using the Quark shortcuts you already know. While I would advise against this (and if you are not concerned about the possible ramifications, i.e. being unable to use your shortcuts on another machine), you can set them in place by going to 'Edit > Keyboard Shortcuts'. In the top-left corner, choose 'shortcuts for QuarkXPress' and click 'OK'. In the same window you can create your own custom shortcuts or edit existing ones for almost any InDesign operation.

Converting PageMaker or QuarkXPress documents

Some Quark and PageMaker documents, depending on the versions used to create the files, can be opened by InDesign. InDesign versions up to CS2 can open Quark documents created in versions 3.3 to 4.1 and PageMaker documents from versions 6.5 and 7.

To do this, choose 'File > Open', browse to the folder and, in the 'files of type' box, choose either Quark or PageMaker. Press 'open'. There may be minor changes, due, for instance, to the different ways in which Quark and InDesign handle things like master-page items, but generally there is little difference.

Undo

InDesign, like later versions of Quark, has a multiple undo feature, which makes it much easier to deal with mistakes that are not caught immediately. To use it, choose 'Edit > Undo' ('apple/control + Z'). Each time you do this, the previous operation is reversed. 'Redo' in the same way, using 'apple/control + shift + Z'. The number of undo operations possible is only determined by the RAM on your system – on most systems it can run into the hundreds.

Saving InDesign files

InDesign files can be saved in document or template format. For either, choose 'File > Save' and then select either document or template from the 'save as type' list.

Documents can be opened and edited; templates, however, cannot be opened. What opens instead is an unnamed copy, which can be edited and saved as a document, or, to update the original template, saved in template format under the same name as the original (thereby replacing it).

2   The InDesign Toolbox

2.1 The Selection tools

The Selection Tool
Used to move and resize objects, this tool cannot edit an object's shape. To select multiple items, hold the 'shift' key and click to select (or deselect). Drag on a frame handle to resize it. To constrain proportions, hold the 'shift' key and drag a corner handle. Hover the cursor just outside a corner of the selection frame to see a curved, double-headed arrow. This is the rotate cursor, and when visible the object(s) can be rotated.

The Direct Selection Tool
To edit the shape of an object, select it with this tool and 'anchor points' appear on its outline. Click and drag on these to change the object's shape. 'Shift-click' to select or deselect additional points, or click and drag to create a bounding box around the points. This tool can also reposition images in a frame (see 'Cropping images', p. 106).
See 'The Selection Tools' movie on the CD for examples.

2.2 The Drawing tools

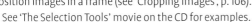

Tip	For many of these tools, double-clicking on the tool button opens a dialogue window that allows the default settings to be changed.

The Pen Tool
A Bézier tool, the Pen tool is used in exactly the same ways in InDesign as it is in Adobe Illustrator. It and the other tools on its flyout are used for drawing and editing lines and enclosed shapes (see p. 58).

fig. 4 The Toolbox.

The Pencil Tool
Again, this tool is exactly the same as in Illustrator (see p. 63).

The Line Tool
To draw a straight line, click and drag with this tool. To draw vertical, horizontal and 45° lines, hold down 'shift' while dragging. Weight and colour can be added using the Stroke, Colour and Swatches windows (see 'Working with Colour', p. 87).

The Type Tool
For details on the Type Tool, see 'Working with Text', p. 92.

The Shape tools
Side by side in the Toolbox, the two shape tools are essentially identical in function. If you click with the Type Tool in a shape drawn with either one, a cursor immediately appears. Alternatively, choose 'File > Place' and browse to, and import, an image. To draw a rectangular frame, select either rectangle tool and click and drag on the page. To constrain the shape to a square, hold down 'shift' as you drag.

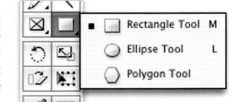

On the flyout menu are the Ellipse Tool, which draws ellipses (or circles if 'shift' is held down), and the Polygon Tool, which draws multi-sided symmetrical shapes. To determine the number of sides, double-click on the Polygon Tool and enter a number. You can also set a 'star inset' percentage, which pulls alternate anchor points in towards the centre of the object.

Tip   **When one of the shape tools is selected, clicking on the screen opens a window showing its current settings, which can then be adjusted. Click 'OK' and the shape is then drawn at that point on the screen.**

2.3 The Transforming tools

All these – rotate, scale, shear and transform – work in the same ways as in Illustrator (see p. 68).

2.4 Other tools

The Eyedropper and Measure tools

Used to pick up the characteristics of one object and apply them to another, this tool is not quite the same as in Illustrator. Here, when an object is clicked on, its appearance changes to indicate that it has soaked up the information, which can then be applied to any number of objects by simply clicking on them. For type, click and drag. Double-click on the tool to see (and edit) the range of characteristics it can pick up.

On the same flyout is the Measure Tool. Click and drag to find the distance between two points on the page.

The Gradient Tool

This is used in exactly the same ways as in Illustrator (see p. 66).

The Hand and Zoom tools

These are really not needed as there are such excellent keyboard shortcuts available. If you have not learned these yet, please do so – if you develop a habit of using the Toolbox tools, it will be hard to break.

The Fill and Stroke icons

These sit towards the foot of the Toolbox (see 'Working with colour' on p. 87). Below these are the Formatting Affects Container and Formatting Affects Object icons. Apply Solid Colour, Apply Gradient and Apply None buttons change the characteristics of the selected object.

fig. 5 The Fill and Stroke icons (right) and Preview and Normal View modes (below).

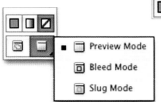

Preview and Normal View modes

At the foot of the Toolbox are two icons: on the left, Normal View Mode; on the right, Preview Mode. Preview visually switches off all guides and frame edges (unless something is selected) and colours the background area, outside the pages, a light grey. This is a valuable feature, as it gives a very clear idea of how the page will look when it is printed.

3   Working with Colour

3.1 Creating a new colour swatch

Creating, editing and applying colour swatches is a little easier than creating, editing and applying paragraph and character styles, so it should be covered first. Select one of the rectangle shape tools in the Toolbox and then click and drag on the screen. The default colour settings are no fill and a 1pt black stroke. To see the available colours, choose 'Window > Swatches' (**fig. 6**).

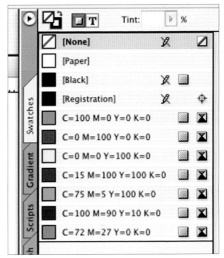

fig. 6 The Swatches window.

The Swatches window contains a list of preset colours and, in the top-left corner, two overlapping icons: the solid square represents fill characteristics and the frame represents the stroke or outline. A red diagonal slash through the Fill icon and the list item 'none' indicates that the selected object – the rectangle – has no colour fill. A black frame shows that it has a black stroke, but it is not possible to tell how thick that stroke is here – for that you would need to check the Stroke window.

To fill the rectangle with a colour, the Fill icon has to be above the Stroke icon. Whichever of the colours is clicked on fills the shape. To fill an object with a percentage tint of a colour, either type a number into the 'tint' percentage window or click on the arrow and use the slider.

To make the stroke a different colour, click on the Stroke icon, so that it overlaps the Fill icon, and pick a colour from the list. Again, a tint percentage can be specified instead of a solid colour.

Both the Fill and Stroke icons are also found near the foot of the Toolbox, where they serve exactly the same purposes.

If you are colouring text rather than a drawn shape, a letter 'T' appears in the Fill icon as a reminder.

Now, let us have a closer look at the other default colours in the list. On the left of each listing is a colour swatch, followed by (in most cases) a CMYK specification rather than a name. There is also a grey box and a coloured square diagonally divided into four segments.

Three of the default colours have next to them what looks like a pencil with a small red line through it, meaning that these colours cannot be edited.

The colour swatch on the left is a visual representation of the colour. The CMYK tint specification is more precise than a name, such as 'light green', and confirms that the colour is, in fact, CMYK format and not RGB. The grey box indicates that the colour has not been designated as a spot colour, which is a special colour mix that is applied with a separate plate in the print run and is not made up of CMYK components. A 'process' colour (i.e. *not* a spot colour) is composed of combinations of cyan, magenta, yellow and black elements that are each printed on four separate plates. If you accidentally create a spot colour and it goes unnoticed, you might receive an extremely surprising bill from the print shop, as the job will have involved printing with a *fifth* plate. If a colour *has* been designated as a spot colour, the grey box becomes a white box containing a small grey circle. The diagonally divided colour square on the right is also an indication that the colour is CMYK format.

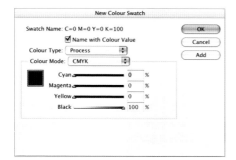

fig. 7 Creating a new colour
swatch.

To create a new colour, click on the 'options' button (the small triangle in a circle at the top of the window) and choose 'new colour swatch' from the list (**fig. 7**).

Use the sliders or type in percentages to create the new colour. By now, you will have noticed that InDesign falls over itself to confirm wherever it can that colours are not RGB. The default setting for all new colours is CMYK, because InDesign was created primarily for producing documents to be printed in commercial print shops, where RGB colours have no place. The RGB colours are represented in the default swatches list, but appear in CMYK format. You can specify RGB if you really want it.

The default setting for new colours is 'process' (not spot), indicating that the colour components will be absorbed into the appropriate part of the four-colour separation information that is sent to the printer.

On the 'colour mode' list you will find RGB (genuine, though useless) and other formats that are useful in a print shop, for example 'Pantone solid coated'. These colours *are* custom mixes and *are* intended to print on a separate plate, hence their spot-colour designation.

Many corporate entities use a Pantone colour for their logos and identity, but want to print them in CMYK because it is much more cost-effective. In fact, only a fairly small percentage of the Pantone range can be duplicated exactly using CMYK colours. However, many of the other colours only change slightly when converted, certainly not enough to warrant the additional expense of a fifth colour. To convert a Pantone to the closest possible CMYK match, choose 'Pantone Solid Colour' from the 'colour mode' list; enter the specific Pantone ink number in the window and then re-select CMYK as the colour mode. The swatch is still named with the Pantone colour, but is now made up to the closest possible match using the CMYK colours.

3.2 Editing a colour swatch

A new colour swatch can be edited at any time, and all the objects to which it has already been applied update to the new specification.

To edit an existing colour, double-click on it in the Swatches window. The Swatch Options window opens, showing exactly the same information as the New Colour Swatch window. Make the required changes and click 'OK'.

Two of the default colours – registration and paper – require some further explanation.

At first glance, registration appears to be exactly the same as black. However, instead of a box indicating that it is a CMYK colour, it has an odd-looking icon like a gun sight. This is the 'registration target', an element usually placed outside the live area (the final trim size) of the page. The targets are in exactly the same position on each of the CMYK plates and are used to fine-tune the position of each colour. When the targets print exactly on top of each other, the job is in perfect register.

However, the actual specification of the colour – 100% of all four CMYK colours – means that it must only be used for very small elements of the job, like registration marks, that appear outside the final trim marks. If it were used to fill type or solid shapes, it would create unbelievable registration problems or cause the job to self-destruct on its way through the press. This is because there is a limit to how much wet ink can be put on a piece of paper before no more wet ink wants to stick to it. If that happens, it has exceeded what is known as the 'maximum ink-density limit' and the ink peels back off the paper and onto the press, wrecking the job.

Paper is set to white as a default. If it is edited to a different colour, the document pages change to display the same tint. This is why it is called paper, in an attempt to show what the document would look like if it were printed on that colour of stock. In reality, unless you are only printing black type, it is not an accurate representation because InDesign continues to display images and other colours as if they are printed on opaque white backgrounds. However, unless you are using a process that uses a very thick layer of ink, such as some screen-printing systems, the colour of the stock will affect the images and other colours. In practice, everything in the document that is anything other than solid black is tinted by the colour of the paper.

See the 'Custom colours' movie on the CD for examples of creating and editing new colours.

3.3 Creating gradient swatches

Swatches of solid colour and gradient swatches are created in much the same way. Gradients are blends of two or more colours, and InDesign allows the creation of two kinds of gradient: linear and radial. Both are extremely effective graphic elements on a page and add more visual interest than the exclusive use of flat colours.

In the examples shown in **fig. 8**, both the linear and radial gradients are made up of just two colours. However, it is easy to create multi-colour gradients and save them as gradient swatches for future use.

To create a gradient swatch, click on the 'Options' button in the Swatches window and choose 'New Gradient Swatch' (**fig. 9**). Name the swatch, and specify linear or radial as its type.

To colour the swatch, go to the 'gradient ramp' at the foot of the window, and click on one of the paint pots underneath the shaded grey bar. Immediately, the colour sliders and the 'stop colour' (the colour mode for that part of the gradient) are activated.

Choose 'Named Colour' ('Swatches' in CS versions) from the 'Stop Colour' drop-down list and then you can select from any solid colour swatch currently listed in the Swatches window.

As with solid colour swatches, the sliders or the percentage windows can be used to create a colour value for that end of the gradient. The grey bar re-colours to show the result. Click on the paint pot at the other end and choose a different colour.

Click on the 'OK' button at this point, and a simple two-colour gradient is created. However, click at another point under the shaded bar

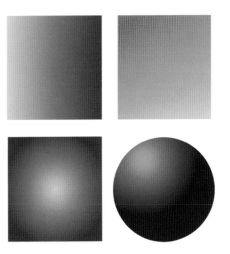

fig. 8 Simple gradients.

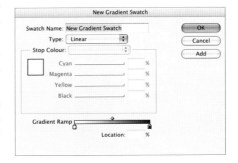

fig. 9 Creating a new gradient swatch.

and another paint pot is added, which can be coloured in exactly the same way. To delete a paint pot, simply drag it away from the bar. You can only delete a pot after there are at least three present, as you cannot have a gradient of only one colour.

The small diamond icon above the bar indicates the mid-blend position between the two adjacent paint pots beneath it. To move the blend position, drag the icon to the left or right. You can also position the diamond icons numerically using the 'location' area.

Gradient swatches are edited in exactly the same way as solid colour swatches, and, again, everything to which they were already applied updates automatically. They can be used on text or graphics, either as fills or strokes. See the 'Gradients' movie on the CD.

3.4 The Stroke window

To apply a specific width to a stroke, choose 'Window > Stroke' (**fig. 10**). If in doubt as to whether all the options are visible, click on the 'options' button and select 'show options'.

The main window allows you to enter a thickness in units of 0.1 of a point. A point is a 72nd of an inch, so, a 36pt stroke is 0.5" thick, an 18pt stroke is 0.25" thick, and so on. A common thickness for image borders is 1pt and for ruled lines 0.5pt.

The 'mitre limit' dictates how corners are drawn. To ensure no unwanted surprises in the way corners are drawn, leave it at a value of 4. 'Cap' buttons determine how the ends of lines are drawn, while the 'Join' decides whether corners (and other changes of path direction) are square, rounded or bevelled. In general, all you need to do here is to enter a stroke thickness for the selected object.

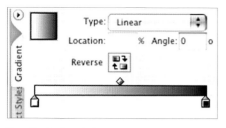

fig. 10 The Stroke window.

3.5 The Gradient window

You can also create (and save) gradients in the Gradient window. Choose 'Window > Gradient' (**fig. 11**). As with the Stroke window, click on the 'options' button and then on 'show options' if all choices are not visible.

Draw a shape and click on the shaded gradient bar at the foot of the window. The object immediately fills with a greyscale gradient. Again, you can choose between linear and radial and also set a gradient angle. The direction of the gradient can be reversed by clicking on the 'reverse' icon. The blend points, above the bar, work as described in 'Creating gradient swatches' on p. 89.

Click under the bar and another paint pot will be added.

But, everything is still grey. To colour this kind of gradient, the Colour window is required. Go to 'Window > Colour', click on the 'options' button, and choose CMYK from the list. With the object selected, click on the gradient bar and then on one of the paint pots. The colours become adjustable using the sliders in the Colour window. You can also click anywhere in the rainbow-coloured bar at the window's foot to select a colour (**fig. 12**, opposite).

fig. 11 The Gradient window.

Do not click in the square with the diagonal red bar, or else the object will have no fill colour at all. You can, however, click on the black or white swatches at the right end of the rainbow bar.

Gradients can also be edited by selecting a paint pot in the Gradient window and 'alt-clicking' on a swatch in the Swatches window.

3.6 The Transparency window

Probably one of the most important and exciting developments ever added to a page-layout program, the ability to create a degree of transparency in objects opens up incredible design opportunities. To open the Transparency window, choose 'Window > Transparency' (**fig. 13**). Opacity is applied as a percentage to any page element, regardless of whether it was created in InDesign or imported from elsewhere. Select an object and enter a value in the opacity area. The object immediately becomes transparent to the specified degree and anything beneath it becomes visible.

Transparency is very simple to use and incredibly effective – there really should be bands playing and flags waving at this point in the book just to underline the fact.

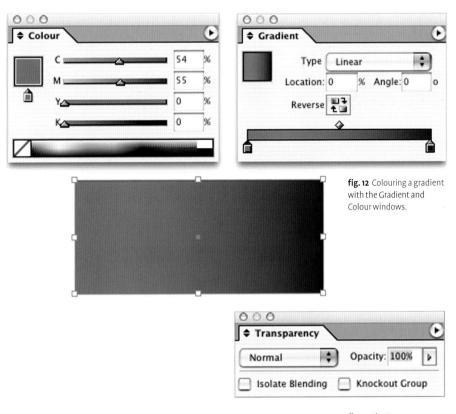

fig. 12 Colouring a gradient with the Gradient and Colour windows.

fig. 13 The Transparency window.

4   Working with Text

4.1 Importing and formatting text

Having seen how to create, edit and apply colours, it is now time to learn the same skills with text. First, however, you need to get the text into InDesign.

If you are typing in the text yourself, type it directly into InDesign; all the necessary typographical controls are there and sticky formatting problems cannot happen. If, however, a Microsoft Word document needs to be imported, one of several things can be done:

1) Draw a text frame and choose 'File > Place' ('apple/control + D'), navigate to the text file and click 'open'.

2) Do as above, but without bothering to draw a text frame first. Imported text automatically flows into a frame that has already been drawn. However, if no frame is available, the cursor changes into a text-loaded cursor, which you can then click and drag, thereby drawing a text frame into which the text can flow.

3) Do as above, and click inside the margins of a document page.

All three options result in the same thing: a text frame, containing text, on a page. However, I would like to offer an alternative method, because of a single, but very good, reason: sticky formatting. Word documents, particularly, like to take their formatting with them when they travel – even if they were not formatted using particular styles. Therefore, by importing text from a Word document – even when using the 'Edit > Copy', 'Edit > Paste' route – you also import (a translated version of) the attributes originally applied in Word. At the very least, there is likely to be a new entry in the Paragraph Style window (see 4.2) called 'normal', with a tiny icon to its right that looks like a Zip disk.

There may be no problems as a result, but the way something looked in Word compared to how it needs to appear in InDesign are usually two very different things, so there is no compelling reason to bring the Word formatting along. And, in fact, it can be positively dangerous to do so.

While it is possible seemingly to get rid of all the attached formatting instructions, it sometimes proves extremely difficult to shed them completely. In one instance, it was some time before everything looked as I wished on-screen. Then, I ran a high-resolution PDF version of the file. Words were suddenly missing.

To avoid this situation, first open the document in Word, and then re-save it in text-only format, creating a file in which all formatting is removed. Import the text-only document into InDesign, and use the original Word document only as a formatting guide, i.e. to check the rendering of words that should be in italic or bold. This may not be a particularly slick fix, but it works. More important, it does not suddenly throw you into a state of panic with a looming deadline.

4.2 Creating and editing paragraph and character styles

Many people unfamiliar with text styles approach text formatting as a straightforward affair, beginning with a choice of typeface. Then, they highlight one chunk of text at a time and apply size and leading (the space between the lines) specifications. Later, if a block of text fills too much or too little space, the process is repeated so that a different point and/or leading size can be applied.

In my experience, most people assume that this must be the way to proceed. In fact, far from being simple and straightforward, this method – or, rather, this lack of method – is time-consuming, potentially inaccurate and totally unnecessary.

Unless you are producing a single-page document – such as a poster, which contains very little text and for which the above 'method' actually works perfectly well – you should spend a few minutes deciding how everything needs to look. For instance, suppose you are beginning work on a multi-page publication (and, by multi-page, I mean *anything* larger than a single-page document) in which there is a hierarchy of related type styles to consider: headings, sub-headings, body copy and photo captions. Imagine how tedious it would be to apply each attribute, separately, to each instance of each one. This approach might also require manually revising them all separately, if, as the project develops, they turn out to be the wrong size or leading.

How much easier it would be if all the attributes for each style were held together as a 'macro' (a single command containing a whole set of other commands), so that they could all be applied simultaneously with a single click. And, when you edit a type style, as when editing colours, any text to which the style has already been applied updates automatically.

Welcome to paragraph and character styles.

InDesign, of course, goes way beyond the specification of basic things like typeface size and leading. In fact, it goes far beyond what most of us will ever need.

Paragraph styles
To open the Paragraph Styles window (**fig. 14**), choose 'Window > Type > Paragraph Styles' (in CS versions, it is a tab on the right of the screen), click on the 'options' button and select 'new style' from the list.

The New Paragraph Style window appears (**fig. 15**). On its left is a list, the first item of which is the current view: 'general'. At the top, give the style a name related to its use, such as 'heading'. Right now it cannot be based on another style, because there *are* no other styles. 'Based on' creates parent or child relationships between styles, in which the child styles are based on the parent styles and automatically incorporate changes made to the parent styles.

It is not yet possible to indicate a 'next style'. If 'sub-heading' could be chosen at this point, then as soon as a line of text on a page had been specified as 'heading' and the 'return' key pressed, the next line would be formatted automatically as 'sub-heading'.

Useful though 'based on' and 'next style' can be, I often create all the styles for a job without using either of them. 'Based on' can be a nuisance, as a number of things change every time you edit the parent style, and 'next style' is only useful if you format text as you type it in.

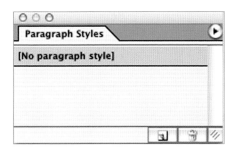

fig. 14 The Paragraph Styles window.

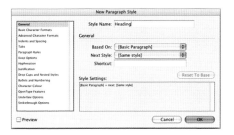

fig. 15 Naming a new paragraph style.

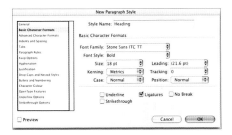

fig. 16 Setting up basic character formatting.

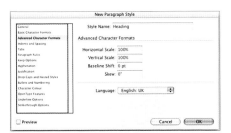

fig. 17 Advanced character formatting.

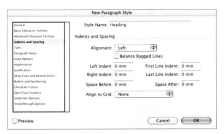

fig. 18 Setting up paragraph formatting (above and below).

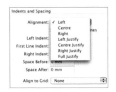

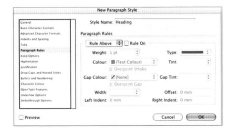

fig. 19 Adding paragraph rules.

Next, click on 'basic character formats' in the list (**fig. 16**).

This window is extremely important. Choose a font from the list and, to the font's right, select a style. Some fonts only have one style, while others have several, such as bold, italic, and so on. On the following line, specify a size in points. Now, either select a leading size or choose 'auto', which is set at 120% of the point size, from the list.

Leave 'kerning' and 'tracking' as they are because neither usually needs adjusting at the style level. Kerning refers to how individual pairs of letters are positioned relative to each other; for example, if a capital 'W' is followed by a lower-case 'e', there may be too much space between the letters. You may want to close up the space a little – but not by making an adjustment here. Instead, it should be made in the Control Bar. Tracking deals with the overall spacing between all the letters and words. Again, it is sometimes useful to adjust tracking to make text fit, but, as with kerning, this should not be done here.

If you want to use small caps (small versions of upper-case letters) or all caps, select the relevant option from the 'case' list.

Leave everything else as is and move on to 'advanced character formats' (**fig. 17**).

If you need, for example, Goudy Condensed, but only have regular Goudy, you could fool most people by using the regular font with a horizontal scale of around 80%. Similarly, if you wanted to create a faux (false) italic, apply a skew value of, say, 15º or 20º. Baseline shift and vertical scale specifications are not generally required.

The 'language' window lists the dictionary chosen when the program was installed and is the one used for spell checking.

Now, go to 'indents and spacing' (**fig. 18**), a very useful area that controls paragraph alignment. Here, as well as the usual list of 'left, centre, right, justify', it is also possible to specify 'centre justify', 'right justify' (which either centres or aligns to the right the last line of a justified paragraph). There is also the option of 'full justify' (sometimes called 'forced justify'), which spreads out the last line to fill the entire column width: a single word is letter-spaced to the full width, while more than one word becomes word-spaced to the full width. In CS2, it is also possible to specify alignments of 'towards' and 'away' from the spine.

Left and right indents apply to the entire paragraph, while first-line indents only apply to the first line of a paragraph. I often create a duplicate of a body copy style, one with and one without a first-line indent. CS2 also offers a last-line indent.

I do not use 'space before' and 'space after', as I use paragraph styles to control the distance between paragraphs. To see this, open 'styles.indd' on the CD and check the settings in the Paragraph Styles window. For the same reason, I do not often use a baseline grid, which can be set up using the 'grids' section in 'preferences'.

In my entire career, I have only used a tab specification as part of a type style once or twice. Unless you deal with a lot of type that all requires the same kind of tab commands, it is not worth setting up tabs as part of a paragraph style. However, tabs themselves are very useful and are explained in detail on p. 97.

Paragraph rules (**fig. 19**, opposite) can be placed before and/or after each paragraph and are also perfect for producing a very particular heading effect that is tedious to create any other way. See 'styles.indd' on the CD.

Do not change anything in the 'keeps options' area, which prevents single lines of paragraphs being left behind on previous pages, or taken forward, alone, to a subsequent page. While this sounds useful, it tends to create havoc with page column depth. This kind of adjustment should not be left to 'auto' settings and is best dealt with manually on a case by case basis.

Default hyphenation specifications can be changed in the 'hyphenation' area (**fig. 20**). To turn off hyphenation completely, uncheck the 'hyphenate' box.

Adobe's 'Paragraph Composer' (found under 'Justification' in CS versions, **fig. 21**) looks at the overall visual balance of each paragraph before making a final decision about where to turn the lines. This results in a better-looking block of text, but it changes its mind constantly as text is entered and can drive you nuts. If it is too distracting, choose 'Single Line Composer' instead, and then change it back again when all the text is keyed in.

Other than setting the Paragraph Composer in CS versions, there is generally no need to change anything in the justification area.

Under (up to v.2) 'Drop Caps and Composer' or (CS versions) 'Drop Caps and Nested Styles' (**fig. 22**), set up a drop-cap style by specifying how many lines deep the drop-cap character needs to sit. To apply it to more than just the first character, enter the required number. In CS+ versions, a nested style – any of the styles saved so far in that document – can be chosen to follow the drop cap for a specified number of words.

InDesign CS2 added 'bullets and numbering options' to format lists, meaning that specific bullet characters can be added and then applied as part of the style.

Using 'character colour' (**fig. 23**), you can specify a fill and/or stroke colour for the type from any colour listed in the Swatches window. Tints can also be selected. Only check the 'overprint' box, for fill or stroke, if you definitely want it to overprint, rather than 'knock out' its shape (i.e. delete any other colour that is directly underneath it). 'Open type features' do not generally require changing.

Click 'OK' and the new, named style appears in the list below 'no paragraph style' (called 'basic paragraph' in CS onwards). Incidentally, this is another way to get rid of unwanted formatting: select the text and click on this listing. Supposedly, all current formatting will be lost (although it will probably not change its appearance) and another style can then be applied. It is a good idea in principle, but, unfortunately, does not always work.

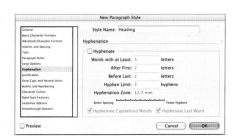

fig. 20 Adjusting paragraph style hyphenation.

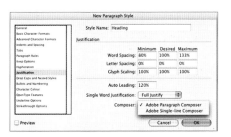

fig. 21 Paragraph Composer controls.

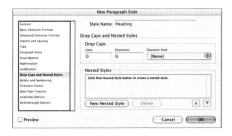

fig. 22 Formatting drop caps and nested styles.

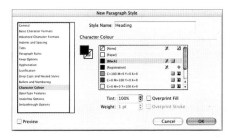

fig. 23 Assigning a colour for a style.

Tip

Tip   **If a small '+' symbol appears next to a style listing, it
means that there is some other formatting still attached.
To delete these unwanted extras, hold down the 'alt' key
and click on the listing again.**

Although most paragraph styles are easy to set up, some are more
involved. See 'styles.indd' in the InDesign section of the CD.

Character styles

The Character Styles window (**fig. 24**) (in the same place as the Paragraph
Styles window) changes the appearance of a single letter, word or phrase
within a block of text to which a paragraph style has already been
applied, for example, when an occasional word needs to appear in italic
or bold. Follow the creation method for paragraph style, but then click
and drag to highlight the word to be changed and select the appropriate
style from the list in the Character Styles window.

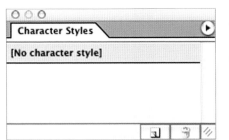

fig. 24 The Character Styles window.

4.3 Linking text frames

To link a contiguous block of text (a 'story') across a series of text frames
and/or paths (see 'path type.indd' and the 'Linking text' movie on the
CD) the text frame icons are used.

If the text begins in this frame, an icon appears at the frame's top-
left corner (**fig. 25**).

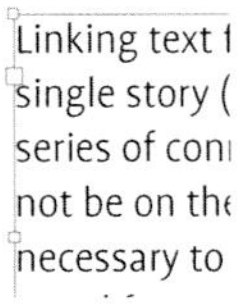

If the text flows into this frame from a previous frame and is linked to a
subsequent frame, icons appear at the top left and bottom right (**fig. 26**).

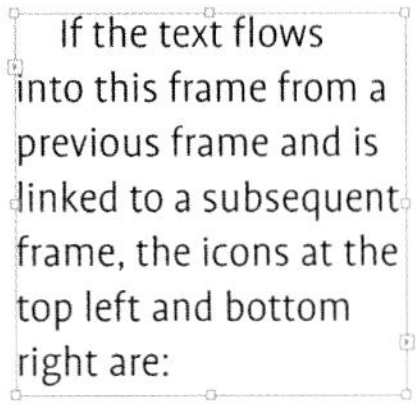

If the text flows into this frame from a previous frame but has not yet
been placed in subsequent frames, an icon shows in the bottom right
(**fig. 27**). This is the 'out port'.

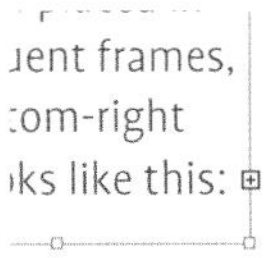

If the initial frame is too small to accommodate all the text, a small
red '+' sign appears in the lower-right corner, as shown in **fig. 27**. Using
the Selection Tool, click on the red '+' sign and the cursor's appearance
changes to indicate that it has text loaded.

There are three ways to place the text in the document:

Manual placement

Click and drag to create a new type box, into which the copy will flow. Or,
simply click within an existing type box.

Semi-autoflow placement

Hold down the 'alt' key as you click on the next column or page to create
linked type frames. As long as this key is held down, you can create as
many linked type frames as required until all the text fits.

Autoflow placement

Hold down the 'shift' key and click in the next frame. The text flows into it
and then automatically into as many additional frames on as many
additional pages as are required to place everything.

fig. 25 Shows the
appearance of the top-left
corner of a frame in which a
block of text begins.

Linking text f
single story (
series of cont
not be on the
necessary to

fig. 26 Text flows into this
frame from a previous
frame and flows out into
another.

If the text flows
into this frame from a
previous frame and is
linked to a subsequent
frame, the icons at the
top left and bottom
right are:

fig. 27 Indicates there is
more text to place.

ient frames,
:om-right
iks like this:

4.4 Text frame options

Under 'Object > Text Frame Options' are several useful controls (**fig. 28**). One, 'Ignore Text Wrap', enables the selected text to appear *within* a text wrap (see p. 106) border. Others here deal with the formatting of the frame itself and the placement of the text within it.

The 'Columns' section creates guides within a text frame. The 'Inset Spacing' defines a buffer zone around the text, while the 'Vertical Justification' controls the overall position within the vertical space.

Click to check the preview window to view the adjustments.

4.5 Using tabs

To apply tabs to a block of text, first decide how it should be formatted, i.e. how many columns are required? I have often been handed a Word document that contained information that should have been tabbed but had not been, and I have had to figure it out for myself. Similarly, I have been given text already separated by tab key commands, which I have had to re-define in InDesign. Last, but definitely not least, I have been handed a block of text in which a fake tabbed appearance has been produced by repeatedly hitting the spacebar to create the necessary spaces. For all the above instances, the solution is more or less the same.

First, click and drag across the entire block of text with the Type Tool.

Tip	Selecting a block of text is easier to accomplish if done from the end of the text.

Then, choose 'Type > Tabs' ('apple/control + shift + T') and the Tabs window appears (**fig. 29**). The window tries to place itself usefully, for example, straddling the column width of the selected block of text. However, depending on the degree of zoom, this may not be possible. The good thing is that it is not that important.

In the top-left corner of the Tabs window are four arrow buttons to control the alignment of one column of text, which specify left, centred, right and aligned on a decimal point (although it can actually be aligned on anything) tabs. To their right is a window labelled 'X', which indicates the position of the selected tab in terms of how far it is from the left edge of the page.

Next is the 'Leader' area, an example of which is the row of dots appearing in a table of contents between the chapter name on the left and the corresponding page number on the right.

Last is the 'Align On' area, where you should key in the character on which that column is to be aligned (if the align tab is chosen).

Decide on the alignment option for the first column of text and click in the horizontal space above the ruler. This places the appropriate tab marker at that point, highlighted in blue. A vertical line appears, running down the page and through the text, whenever the mouse button is held down on the marker. This indicates the position to which that marker will align the text. A marker can be dragged to a new position at any time.

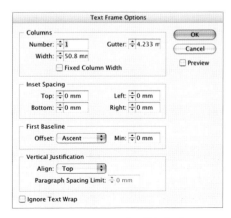

fig. 28 The Text Frame Options window.

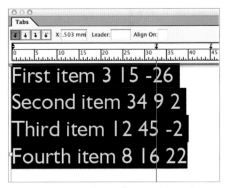

fig. 29 Setting up tabs.

Assume that the first marker placed is for left alignment but the next column needs to be centred. If the centre tab button is clicked on *while the first marker is still highlighted*, the marker will change from being *left*-aligned to *centre*-aligned. To avoid confusion, therefore, it is better to click and place the tab marker in the horizontal space and then click on the button to define it.

Once all the markers are in place, click to place the cursor at the beginning of the text for each column and then press the tab key on the keyboard. Repeat for each row. If text is actually too long to be accommodated by the width of one of the columns, highlight the entire block and drag the markers to wider settings. The position of the text updates as the settings change.

Tip	**Always persevere to the end of each line before deciding that a marker is placed incorrectly. Often, the text only adjusts to its final position as the last tab command is placed. To experiment, see 'tabs.indd' on the CD.**

4.6 Check spelling

While there are obvious dangers in using only a spell checker to proof work, it does find misspelled words and is a very worthwhile first step. It does not matter which tool is selected when the spell checker is activated, but it can make a difference if a text frame is chosen (see below).

Choose 'Edit > Check Spelling'. The Check Spelling window appears (**fig. 30**). At its foot is the 'search' area, in which you decide to check the story, the document or all documents.

A 'story' refers to an entire block of text, regardless of how many frames it is spread across. To choose this option, a text frame must be selected. A 'document' means all the stories in an active document. 'All documents' relates to all the documents in the folder in which the current document has been saved (for details on saving InDesign documents, see p. 84). Whichever option you select, click 'start' to begin the check.

If the checker finds a suspect word, it highlights it in the document and lists possible alternatives in the 'Suggested Corrections' area. If one of these alternatives is suitable, double-click on it to replace the suspect. If none of the alternatives are correct, but you know the correct spelling, type it in the 'Change To' window and click on the 'Change' button to the right.

Should no alternatives be suggested or if you know the word is correct, you can tell the checker to ignore this instance, to ignore all instances of this word or to add it to the dictionary (in which case it will not come up as suspect once you have finished dealing with this instance). Obviously, if you do not know whether the word is correct, this is a good time to look it up.

To add a word to the dictionary, click the 'Add' button. In the Dictionary window (**fig. 31**), again click on the 'Add' button. Do not click

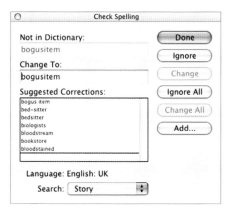

fig. 30 The Check Spelling window.

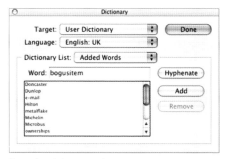

fig. 31 The Dictionary window.

on the 'Hyphenate' button unless you want InDesign to hyphenate it for you, where applicable. There are also options for removing previously saved words and more, but these are rarely needed and are not included here.

After clicking on 'Add', click on 'Done' to return to the Check Spelling window. Tell the checker to ignore this instance and it will move on to the next suspect word.

Incidentally, it is also possible to click within the suspect word on the document page and fix the mistake there. If you follow this route, leave the cursor flashing at that point in the document and, to continue with the check, click again on the 'start' button.

4.7 Find/Change

This utility is invaluable for tracking down incorrect instances of a word or phrase and also for deleting unwanted double spaces in the text. Double spaces are commonly inserted at the beginning of sentences and can be a nightmare. In the days of typewriters, which used fixed-space text (i.e. a capital 'W' was the same width as a lower-case 'i'), double spaces were important visual aids. However, digital type is designed to allow each character its own width (except for Courier, which is a good reason never to use it), making the use of double spaces redundant.

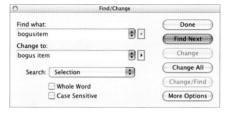

fig. 32 Find/Change window.

The Find/Change window is under 'Edit > Find/Change' (**fig. 32**).

Type the word(s) or characters to search for in the 'Find What' box and the replacement in the 'Change to' area. To search for an obscure character, click on the small arrow to the right of the 'Find What' box and select it from the list.

Instruct InDesign to check the text, to the end of the current story, the document, all documents in that folder or, if a block of text is selected, just within that block. Also decide whether the search should be case sensitive and whether to look for occurrences of the whole word or to find words containing that combination of letters.

Click inside the first text block on the first page (this is not essential, but it helps to prevent going through things for a second time by mistake) and click 'find next' in the window. If what you are looking for exists within the parameters of the search, the first instance is highlighted in the text. Then choose whether to change this instance alone (and continue looking for the next occurrence by clicking 'find next' or 'find/change') or all found instances.

4.8 Tracking controls

Do not be misled by this seemingly unimportant title: tracking controls are very important indeed. Their main use is in getting around two different but closely related problems: widows and orphans. When the last line of a paragraph is a single word, it is know as a widow. An orphan is when the first line of a paragraph is on one page and the rest of it is on the next or when the last line of a paragraph is on the next page. Typographically speaking, these are poor ways to leave things.

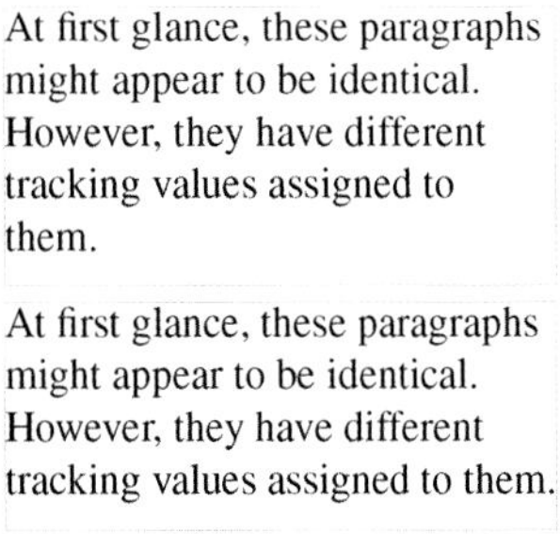

At first glance, these paragraphs might appear to be identical. However, they have different tracking values assigned to them.

At first glance, these paragraphs might appear to be identical. However, they have different tracking values assigned to them.

fig. 33 Solving fitting problems using the tracking controls.

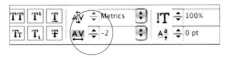

fig. 34 The location of the tracking controls on the Control Bar.

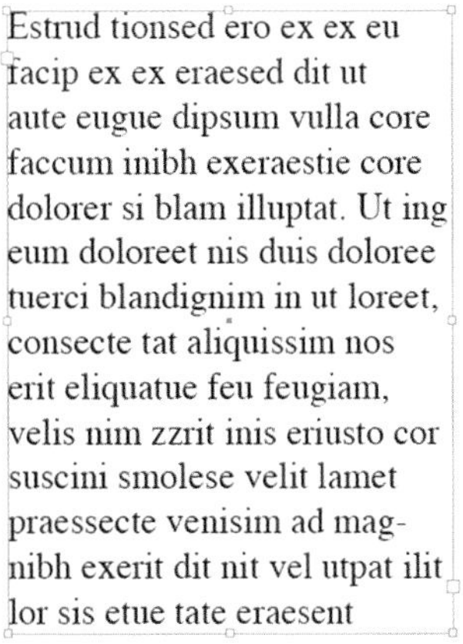

Estrud tionsed ero ex ex eu facip ex ex eraesed dit ut aute eugue dipsum vulla core faccum inibh exeraestie core dolorer si blam illuptat. Ut ing eum doloreet nis duis doloree tuerci blandignim in ut loreet, consecte tat aliquissim nos erit eliquatue feu feugiam, velis nim zzrit inis eriusto cor suscini smolese velit lamet praessecte venisim ad magnibh exerit dit nit vel utpat ilit lor sis etue tate eraesent

fig. 35 An example of placeholder text.

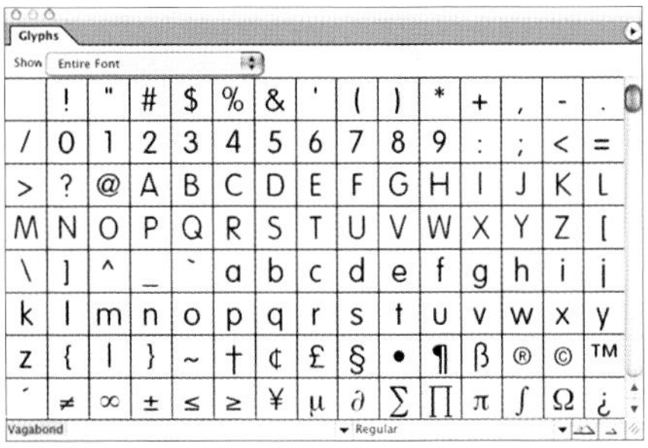

fig. 36 The Glyphs window.

Being able to remedy these also means being able to deal with other text-fitting problems and the results are much better looking.

Look at the blocks of text in **fig. 33**. The text is the same in both instances and the spacing, while different, is perfectly acceptable in both. However, the end of the text in the upper block is a problem, whereas it is not in the lower. A tracking edit is the only difference between the two. The text in the lower block was selected and adjusted using the tracking controls in the Character window ('Window > Type ['and Tables', in CS onwards] > Character' (circled in **fig. 34**).

To try this, highlight some text and click on the up or down arrows in the tracking control field. Each click of the arrow leads to an adjustment in increments of 10 units. While these are very small, it is not advisable to make an adjustment greater or smaller than plus or minus 15 as the results may become visible.

Clicking on the 'down' arrow reduces the overall tracking value in the selected text and solves the problem by pulling up the last line of text into the rest of the paragraph. Alternatively, when this does not work, use the 'plus' arrow to push one or more words down to share the last line. If neither of the above work, try adjusting the horizontal scale from between 97% (to shrink the text) and 103% (to expand the text).

Almost always, these adjustments solve tricky (and typographically ugly) fitting problems.

4.9 Placeholder text

In production situations, designers often need to begin work on a project before editors have handed over the text. In these cases, placeholder text can be used. To do this, create a text frame and choose 'Type > Fill with Placeholder Text' (**fig. 35**).

4.10 Glyphs

Any character in a specific typeface can be found by choosing 'Type > Insert Glyphs' (**fig. 36**). The cursor should be inserted in the text where the character needs to appear. In the Glyphs window, select any typeface on your system and either the whole font or alternatives for a high-lighted selection are displayed. Scroll to the required character, double-click on it and it will appear in the text. See the 'Glyphs' movie on the CD.

4.11 Adding and deleting document pages

To open the Pages window, choose 'Window > Pages'. It can be adjusted (by clicking on the 'options' button and selecting 'palette options') to display page information in different ways. I generally prefer to uncheck the 'Show Vertically' box in the 'Pages' area, as this results in many more page sets being visible in the window (**fig. 37**, opposite).

The Pages window is divided into two areas: the top, which lists the master page(s) and the lower area containing the document pages.

To add pages, click on the 'options' button and choose 'Insert Pages' from the list. In the resulting window, you can decide how many pages to add, and where. If there is already more than one master page, it is possible to select which one to apply to the new pages. Otherwise, the choice is limited to the default master page ('A-master') or 'none'.

To delete a page, highlight it by clicking on its icon in the Pages window and choose 'Delete Page' from the 'options' list. If the affected page contains objects, you will be asked to confirm the deletion. To delete several contiguous pages, click on the first page and then 'shift-click' on the last. The entire block becomes highlighted. Again, choose 'Delete' from the options. If the pages are non-contiguous, delete them by clicking on one, then 'apple/control + click' on the others, one at a time. Delete, as above.

Tip   **Document pages have the 'A-Master' page applied to them as a default, and so their icons, in the Pages window, show the letter 'A'.**

4.12 Getting around in a multi-page document
Once created, all pages within a document are easily accessible from two places:

1) The list of document and master pages in the lower-left corner of the screen (**fig. 38**). Click on the arrow, scroll to the required page and release the mouse button. The screen view changes to the selected page.

2) Their icons in the Pages window. To go to any page, document or master, double-click on its icon (to highlight it) and the screen will immediately show that page.

4.13 Creating and applying master pages
Master pages are the means by which automatic page numbering can be applied to a document. They are also a good way of specifying different guide and margin layouts for certain pages. Additionally, they can contain such things as headers and sidebars as background elements that can be applied to multiple pages. To unlock master-page elements on document pages, 'apple/control + shift + click' on them.

All documents are assigned a default master page, the basic layout of which – size, margins, and so on – depends on the original information entered in the Document Setup window. For instance, if 'Facing Pages' has not been checked, the default master page will be a single, rather than a double, page. A single-page master can be applied to either the left- or right-hand page of a two-page spread.

In a double-page master set, the master page on the left can only be applied to the left-hand page of a document and the master page on the right can only be applied to a right-hand page of a document.

If a mistake is made in the initial setup, it is possible to return to 'File > Document Setup' and change some of the parameters, but not the margins. To change those, go to 'Layout > Margins and Columns'.

To add a new master page, click on the 'options' button in the Pages window and choose 'New Master' from the list. You can specify a name

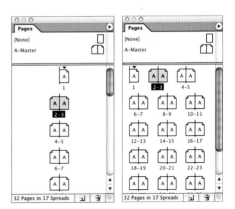

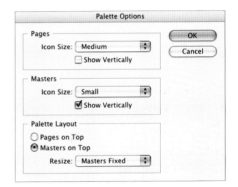

fig. 37 Page display options for multi-page documents (above) and how to change the display (below).

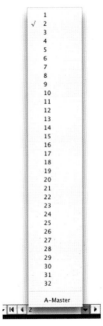

fig. 38 The document and master page list.

and a single-letter prefix and you can base it on an existing master page. You can also decide how many pages it should be. When finished, click 'OK' and it will be added to the list in the Pages window and also to the list in the lower-left corner of the screen. Master pages are deleted using the same method just described for document pages.

To apply a master page to a particular document page, click and drag it – by its name or by its page icon – onto the document-page icon. As that icon's border becomes highlighted, release the mouse button. The icon updates to show the designated letter for that master page (A, B, C, and so forth).

To apply a master page to a sequence of document pages, select the first page in the Pages window and then hold down 'shift' and click on the last page of the set. To select non-contiguous pages, click on the first and then 'apple/control + click' on the others. When the relevant pages are selected, 'alt-click' on the master page you wish to apply.

4.14 Automatic page numbering

In a multi-page document, the ability to generate automatic page numbering is very useful. In the following example, we will set up page numbers to be placed in the lower-left corner of the left page and the lower-right corner of the right page. Once you are familiar with this, you will be able to set them up anywhere.

Set up a 'page numbers' paragraph style to left alignment. For everything else in this style, the settings are up to you. Save the style and double-click on the 'A-Master' name or page icon in the Pages window. They appear on-screen as a double-page spread. If you have zoomed in on a document page prior to doing this, the view of the master-page spread will also be zoomed in. To see the full page view, type 'apple/control + 0' (zero).

Using the Text Tool ('T'), click and drag to create a small text frame, roughly 1cm wide x 1cm tall, on the left page. Then, (Mac) choose 'Type > Insert Special Character' or (PC) right-click inside the frame and choose 'Insert Special Character' from the list. For either platform, select 'Auto Page Number' from the top of the list. Whatever the prefix of the master page (A, B, C) that letter will appear in the text frame.

Pick the Selection Tool and, holding down the 'alt' key, click and drag on that text frame. A duplicate is created. Drag it onto the right-hand page and place it so that it is set within the margins in the lower-right corner, just touching them. Then, position the frame on the left-hand page in the same way, but in the lower-left corner.

It should be easy to position the frames against the margins, as 'Snap to Guides' is a default setting that makes all margins and guides attract objects as they are moved close to them. The feature can be turned off (or back on) easily by going to 'View > Snap to Guides'.

The letter showing in the left-hand page frame is aligned to the left, but so is the letter on the right-hand page (because it is the same style). To change it on the right page, click on the letter (thereby putting a flashing cursor alongside it), and choose 'apple/control + shift + R' to re-align it to the right.

Both the page frames are positioned within the margin area, which means that they could get in the way of page text. To move them, select both (click on one with the Selection Tool, then 'shift-click' on the other) and, using the down-arrow key, nudge them further down the page to a less intrusive position.

Then, click on one of the document pages to which that master page has been applied and you will see the (appropriately positioned) page numbers. See the 'Automatic Page Numbers' movie on the CD.

4.15 Layout/numbering and section options

Sometimes a document, such as a book, requires several different page-numbering formats. For instance, the first few pages may have no page numbers, while other 'front matter' (like the introduction) may be numbered using roman numerals. Page 1 may not appear until the start of chapter 1. Catering for this is easy, as InDesign can create multiple numbering sections within a single document.

To see how this works, open 'booklet.indd' on the CD, a blank, 32-page A5 booklet with an automatic numbering text frame already positioned on the default A-Master pages.

Suppose pages 1 to 4 need no page numbers, a roman numeral section starts on (document) page 5 and chapter 1 begins on (document) page 11. Create the appropriate sections as follows:

Double-click on page 11 in the Pages window.

Choose 'Layout/Numbering and Section Options'. In the window (**fig. 39**), make sure that 'Start Section' rather than 'Automatic Page Numbering' is checked.

Select 'Start Page Numbering At' and enter '1' in the box. Click 'OK'. The default page number style is Arabic, i.e. a conventional Western number format.

Double-click on page 5 in the Pages window, and repeat as for page 1 but, this time, choose a roman-numeral style from the list before clicking 'OK'.

To take care of the first few pages – on which the regular auto page number appears – drag the 'none' master-page icon onto those document-page icons in the Pages window. As there is no automatic page-numbering frame on this master page, any page to which it is applied will not have one.

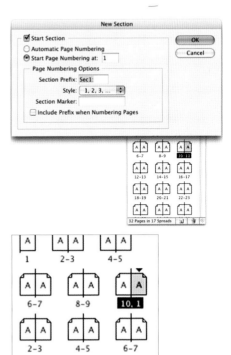

fig. 39 Creating a new section.

Tip   In the above method, it is easier to create the last section first and then work back to the beginning of the book. That way, the numbers assigned to the document pages on which you wish to create additional sections do not keep changing.

5

Working with Images

5.1 Images in a production workflow

Generally, InDesign's tools are geared towards commercial printing – for example, all the colour swatches are in CMYK format. If this is your intention, you should only import TIFF or EPS files. People who know a little about printing probably expect me to now say something like, 'Everything in colour should be in CMYK format, and colour and greyscale images should all have a resolution of at least 300dpi'. However, it does not always make sense to use those formats or that resolution all the way through the production process (see p. 41). Also, the job may be destined for *desktop* laser or inkjet printers (typically found in offices), or commercial digital printers. In the case of desktop printers, the colour format for images almost certainly needs to be RGB, while digital printers may work with RGB *or* CMYK.

If you want to print sample pages in colour on a desktop machine, you are far more likely to get better and more realistic results if you use RGB images. And, if they are 72dpi, they will print much faster, as well as being much faster to work with in the page layout.

Desktop printers generally cannot cope with CMYK images, despite using CMYK toners and inks to print. Translating an RGB file into CMYK, however, is something they do quite well. Send a CMYK file to a desktop printer, and the result usually has a strong greenish tint (known as a colour cast). Obviously, it is not a good idea to send such print-outs to a commercial printer as a guide to how the final result should look.

Also, even though 72dpi is a screen resolution generally assigned to website images, it generates a print with enough detail to see the image's position and composition perfectly well, and is therefore good enough to use for a 'for position only' (FPO) proof print. In such proofs, it is accepted that while everything is in the right place, colours are not completely accurate and images are (probably) low-res versions.

The key in this kind of workflow, therefore, is to use images that are fast to work with and that produce more accurate prints in-house. Then replace them with high-res, CMYK versions just before sending everything out to a print shop.

To determine the best way of setting this up, find out whether your printer will accept native InDesign files or requires PDF versions instead.

If they are prepared to work with InDesign files, all you need to do is create a Photoshop 'action' (macro) that generates RGB, 72dpi copies of your images and saves them into another folder *with the same names as the originals* (see p. 44). Then, use these low-res, RGB versions during the production work. However, when you collect everything to send to the printer, do not include any of the FPO images. Send only the high-res, CMYK versions, together with the InDesign files.

When the plates (or film, in a film-based shop) are being made, the InDesign file searches for the images it needs by *file name*, and thus it will find the high-res, CMYK images.

However, if the printer is only prepared to accept PDF files – which is quite likely – still create low-res, RGB versions in exactly the same way but re-link the InDesign files to the correct, high-res images just prior to making the PDF files (see 'Relinking images', p. 107).

Whichever of the above methods you use, it is critical to remember not to change the physical dimensions of just one of a pair (high-res and low-res) of images. If the low-res image is 10 x 15 cm at 72dpi but the high-res image has been resized or cropped, their relative sizes will be different and the substitution will not work. If you have to change one, make sure you make exactly the same changes to the other.

5.2 Importing images into InDesign

To import images (or text), choose 'File > Place' ('apple/control + D'). In the window, scroll to the image and double-click on the file name.

It does not matter which tool is selected at the time, but it is sensible to check that no other object is selected. For instance, if a frame containing text is chosen with the Selection Tool, the image is placed into it and the text deleted.

If you are actively working within some text with the Text Tool, the image imports at that point – but it will think it is part of the text, which makes it very difficult to work with. However, there are times when you will want to bring a small image or drawn shape, such as a checkbox or bullet shape, into a block of text. These objects are then called 'in-line graphics'. While they are constrained from moving from side to side by their 'text' format, they can be raised or lowered using the 'baseline shift' settings on the Control Bar.

It is very unlikely that a pre-drawn frame will be an exact fit for an image. Usually, images are brought into a document, then the final size and crop are determined in relation to the other elements in the design.

If nothing is selected when you double-click on the image name, the cursor changes to reflect that it now has an image loaded. Click anywhere on the page and the entire image appears.

You may now want to do one of four things with the image: move it somewhere else, scale it to fit into a smaller area, crop it to a different shape without distorting it or wrap text around it.

To move it, choose the Selection Tool, click on the image and drag it to its new position. The other three options are explained in detail below.

5.3 Scaling images

The fifth tool down on the right side of the Toolbox is the Scale Tool. For an example of its use, see the 'Scaling Images' movie and file on the CD.

First, select the imported image with the Selection Tool. Click on the Scale Tool. The only visible change is the appearance of a small star icon in the centre of the image. This is the point of scale. Click somewhere else and the star icon moves to that point. It does not have to stay within the confines of the frame – you can click (or drag) to place it anywhere on the screen.

If possible, position the top-left corner of the image where it needs to be in the final page layout. Then, click on that corner to position

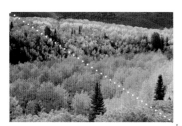

fig. 40 Scaling an image.

the star. Holding down the 'shift' key (this ensures the adjustment is proportional), click and drag towards the star from a point along an imaginary diagonal line drawn from it through the bottom-right corner of the image (**fig. 40**). Once you get the hang of it, it is very easy to do.

Tip   **All objects, including text, can be scaled in the same way.**

5.4 Cropping images

There are two ways to crop an image that has been placed in an InDesign document: by altering the shape or dimensions of the frame or by physically re-positioning the image within the frame.

To change the shape or dimension of the frame
Select the frame with the Selection Tool and click and drag the handles. If the frame is extended too far, a gap may be created between the image and the frame edge. This will look strange if the frame is assigned a stroke specification.

By clicking and dragging on a corner handle, you can re-position two sides at once. Hold down the 'shift' key at the same time and the shape is constrained to being proportional.

To change the shape of the frame beyond this requires the use of the Direct Selection Tool and/or the Pen Tool (see pp 57–58).

To re-position an image within the frame
First, deselect everything. Then, choose the Direct Selection Tool and click on the image – not on the frame. Another dark-brown frame appears, showing the edges of the image itself (and not the frame through which it appears). Click and drag on it to move it around.

5.5 Fitting images to frames and frames to images

When an image is placed into an existing frame, it is very unlikely to fit exactly. Fortunately, InDesign offers several options to remedy this; unfortunately, some are much more useful than others.

The best option, as it does not distort the image, is to fit the frame to the content. Choose 'Object > Fitting > Fit Frame to Content'. Other options found here are sometimes useful, but 'Fit Content to Frame', for example, will almost certainly distort the image.

5.6 Wrapping text around images

The object to which a text wrap is applied can be below or on top of the text that is to be wrapped around it. To create a text wrap, select an object on the page, such as an image, and choose (up to InDesign v.2 and then again in CS2) 'Window > Text Wrap', or (CS1) 'Window > Type and Tables > Text Wrap'. The Text Wrap window appears (**fig. 41**).

The icons along the top indicate different kinds of text wrap. From the left, they are: 'no text wrap', 'wrap around bounding box', 'wrap around object shape', 'jump object' and 'jump to next column'.

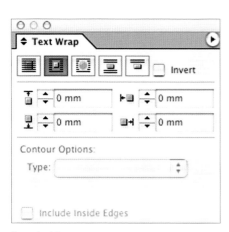

fig. 41 Applying a text wrap.

Click on the one you want to use. Mostly, you will need the 'wrap around bounding box' or 'wrap around object shape'. Should you choose 'wrap around bounding box', the 'outset' windows activate. Click on the arrows to increase the text wrap area beyond the bounding box.

'Wrap around object shape', opens an additional section in the Text Wrap window. Here, it is possible to choose an element on which to base the wrap, for instance, 'same as clipping' (see p. 39) or 'detect edges'.

The shape of a text wrap can be edited using the Direct Selection Tool, but to do this the text wrap has to be visible, which is not always the case. However, if you apply the 'wrap around bounding box' feature, you need to increase the outset values to see the wrap shape. If you apply 'wrap around object shape', then you see the text wrap immediately, as a substantial outset value is given as a default. Text wrap examples can be seen in the 'text wrap.indd' file on the CD.

5.7 Re-linking images

When an image is placed into InDesign, its location on the hard drive is recorded as a link. If that image is moved or modified, update the link in the Links window prior to either printing or generating a PDF file.

To open the Links window, choose 'Window > Links' ('apple/control + shift + D'). The images in the document are listed on the left, with their current status and document page location to the right. If the current status is OK, nothing shows between the name and the page number. However, if a symbol appears between them, a warning message comes up as the Links window opens, offering either to try and fix the links automatically or by using the Links window.

If a file has been modified since it was placed, a yellow triangular icon appears next to its name in the list. This may mean that the link still points to the correct folder, in which case all the 'modified' file links can be fixed at once. Click on the 'Fix Links' button in the warning message, and then on 'OK' in the 'Relink' window.

If a file has been moved, a red circular icon appears next to its name. In this case (or if the above method was unsuccessful), click the 'OK' button in the warning message. Double-click on a 'missing' file name in the Links window, and the 'Link Information' window opens. Click on the 'Relink' button, browse to the new location, and click 'Open'.

If the image cannot be found, cancel the attempt and move to the next image in the list by clicking on 'Next'. When a successful location is found, click on 'Open'. This removes the 'missing' icon, and the relinked item moves to the foot of the list in the Links window.

If other 'missing' images are in the same folder, then, now that a new location has been established, they can all be relinked together. Multiple names on the Links window list can be selected by 'shift-clicking' or 'apple/control + clicking' on them, for a contiguous or non-contiguous selection respectively. Then, either click on the 'Relink' icon at the foot of the window, or click on the 'options' button and then on 'Relink' in the list.

6   More Techniques

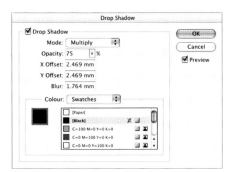

fig. 42 Drop shadow settings.

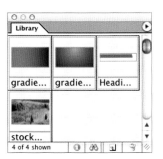

fig. 43 A library.

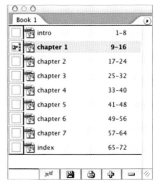

fig. 44 The Book window.

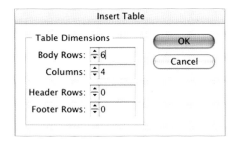

fig. 45 Creating a table.

6.1 Special effects

Three special effects are available: drop shadow, feather and corner effects. All three can be applied to frames or text. Select an object, choose 'Object > Drop Shadow' and check the 'Drop Shadow' box in the top left of the window and the 'Preview' box (**fig. 42**).

The Feather effect produces a soft edge around objects to which it is applied. To use it, choose 'Object > Feather', check the 'Feather' and 'Preview' boxes and set a feather width and a corner setting.

Corner effects can only be applied to such shapes as rectangles. Check the 'Preview' box and enter an effect and a size to see the result.

Multiple effects can be assigned to the same object.

6.2 Creating and using a Library

A Library (**fig. 43**) is a floating window into which blocks of text, logos, coloured objects and images can be dragged. They appear as thumbnail images of the original. Double-click on one to add a description and name. To use a library item, click on it and drag it onto the page.

When a new Library is first created, it has to be named and can then be closed and re-opened as needed. All paragraph or colour styles attached to the objects added to a Library will be added automatically to the document into which these objects are placed.

Libraries are independent of documents and, once opened, remain available on-screen until they are closed again.

Tip	Images and logos placed in libraries link to the original file elsewhere on the hard drive. If the original is moved, the link will be broken and only a screen-resolution copy of it will be placed.

6.3 The Book option

When working on a large project, such as a 300-page book, breaking it up into smaller sections (such as chapters) makes it much more manageable. As long as you use the same document characteristics in each chapter, the Book window (**fig. 44**) enables you to treat all the chapters as a single document while keeping them in separate files.

Book format allows you to create continuous automatic page numbering throughout the entire project and print, with a single command, blocks of pages crossing multiple documents. Also, any one of the included files can be selected as the basis for updating all the paragraph and colour styles for all the other files in the Book.

To explore further, see the 'Book' folder on the CD.

6.4 Creating tables

To create a table, click and drag with the Text Tool to create a frame and choose 'Table > Insert Table' (**fig. 45**). In the window enter a number for the rows and columns. If you already have a block of tabbed text, highlight it all with the Text Tool and choose 'Table > Convert Text to

Table'. You can click and drag with the Text Tool to highlight cells that are vertically or horizontally adjacent, and they can be merged under the 'Table' menu. Similarly, cells can be divided horizontally or vertically. This makes it possible to create almost any table format.

To format the text in a table cell, use paragraph or character styles. For vertical alignment choices and other options, highlight it with the Text Tool and choose 'Table > Cell Options > Text'.

6.5 Using layers

Although layers have been included in InDesign since its early days, there is actually little use for them. The exception is in the creation of a multi-lingual document, when it is very useful to keep the graphics on one layer, the English text on another, the French on another, and so on. Then, by turning the layers on and off, you can print each language version with the common background layer.

To access the Layers window, choose 'Window > Layers' (**fig. 46**). Each layer is colour-coded and when an object on a layer is selected, its frame will be the same colour. Also, in the Layers window, a small square of the colour displays to the right of the pen-nib icon on that layer.

To create a new layer, click on the 'New Layer' icon at the foot of the Layers window or choose 'New Layer' from the 'options' button list. To move a selected object to another layer, drag the small coloured square (to the right of the pen-nib icon) onto another layer.

To merge two layers, click on one to select it, 'apple/control + click' on another and choose 'Merge Layers' from the 'options' list. Delete a layer by selecting it and clicking on the 'Delete Layer' button on the bottom right of the window.

To visually hide a layer, and all the objects on it, click on its 'eye' icon, on the left. To lock a particular layer, so that the items on it can no longer be edited or moved, click in the window next to the 'eye' icon.

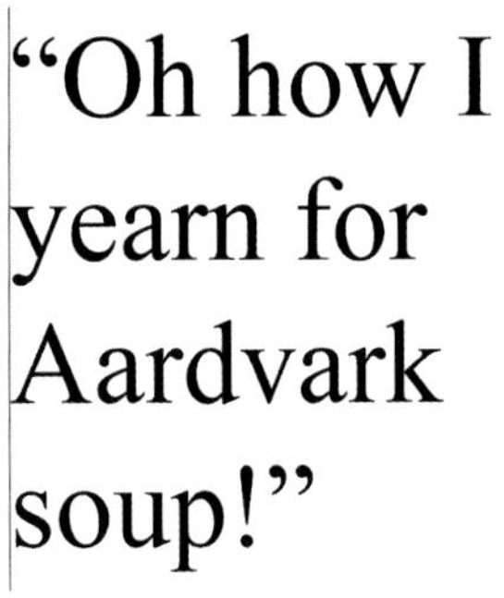

6.6 Optical margin alignment

When you have been involved in graphic design for a while, you begin to notice things – kerning, alignment issues, space issues – that you never noticed before. However, taken too far, it can completely ruin reading pleasure – for instance, regarding the way text is usually aligned on its left-hand margin (**fig. 47**).

This may be what we normally see, but it is less than satisfying visually. Because everything *does* actually align on the left margin, it *appears* to be misaligned. The larger the text, the worse the problem becomes. However, InDesign can help.

Select the text, and then choose 'Type > Story'. In the Story window, check the box for Optical Margin Alignment and choose a point size. It usually works best to select the same point size as the highlighted text.

The result (**fig. 48**) is such that while no two lines actually line up on the left margin, the text appears perfectly balanced.

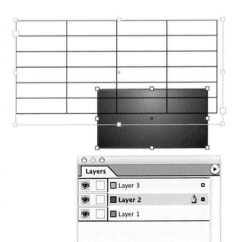

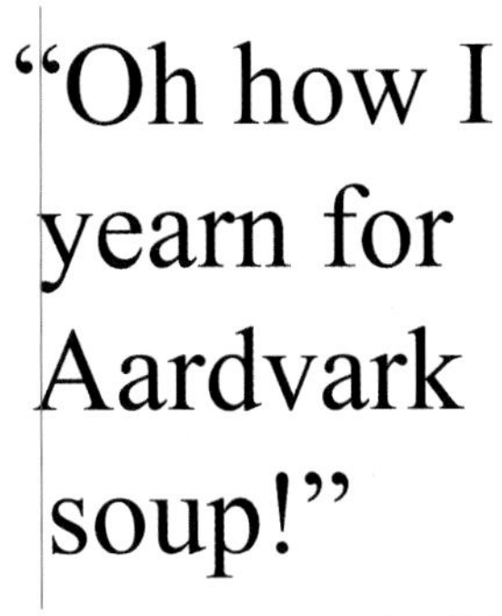

fig. 46 The Layers window.

"Oh how I yearn for Aardvark soup!"

fig. 47 How text is usually aligned on its left-hand margin.

"Oh how I yearn for Aardvark soup!"

fig. 48 The same text aligned using optical margin alignment.

Chapter 4

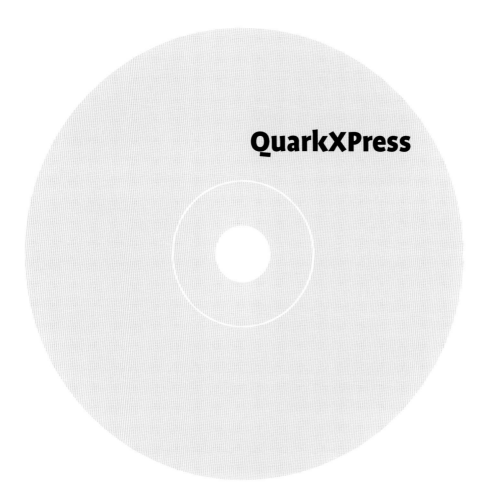

Quark is a very easy program to learn and use and is widely supported by printers worldwide. For many years it has been the page-layout method of choice, allowing the user to create just about any kind of page design for just about any kind of document. Recent versions have the ability to create tables, layers and web pages, while v.6.5 saw the addition of some Photoshop-style image-editing features, which have been taken slightly further in v.7. Also new in 7 are such features as transparency and glyphs, both of which have been available for some time in Adobe InDesign, and the ability to allow several users to work on the same document simultaneously. Whether these developments will allow Quark to hold on to its enviable market position remains to be seen.

The images in this chapter were generated using QuarkXPress v.6.5.

1   The Quark Environment

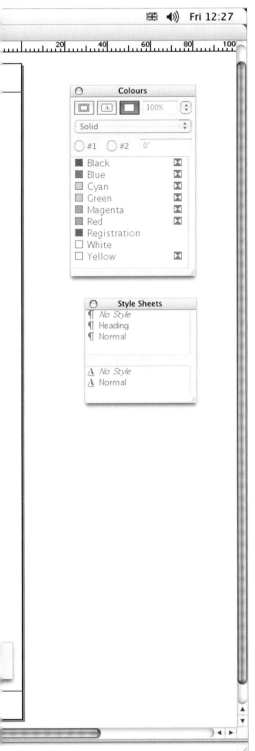

fig. 1 The Quark screen.

1.1 The Quark screen

Straightforward in appearance, the Quark screen (**fig. 1**, previous page) devotes most of its space to the document area. Along the top of the screen are the menus, above which is a title bar showing the name of the open document. Default settings place the Toolbox on the left side of the screen and the Measurements window somewhere near the foot. Other floating windows are found either under the View Menu (up to and including v.5) or under the Window Menu (in versions after 5).

Whenever a document is open, a percentage field appears in the lower-left corner of the screen, which can be highlighted and changed to zoom in or out of the document. Next to this, a small box lists the page of the document you are on; to move to another page, click on the arrow at the right-hand end of this box and select from the list. Scroll bars are positioned beneath and to the right of the document area.

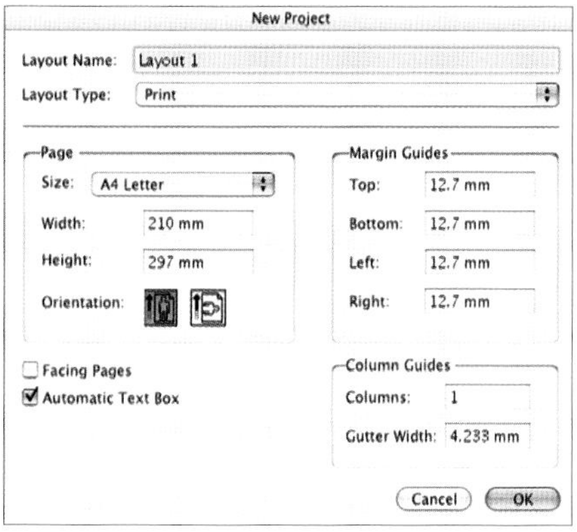

1.2 Setting up a new document

Up until v.6, Quark used the term 'document', but from 6 onwards Quark refers to setting up a new 'project', which can be developed into a page layout or a website. Here, the focus is on page layouts and the creation of documents (not projects) to avoid confusion. For all versions, the process begins in the same way: 'File > New > Project' ('apple/control + N') and the New Project window appears (**fig. 2**).

The 'Page' area contains a list of preset sizes, visible by clicking on the arrow at the right of the 'Size' field and selected by clicking on your choice. If you require a different size, enter the desired width and height and select the orientation of the page – portrait (taller than it is wide) or landscape (wider than it is tall).

The 'Margin Guides' are purple lines appearing on the default master page (see p. 132) and also, therefore, on all the document pages to which that master is applied. They do not print and are simply intended to help position page elements in a consistent way. The measurements specified here indicate the distance between a margin and whichever edge of the page it refers to.

At the foot of this window is the 'Facing Pages' checkbox. If checked, the document is laid out like the pages of a book or magazine: page one is a right-hand page, pages two and three appear as a left- and right-hand set, and so on (see p. 116). The margin names also change to read 'inside' and 'outside' (not 'left' and 'right'), the 'inside' being the binding (or spine) edge. If the box is unchecked, document pages appear as single pages.

'Column Guides' allow you to set additional guidelines within the space determined by the margin guides, dividing that space into equal columns. The 'Gutter Width' is the space between the columns.

If checked, the 'Automatic Text Box' creates a text box on the default master page that fills the area enclosed by the margin guides and also appears on all the document pages to which that master page has been applied. If all, or most, pages need a text box, or if you need to

fig. 2 The New Project window.

import a large amount of text and all your pages will have a similar layout, check this box. Then, when you import text onto page 1, additional pages with automatic text boxes are created automatically until all the text has been placed. (Otherwise, do not check this box, as the result will only be a hindrance.)

Tip   **Quark master page elements can be edited on any document page on which they appear. For example, the contents of a 'running header' text box at the top of the master page, which needs to be edited to hold different text in different chapters within the document, can be changed from within the document in just the same way as any text box can be altered. Conversely, in InDesign, master-page elements are, as a default, locked on the document pages: they appear on them, but cannot be moved or edited unless their status is changed. Changes have to be made on the master page, which then updates all relevant document pages.**

1.3 Zoom and scroll

The ability to zoom in, fix something and scroll across the page to check something else before zooming back out to see the overall effect, is needed *all the time* during page layout. Take care to learn a good method for these operations and *do not* let yourself pick up bad habits. Good methods of working pay off every time you use them and will speed up your production time greatly. Try to avoid using the zoom function in the Toolbox as it breaks workflow. You would have to stop, select the Zoom Tool, use it, and then reselect the tool you were using before.

To test the zoom tools, it helps to have an object on the page. Click on one of the two Rectangle Box tools in the Toolbox and then click and drag on the page to draw a rectangle (see p. 117).

To zoom in, hold down 'control + shift' and click. To zoom out, hold down the 'alt' key *as well* and click. On a PC, use 'control + spacebar'.

To zoom out to a full page view, choose 'apple/control + 0' (zero). To zoom to actual size, choose 'apple/control + 1'. To toggle in and out of a 200% view, hold down 'apple/control + alt' and click – wherever you click becomes (approximately) the centre of the next screen. Other keyboard shortcuts allow you to access more zoom settings, which can be found under the View menu.

To scroll around the page, hold down the 'alt' key and click and drag with the mouse.

1.4 The rulers

Across the top and down the left-hand side of the document window are two rulers. If they are not visible, choose 'View > Show Rulers' (this is a hide/show toggle, so the same process removes them from view). Click inside one of the rulers and drag it onto the page to place a guide.

fig. 3 The zero point.

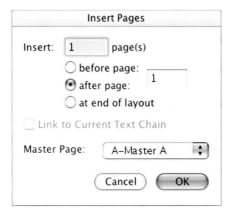

fig. 4 Inserting pages.

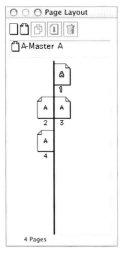

fig. 5 The Page Layout window.

These can be toggled on and off under the View Menu ('Show > Hide Guides', or by pressing the 'F7' key).

The units on the rulers depend on selections made in the 'Preferences' area: under (Mac) 'QuarkXPress > Preferences' or (PC) 'Edit > Preferences'. Ruler units can be changed in the 'Document > Measurements' area on both platforms. (For more useful changes that can be made in the Preferences area, see 'Runarounds' on p. 130.)

The zero point (**fig. 3**), a small box containing two crossed lines, is positioned where the two rulers meet at the top left corner of the document. It can be dragged onto the page and released, thus re-setting the zero point for both rulers, which makes it much easier to measure from a given point on the page. To return the 'zero' to the top-left corner of the page, double-click in the small box.

1.5 Using guides

Drag from either ruler onto the page to position either a horizontal or a vertical guide.

Tip	Many people think that they should click and drag from the very edge of the ruler, but this is not the case, and, by doing so, they are much more likely to move something on the page by mistake. Instead, put the cursor in the middle of the ruler's width, and drag from there.

Guides are there to aid the designer. Under the View Menu are some options regarding their use, such as 'Hide Guides' (to get a clearer view of the page layout) and 'Snap to Guides' (whereby the guides exert a very slight magnetic pull on nearby objects and can be used to align things). If you do not wish to see the guides, choose 'View > Hide guides' ('F7').

If you drag a guide onto a document and release it outside the page area, the guide appears across the entire screen view. However, if you release it on the page area, it only appears on the page itself. If you no longer need a guide, select the Item Tool (the top tool in the Toolbox) and click and hold on the guide. The cursor changes form, at which point you can drag the guide back into the ruler and release it.

1.6 Adding and deleting pages, and the Document Layout window

There are two ways to add pages to a document:

1) Choose 'Page > Insert Pages' (**fig. 4**). Specify how many pages you intend to add and where you wish them to go. If you want to apply a master page (see p. 132) to these new pages, select one from the list.

2) Use the Page Layout window by going to 'View > Show Document Layout' or, for v.6 onwards, 'Window > Page Layout' ('F10' on a Mac, 'F4' on a PC) (**fig. 5**).

The Page Layout window is divided horizontally into two sections. The lower section shows page icons for the entire document, while the upper section shows the current master pages. At the top of the window are buttons controlling the creation, duplication and deletion of pages.

To add pages to a document, click and drag the master-page icon (default name, 'A-Master-A') from the top to the bottom half of the window and drop it at the end of the document.

Care must be taken as it is easy to thoroughly confuse a layout by dropping in a new page at the wrong place. However, it is (probably) possible to fix any mistakes because page icons can be dragged to new positions in the lower half of the window. But, left and right pages in a facing-page document have different side margin settings. So, if a single page (rather than a double-page spread) is introduced part way through a facing-page document, every subsequent page will have its original left or right orientation switched. In such a case, it is very likely that the text frames on the pages no longer fit within the page margins.

To go to a particular page in your document, double-click on its page icon (or use the key command 'apple/control + J' and type in the relevant page number). See the 'Adding Pages' movie on the CD.

1.7 The Measurements window

One of the most useful floating windows in Quark, the Measurements window is accessed via either 'View' or 'Window' and 'Show Measurements' ('F9') (**fig. 6**). Depending on the object selected, the details showing in the window allow you to format text, scale text and picture boxes, scale images and rotate and skew objects. As it does not take up much space, it is worthwhile having it open all the time.

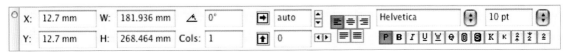

fig. 6 The Measurements window.

1.8 Basic work methods

At this stage, I would like to introduce some common working methods that are used frequently and will prove invaluable.

Creating text and picture boxes
There are two tools in the Toolbox for drawing boxes into which either text or pictures can be placed. Each is on a flyout menu, indicated by the small arrow pointing to the right on the tool button, which is activated by holding down the cursor on the arrow and, when the flyout opens, dragging along it and releasing the mouse on the desired tool. Then click and drag on an empty area of the page to create a text or picture box. For more information about the Text and Picture Box tools, see p. 120.

Grouping and locking items
Sometimes it is necessary to move several items together while retaining their relative position to each other, and grouping them is a

practical way to do this. Select all the objects you wish to move, either by clicking and dragging the cursor to create a bounding box whose border touches all the objects to be grouped or by clicking on one item and 'shift-clicking' on all the others (this is a toggle, and can be used for selecting or deselecting objects).

When everything is selected, choose 'Item > Group' ('apple/control + G'), which ensures that grouped items move together when selected and dragged or scale simultaneously when resized. To ungroup, select the group and choose 'Item > Ungroup' ('apple/control + U').

Items are locked into position by selecting them and choosing 'Item > Lock' ('F6'). Unlock them in the same way, when the command will read 'Item > Unlock'. See the 'Arrange, Group and Lock' movie on the CD.

Bring to Front and Send to Back

The last object drawn or placed on the page appears in front of all other objects. To change the hierarchy, select the object and choose 'Item > Send to Back' ('shift + F5') or 'Item > Bring to Front' ('F5'). The commands 'Bring Forward' and 'Send Backward' move the selection through a single layer of the existing order and are less useful, especially on a complex page. See the 'Arrange, Group and Lock' movie and file on the CD.

The Undo command

Up to v.5, Quark offered only one level of Undo, so it is important to fix mistakes immediately. The Undo command is under 'Edit > Undo' ('apple/control + Z') and works as an Undo/Redo toggle. From v.6, a multiple Undo is included, so that repeated applications of 'apple/control + Z' undoes a series of operations. Or, use the 'undo' and 'redo' buttons in the lower-left corner of the screen.

Saving a document

Quark allows you to save documents in two formats: as a document (up to v.5) or project (v.6), or as a template (up to v.5) or project template (v.6). Documents and projects can be opened and edited. When a template is opened, a copy of it opens, rather than the original, thereby making templates much more secure and harder to update by mistake.

To save a Quark document (or project), choose 'File > Save' ('apple/control + S'). The first time this is used, the Save As window opens, allowing you to name the document and specify its location. Click 'save' to complete the process. If further edits are made, use the same command to update the saved version.

To save a document as a template, go to 'File > Save As' ('apple/control + alt + S') and choose 'template' (or 'project template') from the 'Save as Type' list. Name it, specify a location, then click 'Save'.

Quark files can be saved back one version, for example, a Quark 5 document can be saved in Quark 4 format. However, it is important to remember that more recent developments, such as tables and layers, were not available in Quark 4 and, therefore, would not be saved.

2   The Toolbox

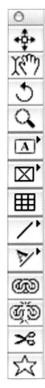

The Toolbox, shown in **fig. 7**, usually appears down the left side of the screen. As with all floating windows, it can be moved by dragging on the shaded bar at its top. It is closed by clicking on (Mac) the dot in the top-left corner or (PC) the 'X' in the top-right corner.

Clicking on an icon selects that particular tool. You will use some of these tools constantly, whereas others are much less important for general day-to-day work.

| Tip | If you select any tool other than the Item and Content tools (the top two in the Toolbox) then, after a single use, the selected tool reverts back to whichever of the Item or Content Tool was last used. Hold down the 'alt' key when choosing a tool if you want to implement multiple uses of it. |

2.1 The Item Tool

This tool is mostly used for moving and resizing objects. Click on an object, and handles appear on the object's corners and at the centre of each side. Drag these to change shape and size. 'Shift-click' to select/deselect additional objects or click and drag to touch objects with a bounding box. Place the cursor over an object, and when it changes to the tool symbol, the object can be moved. See the 'Item and Content tools' movie and file on the CD.

If you select several objects and group them ('Item > Group' or 'apple/control + G'), they will share a single set of corner and centre-side handles, allowing the objects to be resized or moved together.

fig. 7 The Toolbox.

To constrain the proportions of an object while resizing, drag on a corner handle while holding down the 'shift' key.

Selected objects can be deleted with the 'backspace' or 'delete' keys.

This tool must be used when copying and pasting all objects other than text, for which the Content Tool should be used instead.

2.2 The Content Tool

This tool has two main uses: inserting text and repositioning an image within a picture box. See the 'Item and Content tools' movie on the CD.

If this tool is placed within a text box, text can be entered. Or, text can be highlighted, by clicking and dragging across it, and then deleted, replaced or formatted.

Using the grabber hand, on an image in a picture box, allows the image to be dragged to a different position.

When this tool is selected, it can be toggled back into the Item Tool by holding down the 'apple/control' key.

To delete a text or picture box with this tool, use 'apple/control + K'.

2.3 The Rotation Tool

This tool rotates objects manually. The angle of rotation is tracked in the Measurements window (see p. 117), where it can be adjusted or cleared. Select an object and then click on the Rotation Tool. Click and drag on or near the object to define a point of rotation and a lever. As the cursor, to which the lever is attached, moves, the object rotates. The longer the lever, the more precise the rotation.

2.4 The Zoom Tool
As the keyboard shortcut (see p. 115) for this command is so much faster, this tool should not be needed. If it *is* required, click and drag to zoom in.

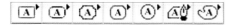

2.5 The Text Box tools
This is the first of the flyout menu tools (see p. 119). When you have selected the appropriate text-box shape, click and drag on the page to create the box. Holding down the 'shift' key while clicking and dragging constrains the shape to a square or circular (rather than rectangular or oval) format, except in the case of the Bézier and freehand text boxes (see 'Creating/editing custom shaped boxes [and lines]', p. 136).

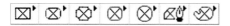

2.6 The Picture Box tools
On another flyout menu, the picture box tools create boxes to hold images. They are drawn in the same ways as text boxes (see 'Working with images' for more information on such things as image placement, p. 135).

2.7 The Tables Tool (v.5+)
See 'Creating and formatting tables' on p. 141.

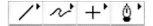

2.8 The Line tools
The Freehand Line Tool (represented by a squiggly line) creates a line following where you have dragged the cursor on the page.

The Bézier Line Tool (nib symbol) draws in exactly the same way as when drawing a Bézier text or picture box (an operation that is discussed in detail in 'Creating/editing custom-shaped boxes [and lines]', p. 136).

The other two tools – the Orthogonal Line Tool for drawing vertical and horizontal lines and the Line Tool for lines drawn at other angles – are in fact both contained within the Line Tool by holding down the 'shift' key as the line is drawn, to constrain it to horizontal, vertical or 45° angles.

To draw a line, click, drag and release the cursor; colour and width can be edited while the line is selected using 'Item > Modify > Line'. If you decide on a dotted-line style in this window, you can also select a colour for the gap between the dots. The colour of a line can be changed using the Colour window ('F12').

2.9 The Text-Path tools
See 'Text on a path' on p. 131.

2.10 The Link and Unlink tools
See 'Linking and unlinking text boxes' on p. 127.

3   Working with Colour

3.1 Applying colour fills and strokes

The Colours window – (up to Quark v.5) 'View > Show Colours' or (Quark v.6 onwards) 'Window > Show Colours' ('F12') – is inactive until the page contains an object to which colours can be applied (**fig. 8**). So, draw a shape on the page; it does not matter whether it is a text or a picture box. While it is selected, click on one of the buttons in the top-left corner of the Colours window.

These buttons will vary slightly depending on whether you drew a text or picture box. In both cases, the button on the left is called the 'frame colour', allowing you to colour the outline, or stroke, of the box. The button on the right applies fill colours. For a picture box, the central button is inactive until either a bitmap or greyscale image is placed in it (see p. 21). In the case of a text box, the central button shows the letter 'A' and is inactive until the Content Tool is selected.

To colour the text within a text box, first select the text by clicking and dragging over it with the Content Tool, then press the central button in the Colours window and click on a colour. While highlighted, the text seems to change to the exact opposite of what you selected, but that is only because the action of highlighting text reverses the view of its colour, causing, for example, black text on a white background to appear as white text on a black background. As soon as you click elsewhere (thus no longer highlighting the text), it appears correctly.

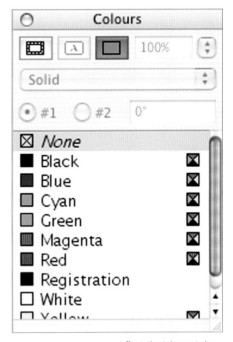

fig. 8 The Colours window.

Tip   **You cannot add a stroke to editable text. And, no, clicking on the 'outline' icon in the Measurements window does not do it either. Instead, the text must first be transformed into a 'text box', meaning that it is no longer text, merely a vector path that has the same shape as the text. At that point, it can be treated like any other shape and filled with solid or blended colours, given a stroke or filled with an image. See 'Adding a stroke to text', p. 126.**

If you have created a picture box, the central button at the top of the Colours window has a different use and appearance. If the box holds a bitmap or a greyscale image, then clicking on a colour while this button is selected turns all the black and grey pixels in the image to the appropriate shade of the selected colour. The 'fill' button changes the colour of the background, as if the rest of the image were transparent (**fig. 9**). This feature does not affect RGB or CMYK images.

Regarding the colours themselves, it is very important to understand that some of the default colours in this window are OK to print, while others are not. Red, green and blue are RGB and, therefore, completely unsuitable for inclusion within a document destined for print, whether to your own desktop printer or to a commercial offset litho shop. These colours do not exist in the CMYK range and, to reproduce them using CMYK inks or toner, they have to be converted, usually to something quite different from what you might expect. So, to

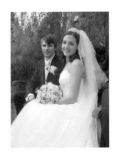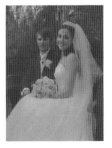

fig. 9 Changing the colours in a greyscale image.

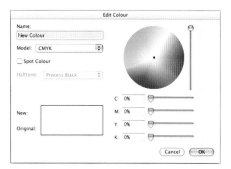

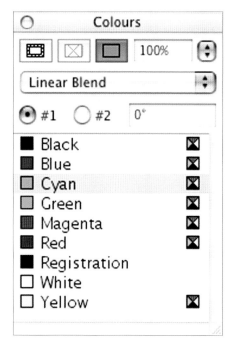

fig. 10 The Edit Colour window.

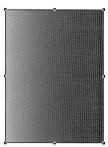

fig. 11 Creating a blend.

avoid using them accidentally, they should be deleted. Choose 'Edit > Colours' ('shift + F12'), click on each of them in turn and press the 'delete' button.

3.2 Creating colour styles

To create a new colour, go to 'Edit > Colours', click on the 'new' button and the Edit Colour window appears (**fig. 10**).

Enter a name for your colour in the window at the top.

Under 'model', choose CMYK or Pantone. If you choose CMYK, uncheck the 'spot colour' box. A spot colour is regarded as being separate from the CMYK colours and there is a chance that if this box is left checked, what should be a 4-colour job will end up producing 5 plates or more. If, however, it is unchecked, the colour will be divided up into its CMYK components and will be output as part of the information on the cyan, magenta, yellow and black plates.

If you select Pantone, and you do actually intend to use a Pantone ink to print the job, leave 'spot colour' checked. Should you wish to convert a Pantone colour to its closest CMYK equivalent, then, after choosing it, uncheck the 'spot colour' box and re-select CMYK from the 'model' list. This converts the colour to the closest possible CMYK tint.

To actually create a new colour, enter values in the percentage windows, or drag the sliders, or click on the colour wheel. When using the last option, darker and lighter shades of the colour can be added by dragging on the vertical slider to its right.

Click 'OK' to return to the Edit Colour window, where you should either click on 'save' or continue to create new colours. All colours listed in the Colours window can be applied to fills, strokes and text.

3.3 Editing colours

To edit an existing colour, go to 'Edit > Colours', click on a colour to select it, then click the 'edit' button and change whatever you wish. As you click on the 'save' button, every use of that colour in the document is updated automatically. See the 'Colour Styles' movie and file on the CD.

3.4 Colour blends

Aside from working with solid colour, it is also possible to create blends between any two of the swatches available in the Colours window. To try this, draw a shape on the page and, with it selected, open the Colours window ('F12'). Click on the arrow to the right of 'solid' and choose a blend type from the list. The 'radio button' for the first of the two colours is selected automatically. Pick a colour from the list, then click the second radio button and select colour number two. The shape fills with colour as you make your choices (**fig. 11**).

Tip	**Blends cannot be saved as colour swatches.**

4   Working with Text

Creating, applying and editing paragraph and character styles follows a very similar process to working with colour. However, while creating new colour styles is a pre-requisite to using them in a document, many people use the Measurements window (see p. 117), rather than paragraph styles, to format their text.

If you are producing anything other than a single-page document, such as a poster containing only a very small amount of text, it is almost certainly better to create and use paragraph (and, to a lesser degree, character) styles. As with colour edits, any edits made to a paragraph style updates any text to which that style has already been applied. In addition, whereas a colour is a simple element, a text style is much more complex and can contain information relating not only to font, size and leading, but to tabs, paragraph rules, hyphenation, colour, and more. To update multiple blocks of text using any other method wastes a great deal of time and is not worth contemplating.

At the beginning of a layout job, create all the colour and paragraph styles that you will need. That way, imported text can be formatted immediately and all the colours are already available. If, for example, the text is then found to be slightly too large, it is an easy matter to edit the style to progressively smaller sizes until the problem has been fixed.

This is not to imply that the Measurements window is of no use for text formatting. It is particularly useful for inputting character-style edits, rather than creating actual character styles. For example, if a single word or phrase needs to appear in italic, then as long as the 'italic' version of the font is available without needing to specify a different font (i.e. the entry in the font list in the Measurements window points to a font *family*, such as 'Arial', rather than to something more specific, such as 'Profile-Light'), it is easier to use the Measurements window to format the word than it is to create an italic character style. It is more efficient, too, in the case of subsequent style edits. If italics have been added using the Measurements window, and the size specification in the applied paragraph style is then changed, the italics update too – whereas a character style would not, as it cannot be based on an existing paragraph style. Otherwise, however, it is preferable to create a character style that points to the exact font needed.

The Measurements window should not be used to specify paragraph formatting, unless only one or two paragraphs in an entire document require special treatment.

4.1 Paragraph and character styles

Paragraph styles

First, choose either (up to Quark v.5) 'View > Show Style Sheets' or (Quark v.6 onwards) 'Window > Show Style Sheets' (**fig. 12**). Then, select 'Edit > Style Sheets' (**fig. 13**) (the shortcut for the Styles window is 'F11' and for the Style Sheets window it is 'shift + F11'). In the Style Sheets window, choose 'New > Paragraph Style' to open the Edit Paragraph Style Sheet

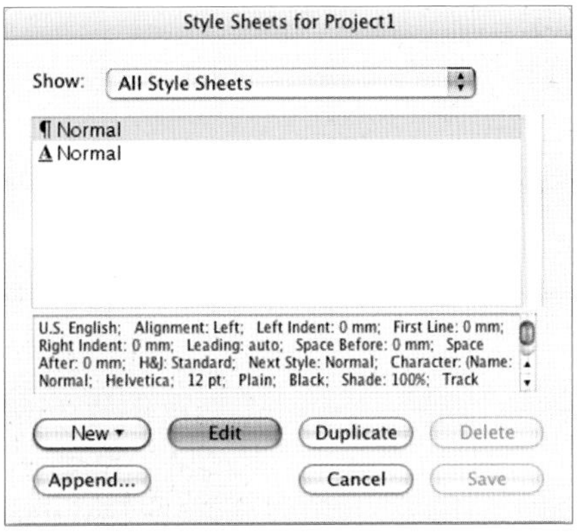

fig. 12 The Style Sheets window.

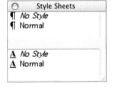

fig. 13 Creating new style sheets.

fig. 14 Beginning the
creation of a new
paragraph style.

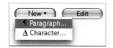

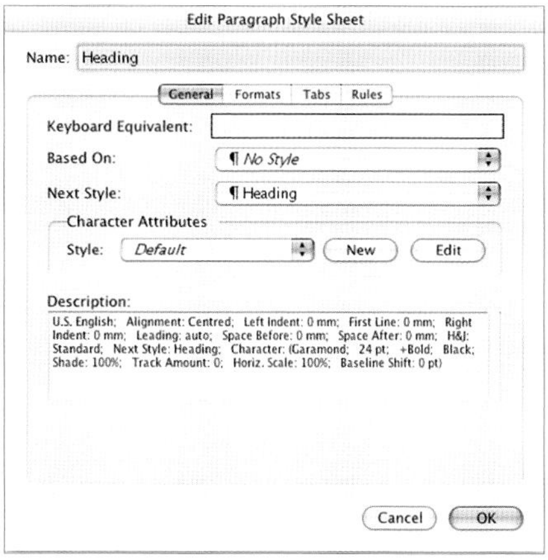

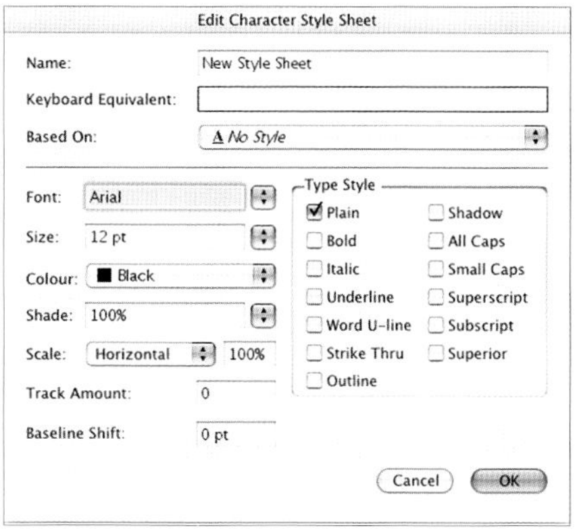

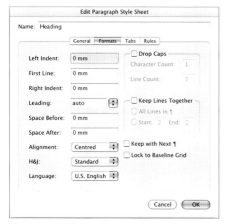

fig. 15 Character formatting.

fig. 16 Paragraph formatting.

window (**fig. 14**). Name the new style and click on the 'Edit' button to set the character attributes (**fig. 15**).

Here, you can choose from all the fonts currently installed on your system; if such styles as bold or italic are available, you can check the appropriate boxes in the right half of the window. In this area, you can also set 'all caps' or 'small caps' (smaller versions of regular capital letters), superscript (as in '4^2') and subscript (as in 'H_2O'). As the latter two formats are rarely required for an entire type style and as they can be applied easily where needed through the Measurements window, it is unlikely that you will wish to apply them here. The same is true of underline and word underline, although editors may find these functions useful if they wish to show text that has been replaced.

Choose a point size for the style: as a guide, there are 72 points to the inch, so 36pt type measures $\frac{1}{2}$", or about 2.5cm, from the top of a letter 'h' to the bottom of a letter 'y'.

Select one of the colours currently available in the Colours window and also choose a tint, but remember that in offset printing, lighter shades are rendered as dots of solid colour. If the text is small, the definition of the letters may suffer from this conversion.

If you desperately need a condensed style but do not have one, set an 80% horizontal width in the 'Scale' box. It will not be a true condensed font, but it might be OK as a temporary substitute.

'Track Amount' means the spacing between letters and words; usually the default is fine, but it can be changed as needed. 'Baseline Shift' is not usually an important setting when creating a style, although it can be useful elsewhere. The baseline shift raises or lowers the selected text in relation to other text sharing the same (base)line.

Tip   **A quick way of setting the character attributes for a new paragraph (or character) style is to apply first the desired specifications to a few words of text. Highlight it with the Content Tool, and choose 'Edit > Style Sheets' as described above. All formatting assigned so far will already be in place.**

Click 'OK' to close this window when you have finished and then go to the 'formats' tab (**fig. 16**). The Formats window determines the paragraph attributes. Left and right indents apply to the whole text, whereas first-line indents only affect the first line of each paragraph.

'Leading' is the space between lines of text. Auto leading is set at 120% of the specified style size, so, if the type was set at 10pt, the leading would be 12pt.

'Space Before' and 'Space After' apply a fixed amount of space between each paragraph. I do not usually use these, as I have another method that I prefer (see 'space styles' on p. 125).

'Alignment' offers five choices: left, centre, right, justify and forced (in which the last line of a paragraph, usually shorter than the others, is spread to fill the entire width of the column). Forced alignment can be a very effective and classy heading style in which a serif (i.e. stylized corners on the letter shapes) typeface is specified in small caps with a spacebar space inserted between each letter and a couple of extra spaces between each word.

'Drop Caps' are large initial capital letters that appear at the start of a chapter or section. Here, you can specify how many characters and how many lines are to be affected.

Other specifications listed here are not usually very important.

'Tabs' are extremely useful within a block of text that needs them, but are rarely helpful as a paragraph style specification. In the last 10 years, I have only used this function once as part of a paragraph style; the more common usage of tabs is covered on p. 129.

'Paragraph rules' can be used to place a horizontal rule of a specified thickness and colour between each paragraph. This is of very limited use, except when creating the effect shown in 'ruled heading style' on the CD. If this kind of appearance is needed, a rule is a very good way to produce it, as separate coloured boxes would not reflow when text is edited.

Rules can be applied in any colour available in the Colours window or as a percentage tint of full strength.

When the style specifications are complete, click 'OK' to close the window. You can then create new styles, or, click 'save' and the new style(s) are added to the list in the Style Sheets window.

To apply a paragraph style, it is not necessary to highlight the entire paragraph. As long as the cursor insertion point is within the paragraph, it will all be formatted in the selected style.

To assign a style to an entire story (all the connected text, whether or not it has all been placed on the page), click within the text and choose 'apple/control + A'. This selects all the text, visible or not, and the style you then choose will be applied to the whole story.

Character styles

These are created in exactly the same way as paragraph styles, but the choices offered exclude all the specifications that only relate to paragraphs (**fig. 17**) and the application is slightly different.

A character style needs to be shown exactly where it is to be applied, and it is therefore necessary to click and drag to highlight all the relevant text before clicking on the style. Character styles can be applied to text that has already been formatted with a paragraph style.

Space styles

Specific spaces between paragraphs can be created using space styles. These are like regular paragraph styles, but with one exception: they only govern the leading specification of a line of space and never format text.

To create a 2pt space style, follow the method, outlined above, for creating a paragraph style, but enter only a value of 2pt for the leading (other values are unimportant). Having saved the style, create a line space between two paragraphs of text, place the cursor on that line and

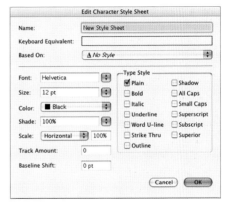

fig. 17 Setting up a new character style.

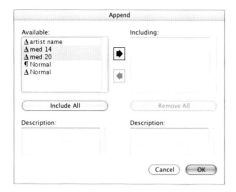

fig. 18 Appending styles
from another document.

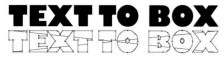

fig. 19 Converting text into a graphic.

click on the 2pt style. For a 4pt space, simply press 'enter', while the cursor is still there, thereby adding a second 2pt line. Alternatively, you can create another style using 4pt as the leading value.

For examples of space styles and more, see 'small caps and space styles' and 'hanging indent styles' on the CD.

4.2 Appending styles from other documents

To import style sheets from another document, choose 'Edit > Style Sheets' and click on the 'append' button. Browse to the file containing the styles you wish to import and click 'open'. The Append window appears (**fig. 18**), split vertically into two halves.

The left side lists the styles available in the indicated document; click on those you wish to import. To select them all, click on the 'Include All' button. To choose a few styles, click on the first one you wish to add and then 'shift-click' on the others, one at a time. When the styles are all selected, click on the right-pointing arrow to copy them to the current document.

4.3 Adding a stroke to text

A stroke cannot be added to editable text. However, if the text is *not* text, but a vector path with the same *shape* as text, a stroke could be added. Vector paths can be filled with colours, blends and images (because the box containing the vector will have been converted into a picture box).

To change text into a graphic, first draw a text box, click inside it with the Content Tool and type a few letters. Click and drag across the text with the Content Tool to highlight it and choose 'Style > Text to Box'. Immediately, a graphic with the same shape as the text appears beneath it. Move the original text box out of the way using the Item Tool and zoom into the graphic for a closer look (**fig. 19**).

Two diagonal lines appear throughout the text shape, indicating that the whole graphic, while made up of separate elements, forms some kind of a group. These are compound paths, and create holes in an object anywhere the paths overlap. To try this, draw two rectangles, one inside the other. Select both of them, then choose 'Item > Merge > Difference'. The inner rectangle becomes a hole in the outer's shape. If you fill the object with a colour, and place it over another shape, you will be able to see through the hole to the object(s) beneath.

Text that has been converted to a 'box' can be treated just like any other shape and filled with solid or blended colours and given a stroke.

Tip	The above method of adding a stroke can only be applied to one line of text at a time.

4.4 Importing text

Adding text to a document can require creating a text box, clicking inside it with the Content Tool and typing. Often, however, text is supplied to a designer in Microsoft Word format. Word formatting is very difficult to remove completely, and, whenever text is imported, existing formatting is likely to introduce new, and quite possibly unwanted, paragraph styles. These will appear in the Style Sheets window with a disk icon on the right. It is easy to edit these styles, but it is preferable to import the text in a way that leaves behind previous formatting. To do this, re-save the Word document as text only, and copy and paste it from there into the Quark document.

Previous formatting commonly causes problems when you try to apply a new paragraph style. If nothing happens when you try to apply the style and a small '+' sign appears next to the style name in the list, the previous formatting is blocking the new instruction. To clear the block, click on the style name while holding down the 'alt' key.

To import text directly into a document, rather than copying and pasting it, create a text box and go to 'File > Get Text' ('apple/control + E').

In the Get Text window (**fig. 20**) are two useful check boxes:

1) 'Convert Quotes', which turns all instances of single or double straight quotes into typographer's (or smart) quotes (i.e. " and " rather than ") and all double hyphens to em dashes. An em dash is the same length as the number of points in the selected type size, i.e. in 24pt type, it would be 24pt long.

2) 'Include Style Sheets' enables formatting styles to be imported (but does not always prevent them from being imported, even if left unchecked). Browse to the text file, open it; text flows into the text box.

4.5 Linking and unlinking text boxes
To control the flow of text into a document, links between text boxes can be created manually. For a visual example of this, see the 'Linking and Unlinking Text' movie and file on the CD.

On page 1 is a single column of text. At its foot is a small red box containing a red 'x', on the right side. This indicates that there is more text to be placed than is currently visible.

These red boxes do not print and are only guides to show there is more text that has not been dealt with. It is useful to remember that the boxes can be caused by empty lines produced by a few hits of the 'enter' key. While these are not a problem in themselves, it is vital to check that there really is no missing text. Unnecessary returns can also lead to unwanted pages at the end of the document.

Open the Preferences section (under the QuarkXPress Menu on a Mac and the Edit Menu on a PC), choose 'Document' and select the 'General' tab. On the left is 'Auto Page Insertion'. Choose 'Off' from the list, otherwise, if a red box appears in the document, a page is very likely to be added at the end to accommodate whatever has not been placed (even if it was empty lines of space).

Another useful preference to change is on the right side of the same window. Uncheck 'Greek Below' and the document will not display small text as a grey bar, but as text. This helps you to maintain your view of a page design, even when the text is too small to read. Setting a preference

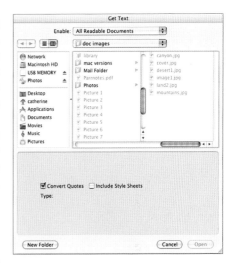

To control the flow of text into a document, links between text boxes can be created manually. Try this by opening 'Linking Text' in the QuarkXPress section of the CD.

On page 1 is a single column of text. At its foot is a small red box containing a red 'x', on the right side. This indicates that there is more text to be placed than is currently visible.

These red boxes do not print and are only guides to show there is more text that has not been dealt with. It is useful to remember that the boxes can be caused by empty lines produced by a few hits of the 'enter' key. ⊠

fig. 20 Bringing text into a document.

while a document is open only makes it the default setting for that document. Doing so while no documents are open changes the setting for all subsequent new documents, although it does not affect previously saved documents (see p. 130 for more useful changes to default settings).

To control the flow of text into a document, links between text boxes can be created manually. Try this by opening 'Linking Text' in the QuarkXPress section of the CD. On page 1 is a single column of text. At its foot is a small red box containing a red 'x', on the right side. This indicates that there is more text to be placed than is currently visible.

These red boxes do not print and are only guides to show there is more text that has not been dealt with. It is useful to remember that the boxes can be caused by empty lines produced by a few hits of the 'enter' key. While these are not a problem in themselves, it is vital to check that there really is no missing text. Unnecessary returns can also lead to unwanted pages at the end of the document.

Open the Preferences section (under the QuarkXPress Menu on a Mac and the Edit Menu on a PC), choose 'Document' and select the 'General' tab. On the left is 'Auto Page Insertion'. Choose 'Off' from the list, otherwise, if a red box appears in the document, a page is very likely to be added at the end to accommodate whatever has not been placed (even if it was empty lines of space).

Another useful preference to change is on the right side of the same window.

fig. 21 The Link Tool (top) and linking text across multiple frames (below).

Draw another text box on the right of the page and click on the Link Tool near the foot of the Toolbox. Click once inside the text box on the left. The cursor becomes a link icon and the border of the text box turns into 'marching ants' (moving dotted lines). Click inside the second text box. An arrow momentarily appears, indicating the direction of text flow, and the additional text flows into the second box (**fig. 21**).

It does not matter whether the boxes to be linked are on the same page or not as long as they are in the same document, do not already contain text and are not already part of a text string (one of a series of linked boxes into which text has already been flowed).

Now, go to pages 2 and 3 of the 'linking text' document. There are several text boxes, but only the box on the left contains text. Select the Link Tool and hold down the 'alt' key to prevent the selected tool from reverting to either the Item or Content tools after only a single use.

Click on the text-filled box on the left, then on the next box, then on the next one, and so on. There should now be a series of linked boxes.

Select the Item Tool, click on the first box in the chain and press the 'delete' key. The box is deleted, but the text is not – it simply flows into the next box. To see the direction, or thread, of text flow, click on any one of the boxes with the Link Tool and arrows showing the flow appear, running from the foot of one box to the top of the next.

Now, try unlinking. Select the Unlink Tool and click on one of the text boxes. Again, the arrows appear. Click on the base of one of the arrows, and the flow is broken at that point.

In a series of linked boxes, you can remove only one box from a thread. Select the Unlink Tool and click on one of the linked boxes. Choose a box, other than the first or last in the chain, and click on the base of the connecting arrow that points away from it while holding down the 'shift' key at the same time.

Tip   **To check the direction of text flow between several text boxes, select them with the Unlink Tool. If you use the Link Tool and accidentally click in one of the boxes, you may cause text to reflow, with possibly disastrous results.**

4.6 Hyphenation and justification

Quark has a default hyphenation setting. To turn it off, you need to create a new hyphenation and justification (H&Js) style, which can then be applied to any existing paragraph style.

Go to 'Edit > H&Js' and a window very similar to the Style Sheets window appears. Click on 'New' and give this style a name (for example, 'Off'). Uncheck the 'Auto Hyphenation' box near the top-left corner, click

'OK' and then 'save' (**fig. 22**). To apply this new setting to an existing paragraph style, choose 'Edit > Style Sheets', select the style you wish to update and click on the 'Edit' button. Select the 'Formats' tab and, in the bottom-left corner of that window, choose the new H&Js style from the drop-down list.

Click 'OK' and 'Save', and the paragraph style no longer allows words to be hyphenated. You can still add 'discretionary' hyphens if needed by positioning the cursor at the relevant point, holding down 'apple/control' and pressing '-' (the hyphen key). See the movie on the CD.

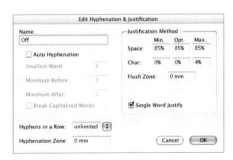

fig. 22 Creating a custom hyphenation style

4.7 Tabs

As long as two simple rules are adhered to, it is quite straightforward to apply tabs to separate a block of text into columns. First, allow enough space for the text. Not doing so does not result in a disaster, but it does produce confusion. It is much easier to remove excess space than it is to deal with too little. Second, having set up the tabs, do not panic if, when you click the 'Tab' key, the text does not move immediately to the position you think it should. Keep entering tab commands until you have completed them for the entire line and usually you will find that everything sorts itself out; if not, you probably did not allow enough space.

On the CD, open the file called 'Tabs'.

It is a good idea to turn on the 'Invisibles' when setting tabs. To do this, go to 'View > Show Invisibles' ('apple/control + I' ['i']). This is a toggle command, so they can be turned off in the same way. Invisibles display otherwise hidden commands, such as hard returns and tabs, thus allowing you to see if you have entered a tab command twice.

On the page are three blocks of text, representing the three most likely ways in which copy requiring tabs will be presented to you.

At the top is the worst case scenario: there are no tab commands and no instructions as to how many columns the text should be divided into. (Page 2 of the document shows all the blocks tabbed correctly, but try to figure it out for yourself first.) Zoom in until all the text is clearly visible. Then, starting from the end of the block, click and drag back to the beginning with the Content Tool. It is generally easier to highlight text from the end rather than from the beginning, as the edge of the text box does not get in the way.

When the text is highlighted, choose 'Style > Tabs' ('apple/control + shift + T'). A ruler with a horizontal space above it appears across the top of the text (**fig. 23**) and the Paragraph Attributes window opens to display the different tabs. The 'Left-Aligned' tab is selected as a default.

A click inside the horizontal space above the ruler places a tab marker. While the marker is selected, it can be changed to one of the other markers by clicking on the appropriate button, or it can be dragged to a new position, or it can be pulled out of its window to delete it.

Click to position the other tab markers that you think you will need. Decide what kind of tabs they should be – either left- or centre-aligned will probably work best in this case. Remember that whichever button is

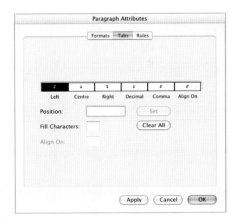

fig. 23 Tabs.

selected in the window dictates the alignment of the next tab marker unless it is changed.

When you have finished, click inside the text with the Content Tool at the position where the first tab command is needed. Press the 'tab' key (positioned above the 'caps lock' key on the left side) and repeat the process to designate each column in the line.

The text should end up being separated clearly into four columns. If the text in one of the columns is uneven, check whether the tab command was accidentally placed to the left of a space. If some of the text seems to miss out a column completely, jumping instead to the next tab position, then either the column width for the previous column was not wide enough and has pushed the text further out, or there are two tab commands instead of one.

If a column is too narrow, highlight the entire block again and go to 'Style > Tabs'. Drag the existing markers further to the right to allow more space between the columns, and then press the 'apply' button. The text moves to the new positions and you can see whether the problem is solved.

The second block of type represents a much better scenario, in that tab commands have already been placed in the text. All that is needed is to highlight the text, open the Tabs window, reposition the tab markers and press 'apply'.

The last example is, unfortunately, very common. Rather than using tabs to separate the text, the author has simply held down the spacebar until everything is more-or-less lined up. In this situation, follow the method outlined for the first block, but instead of simply entering tab commands in the text, click and drag to highlight all the space first and *then* press the tab key. That way, the space is removed at the same time as the tab command is placed.

| Tip | To see a live update when re-adjusting tabs, hold down the 'alt' key as you press the 'Apply' button in the Tabs window. It will then allow you to see the results of any edits as they are made. |

4.8 Runarounds

Also known as text wraps, runarounds force text to get out of the way of something else. Unfortunately, a runaround setting is the default in Quark and applies to all text and picture boxes until it is changed. Another irritating default setting in Quark gives all text and image boxes a solid white fill (it is easy enough to apply a white fill, or a fill of any other colour, when and where needed).

These two defaults can be dealt with at the same time and in the same place. I strongly recommend closing down all active documents before making these changes, otherwise they will only apply to the open documents, and nowhere else. If no documents are open when these settings are changed, they will apply to all documents created from that point.

Click on (Mac) the QuarkXPress Menu or (PC) Edit Menu and choose 'Preferences > Document > Tool'; alternatively, double-click on the rectangular text tool button. A list of all the shape- and line-drawing tools appears in the window (**fig. 24**). Select the rectangular text box icon and then press 'Select Similar Types' to highlight all the other text-box tools. Now, press 'Modify'. In the Modify window, on the 'Group' tab, choose 'None' as the new box colour and click 'OK', thereby solving the problem of the solid white fill. Unfortunately, to deal with the runaround, the tools have to be selected individually. Select the rectangular text box tool icon once more, click on 'Modify', then the 'Runaround' tab. At the top, opposite 'Item', choose 'None', click 'OK' and do the same for the next tool, and so on.

It is also possible to change the solid fill setting for the picture-box tools as a group, but again you must change their runaround values individually.

When finished, click 'OK', and you have a new and more generally useful default for all future documents.

Runarounds can be applied to text and picture boxes by choosing 'Item > Runaround'. The basic choices for the type of runaround are 'None' or 'Item'. When 'Item' is chosen, additional outset values (a buffer zone extending beyond the box itself) can also be specified.

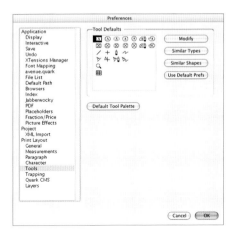

fig. 24 Using the Preferences window for modifying such tool attributes as 'Runarounds'.

4.9 Text on a path

Text can be placed on paths as well as in text boxes. To do this, choose one of the text-on-a-path tools and draw a line on the page.

The default specification for lines drawn with these tools is for no thickness and no colour, so that the text placed on them appears to be floating on the page. You can, however, specify stroke characteristics, just as with any other line.

When the line is drawn, the tool selection immediately reverts to the Content Tool and a cursor insertion point appears. Text can be typed in manually, pasted in or imported by going to 'File > Get Text'. Once in place, it can be formatted in any of the usual ways. Text can be linked from the end of a line into a text box or the line can be edited to accommodate more text. To edit the shape of lines and box outlines, see 'Cropping and repositioning images' on p. 136.

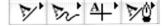

4.10 Creating a table of contents

A table of contents can be generated using a list. If, for example, you have created a paragraph style for the chapter headings of a book and another for the sub-headings, both styles can be included in a list that allows you to duplicate, elsewhere in the document, all the text appearing in both styles.

To set up a new list, go to 'Edit > Lists' and choose 'New'. The Edit List window appears (**fig. 25**), showing all the paragraph and character styles

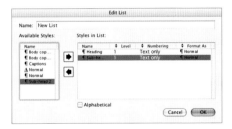

fig. 25 Creating a table of contents.

in your document. Select those you wish to include in the list and click the arrow pointing to the right.

Tip   All text that has been formatted with the selected styles is included in the list.

There are three numbering options on a table of contents: none, the entry followed by the page number and the page number followed by the entry. You can also specify one of eight levels of hierarchy and a different type style, using the 'Format As' column. Check 'Alphabetical', if required. When finished, click 'OK'.

To generate a table of contents, choose 'View > Lists', select the list from the 'List Name' and click 'Update'. The list appears in the lower part of the window. To place the list in the document, draw a text box, click inside it with the Content Tool and click 'Build' in the 'Lists' window.

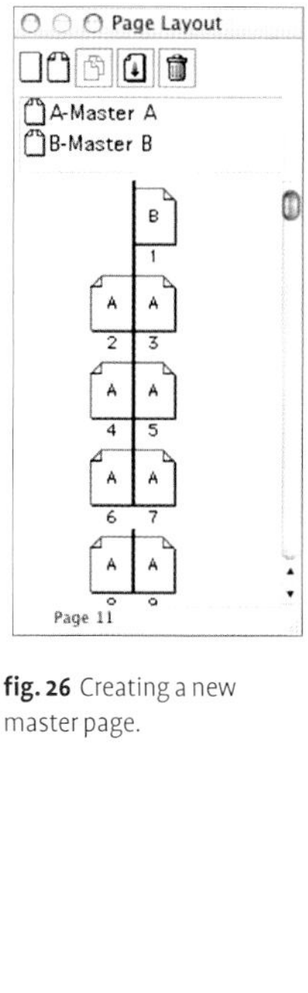

4.11 Master pages and sections

fig. 26 Creating a new master page.

Master pages are a way of applying automatic page numbering and placing objects that need to display on several document pages in the same, or a similar, way. See the 'Master Pages' movie on the CD.

All documents have a default master page, called 'A-Master A'. The name of this and any other master page can be changed by double-clicking on it and typing in something else.

To create a new master page, click on either the single or facing master-page icon in the top-left corner of the Page Layout window (**fig. 26**) and drag it down into the upper section. It automatically takes the next available alphabetical name (B-Master B).

If you have a facing-page document and you create a new single-page master, you can apply the master to a left- or a right-hand page in the document.

If you create a new double-page master, the left-hand page can only be applied to left-hand document pages and the right-hand page only to right-hand document pages.

To see a master page on-screen, double-click on the page icon next to its name; alternatively, choose it in the 'Page' field in the bottom-left corner of the screen. Master pages show a 'link' icon in the top-left corner to distinguish them from regular document pages.

As far as content is concerned, objects can be placed on master pages in exactly the same way as on document pages. There is one exception: automatic page numbers, which can only be created on a master page. To do this, open the file called '16-page layout' on the CD.

Two different master pages have already been created for this document: 'A-intro pages' and 'B-chapter pages'. Master page A is currently applied to all the document pages.

Double-click on the page icon for the 'A-intro pages' master to see it on-screen. It holds the layout guides and margins for the introductory section of a book. Create a small text box on the left-hand page, click inside it with the Content Tool and choose 'apple/control + 3'. An odd set of characters appears: '<#>' (**fig 27**). These are replaced by the automatic page numbers within the document.

fig. 27 The automatic page numbering symbol.

Using the Item Tool, copy and paste this text box onto the right-hand page of the master. Drag both text boxes to the lower-left and lower-right corners of the margin areas on their respective pages. Then, select them both and nudge them further down with the keyboard arrow keys. This is an easy way of placing objects on opposite pages at the same horizontal level.

Tip **As a time-saving alternative to using the copy and paste commands repeatedly, use 'apple/control + D' to duplicate the most recent operation.**

The characters within the text boxes can be formatted using any existing paragraph or character style, or through the Measurements window.

Highlight the text in the box on the right-hand page, then press 'apple/control + shift + R'. This is a keyboard shortcut that aligns the text to the right (you can also align to the left with 'L', centre with 'C' and justify with 'J').

Now, double-click on one of the document page icons to see how the page numbers look in the document. If you wish to change the numbers' appearance, return to the master page and do so; otherwise, proceed to the next step.

The auto page number boxes also need to be copied and pasted onto the B-master. To copy them, re-open the A-master, select both boxes and press 'apple/control + C'. Then, if you are using v.6 onwards, open the B-master, and choose 'Edit > Paste in Place'; on earlier versions, use 'Edit > Paste' and position the numbers manually in the same place as on the A-master.

To apply a master page to a single document page, click and drag the master page, by either its name or icon, and drop it onto the document page. The page icon becomes highlighted when you are in the correct drop zone. To apply the same master to a sequence of pages, click on the first document page icon to select it and then 'shift-click' on the last – all the page icons in between also become highlighted. Or, to select a non-contiguous set of pages, 'apple/control + click' on them one at a time. In this case, select pages 9 to 16, hold down the 'alt' key and click on the B-master listing, thereby immediately applying that master to all the selected document pages.

At the very beginning of a book, page numbers do not normally feature. Then, the introductory section often uses roman numerals, while regular page numbers usually start on the first page of the first chapter.

Different numbering systems can be created in the Section window, but first another master page, with no page numbering boxes, needs to

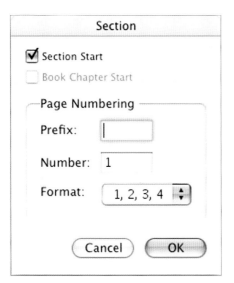

fig. 28 Creating a new section.

be created. Drag down the single- or the facing-page icon from the top-left corner of the Document Layout window and release it in the master-page section. Rename the new master as 'C-blank' and then apply it to pages 1, 2, 3 and 4 of the document.

It is easier to define sections by working backwards from the end of a book, rather than working forwards from the beginning, as all the assigned page numbers change as you go. Therefore, begin by defining the start of chapter 1 on (document) page 9 by double-clicking on page 9 in the document window and choosing 'Page > Section'. In the Section window (**fig. 28**), check the 'Section Start' box but leave everything else as it is. Click 'OK'. What was (document) page 9 is labelled now as page 1.

Double-click on (document) page 5 and again go to 'Page > Section'. As before, check 'Section Start'. This time, leave 'Number' as 1, but choose one of the roman numeral choices from the 'Format' list. Then click 'OK'. The first four document pages now have no page numbers; document pages 5 to 8 display roman numerals, beginning with 'i'; and regular page numbers, starting with 1, begin on (document) page 9.

4.12 Converting a text box to a picture box

To do this, open the 'text box to picture box' file on the CD, and choose 'Item > Content > Picture'. A warning will indicate that you are about to lose the contained text. If you click 'OK', the text box is immediately converted the text box is converted into a picture box. Picture boxes can be changed to text boxes in the same way.

5   Working with Images

5.1 Importing an image

Draw a picture box on the page, and in the same way as when importing text, choose 'File > Get Picture' ('apple/control + E'). Browse to the image, click 'OK' and the image appears in the box.

5.2 Resizing images

When an image is too large for its picture box, only the top-left portion is visible. Even though it is not listed in any of the menus, in all versions up to 5, you can choose 'apple/control + shift + F' to fit a picture to a box (although this is bound to distort it, so is not a good idea). In v.6, the same command fits the picture to either the height or width of the box, but does not distort it. To fit the picture to the box proportionally, use 'apple/control + shift + alt + F'. While better, this is still of limited use. The most useful command, 'Fit Box to Picture', is only available from v.5 and does not have an assigned keyboard shortcut. It is found, along with the other commands just mentioned, under the Style Menu.

There is also a very useful shortcut that enables you to enlarge or reduce an image in increments of 5%: hold down 'apple/control + shift + alt' keys and press the '<' key to reduce or '>' key to enlarge. The Measurements window tracks changes in size as you work and can also be used for making scale adjustments to images in units of 1%.

See the 'Scaling Images' movie on the CD.

Tip   **It is not a good idea to increase the original image size by more than 20% as all you are doing is spreading the original level of detail over a larger area. To reduce an image, on the other hand, presents no problems – aside from the fact that its file size may be much larger than is necessary for the size at which it is being used.**

5.3 Linking images to a Quark document

Linking means that the document holds a screen representation of the images used and not the actual images, which exist as separate files. Only the actual images are capable of providing the printer with the full level of detail to print. When an image is imported, the link information created at that point tells the document where to find it later. To print correctly, *all* the images *and* the document file have to be sent to the printer. Otherwise, the document will not reproduce properly.

The difference between 72dpi and 300dpi (the required resolution for offset printing) may not at first seem too bad: a ratio of roughly 1 to 4. However, if you square the numbers to find the actual difference between the number of pixels in a 1" image at 72dpi and another at 300dpi, you will find that the 72dpi image has 5184 pixels, whereas the 300dpi image has a staggering 90,000 pixels – 19 times more detail.

If the images are kept in the same folder as the Quark document, there is no problem linking the screen representation with the actual image. However, very often during the design process, images are

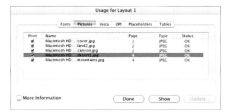

fig. 29 Keeping track of images with the Usage window.

brought into a document from various places on the hard drive. Then, when the job is ready to be sent out, they must all be found.

Details of the images in a document are found under 'Utilities > Usage'. Click on the 'Pictures' tab (**fig. 29**) and the window lists all the images in the document, detailing what page each one is on, what type of image it is and its status.

An image that cannot be located is listed as 'Missing'. If it can be found, but has been edited since being placed in the document, is listed as 'Modified'. Only if there are no problems is it listed as 'OK'.

If an image appears as missing or modified, select it in the list. If you are not sure which image is being referred to, click on 'Show' to select it on-screen. To find or update the link, click 'Update'. Browse to the folder in which the image is located and click 'Open'. If other missing images are also in this folder, Quark prompts you to allow it to update the status of those at the same time.

If all other work is complete and the document has located all the images, the file is ready to send to a printer. Unless it is being sent in PDF format, the document, the images and the font information must be collected together (see Using 'Collect for Output', p. 140).

| Tip | The Usage window can also be used to tell you which fonts have been used in a document. |

5.4 Cropping and repositioning images

To make only part of an image visible, a picture box can be cropped to a new size using the Item Tool, and made into a new shape using the Content Tool. When a picture box containing an image is selected, the Content Tool can move the image within the box. Hold the cursor over the image and it changes to a grabber hand. Then, click and drag.

5.5 Creating/editing custom-shaped boxes (and lines)

Draw the shape you need using the Freehand or Bézier Text Box tools. The Freehand Text Box Tool looks like a classical artists' painting palette, while the Bézier Tool is in the form of a pen nib.

To create a freehand shape, click and drag on the screen. To use the Bézier Tool, click, move and click again to draw straight line segments or click, move and click and drag to produce curved line segments.

To customize an existing shape, select it with the Content Tool, then go to 'Item > Shape' and click on the 'Freehand' shape in the list (**fig. 30**). Choose 'Item > Edit' and click on 'Shape' ('F10'). The 'handles' around the box shape are replaced by four anchor points, one in each corner. The Content Tool can now move these. 'Shift-click' on additional points to select them if you want to move them together. If the cursor is held on the box outline, entire sides can be moved.

Holding down the 'alt' key allows anchor points to be deleted or added: place the cursor over an existing point and click to delete, or click on a line segment to add a point.

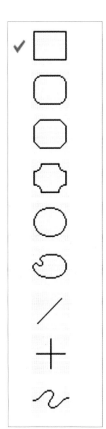

fig. 30 Changing the shape of a text or picture box.

Anchor points can be one of three types, each supporting a different kind of shape within the adjacent line segments. A corner point allows the line segments on either side of it to connect with it from any angle. A smooth point forces the line to cross it in a smooth curve. The Bézier handles, which attach to the anchor point, act as a see-saw, but can be of different lengths. A symmetrical point also holds the line to a smooth curve, but the Bézier handles must be of the same length.

To change an anchor point from one of the above designations to another, select it with the Content Tool, go to 'Item > Point > Segment Type' and select from the list. Multiple anchor points can be selected and changed at the same time. See the 'Editing Shapes' movie on the CD.

Bézier handles pull lines into curved shapes. Using a combination of anchor points, Bézier curves and straight lines, it is possible to create any 2-D shape. Line segments can be changed to straight lines or curves. Click on a line segment between two anchor points, go to 'Item > Point > Segment Type' and choose straight or curved.

Drawn lines can be edited in the same ways as described above. Freehand lines do not need to have their 'shape' designation changed first.

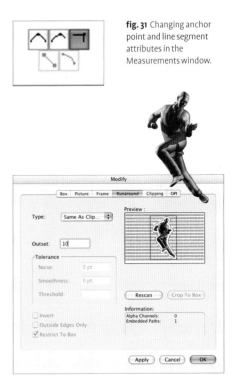

fig. 31 Changing anchor point and line segment attributes in the Measurements window.

Tip   Selected anchor points and line segments can be changed using their icons in the Measurements window (fig. 31).

5.6 Embedded clipping paths

Sometimes images have clipping paths attached to them, which can be used to crop an image in the same way as a custom picture box. Anything outside the path is unable to display and the clipping path acts as a mask. Clipping paths are usually created in such applications as Adobe Photoshop. They are vector outlines and can sometimes make an image look as if it has been cut out and pasted into place. This is because vectors are not based on pixels and actually ignore them.

When an image with a clipping path is imported, select it and choose 'Item > Modify'. Click on the 'Runaround' tab. In the Modify window (**fig. 32**), select 'Same as Clipping' as the type and set an outset value. This shows as a pink line around the visible image, which acts as a buffer zone between the image and the surrounding text.

For a runaround to work, the image has to be placed on top of the text. To do this, select the image and go to 'Item > Bring to Front'. The text over which the image is now placed is forced to wrap around it according to the clipping path and its outset value.

fig. 32 Defining the outset value on a clipping path.

5.7 The Merge command

Another way to create custom shapes is via the 'Merge' command. Draw two overlapping boxes, select both, go to 'Item > Merge' and select from the list the effects you want. To create a single large shape that combines both outlines, choose 'Union' (**fig. 33**). Examples of merging and splitting objects can be found in the 'merge and split' file and the 'Merge' movie on the CD.

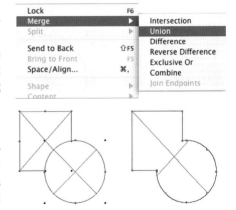

fig. 33 Using the 'Merge' command.

6   Utilities and Pre-Press

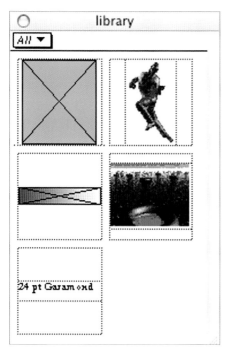

fig. 34 Using a Library.

6.1 Creating and using a Library

Under 'File > New' select 'Library'. Libraries are useful for storing items that you are likely to use often, such as logos, paragraph styles and colours. Give the Library a name and a location and click 'Create'.

The new Library window appears (**fig. 34**). It is independent of Quark documents, which can be created, opened and edited without affecting the Library at all.

Any element on an active document page can be dragged and dropped in the Library window. As a result, the Library will hold a copy, which it displays as a miniature of the original.

If you want to transfer a colour or a blend from one document to another, or to create multiple copies within a single document, simply drag the item from the Library onto that page and drop it.

Any custom colour styles contained within it are immediately added to the 'Colour Styles' list and any paragraph or character styles are added to their respective lists.

Tip	**Images that are placed in libraries are merely visual references to their original location on the hard drive. If that location is changed, then, in any documents into which that library item has been placed, the image will appear on the 'Utilities > Usage > Pictures' list as missing, and will only print at 72dpi. To print correctly, the link to the original image must remain unchanged.**

6.2 Creating and using a Book

Large documents may be easier to manage if they are broken down into a series of smaller, linked documents, designated as a Book. In this umbrella format, one document acts as the master and all paragraph, character and colour styles in it can be synchronized across all the other included documents. Page numbers flow through all the files and update automatically as individual documents continue to be edited.

To create a Book from a series of related files, such as individual chapters, choose 'File > New > Book'. In the New Book window (**fig. 35**), enter a book name and location, and click 'Create'.

In the next window, click the 'Add Chapter' button (top left) and select the file that you wish to assign as the master. This should contain the styles, colours, H&Js and any other settings that you want all the book files to share. It should also have automatic page number boxes.

Other documents can be selected by clicking on the 'Add Chapter' button. Browse to the document and click 'Add'. If no document name is highlighted when 'Add' is clicked, the new document is inserted at the end of the current list; otherwise, it is added directly above the one highlighted. When the list is complete, click the 'Synchronize' button and choose the styles to add to the document files.

The order of the chapters can be changed by holding down the 'alt' key and dragging them to a new position in the stack.

fig. 35 Creating a Book.

Additional style sheets can be added to any of the documents, but cannot be synchronized across the entire Book unless they are added to the master file.

Any of the enclosed documents can be edited in the normal way.

6.3 'Check Spelling' and 'Find/Change'

These are two essential functions. The spell checker is found under the Utilities Menu, while 'Find/Change' is under the Edit Menu.

The spell checker relies on the XPress Dictionary, which contains 120,000 words and is installed at the same time as the software. It cannot be edited. However, you can use it in conjunction with 'auxiliary' dictionaries that you create yourself and to which you can add words as needed. To do this, choose 'Utilities > Auxiliary Dictionary', and give it a name and location.

You can check the spelling of a word, a story or the entire document. To check a word, highlight it with the Content Tool; for a story, click in a paragraph with the Content Tool. If nothing is selected, the whole document is checked.

When you make your selection, the Word Count window appears (**fig. 36**), listing the total number of words checked, the number that are unique (i.e. that only appear once) and the number of suspect words, which do not (yet) feature in the dictionary.

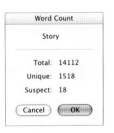

fig. 36 The Word Count window.

Click 'OK' and the Check Document/Story/Word window appears.

Each suspect word is then listed in turn.

When a word is flagged as not being in the dictionary, you can add it, skip it, change it to one of the suggested alternatives (if any), or correct its spelling and replace it.

'Find/Change' searches for the characters typed into the 'Find What' field, either in the story (the default setting) or the document (**fig. 37**). Choose whether to ignore case and/or attributes; examples of attributes are font and size, which can be searched for specifically by unchecking the 'Ignore Attributes' box and thus expanding the window.

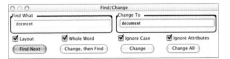

fig. 37 The 'Find/Change' window.

In the 'Change To' field, type whatever you want to replace the found item, then click to enter a cursor insertion point at the beginning of the document or story and press the 'Find Next' button. Depending on your search, you may wish to check each occurrence individually. However, if you are searching for double spaces to replace them all with a single space, for example, 'Change All' is a quicker way to proceed.

6.4 Saving a page in EPS format

Any page in a Quark document can be saved as an Encapsulated PostScript (EPS) file via 'File > Save Page as EPS'. The result can either be imported into a different page layout or opened in Illustrator or Photoshop. If it is brought into Illustrator, vector information is retained; Photoshop, however, asks for a size, resolution and colour mode and then converts it into a bitmap.

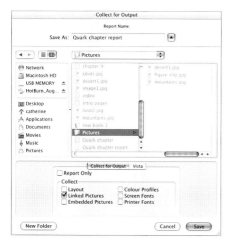

fig. 38 Using 'Collect for Output'.

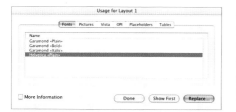

fig. 39 Keeping track of font usage.

6.5 Using 'Collect for Output'

Quark documents record the original location of each placed image and, provided this has not changed, it is possible to assemble all images using 'File > Collect for Output' (**fig. 38**).

If any link locations have changed, Quark offers to list the affected images and allows them to be re-linked. It also offers to save the file, if this has not been done already. Choose a location – preferably an empty folder – and click 'Save'. A report is always created in the same folder, but there is little need to send it to the printer as they are unlikely to refer to it.

Tip   **While the Quark document and all images are collected in the named location, fonts can only be collected in v.5 onwards, and only then if the 'Font' checkbox in the Collect for Output window is checked. However, most font licensing does not permit you to send fonts to a printer; instead, it requires the printer to buy their own copy. In practice, this is often ignored, but technically it is a copyright infringement.**

6.6 Using 'Utilities/Usage'

To view the status of all images and fonts in a document, choose 'Utilities/Usage' and click on the 'Fonts' and 'Pictures' tabs (**fig. 39**). Often, a font is listed that you do not expect to see, in which case use the 'Show First' button to locate its position. Usually, only a few blank lines of space are indicated, which probably means that one of the default fonts on your system remains in place on those lines. Using the 'Replace' option, you can specify a font that is actually used within the document. If it is a very common font, such as Arial, it should not pose a problem as the printer is bound to have it installed and no warning flags will be raised.

To check the status of images, see 'Linking images to a Quark document' on p. 135.

7   More Techniques

7.1 The Layers window

Although layers are a much-trumpeted addition from Quark 5 onwards, there is actually little use for them within a page-layout program, unless you are creating a multi-lingual document. In that case, it is extremely useful to keep all the graphics on one layer, the English text on another, the French text on another, and so on. Then, by turning the layers on and off, each language version can be printed together with the common background layer. For an example of layers, see the 'layers' file on the CD.

The Layers window is under (v.5) 'View > Show Layers' or (v.6+) 'Window > Show Layers' (**fig. 40**). In it, each layer is assigned a colour. Any selected object displays a small square of colour to the right of its name to show which layer it is on and its selection frame is the same colour. To create a new layer, click on the 'New Layer' icon, the top-left button in the Layers window.

To move a selected object to another layer, use the 'Move Item to Layer' button or select the object and drag the small coloured blob, showing to the right of the pencil icon on that layer, to another layer.

To merge two layers, click on one layer to select it, 'shift-click' on the second layer and click on the third button from the left in the window. To delete a layer, select it and click on the 'Delete Layer' button.

It is possible to lock items on a particular layer so that they can no longer be edited or moved. To do this, click in the padlock column alongside the relevant layer's name. To visually hide a layer, and all the objects on it, click on its eye icon, on the left.

7.2 Creating and formatting tables

From v.5 onwards, it is possible to create tables automatically rather than relying on imports from other applications or by laboriously drawing them with the Line tools. Choose the 'Tables' button in the Toolbox and click and drag on the page.

A window opens in which basic row and column information can be entered. In the same window, you can also specify whether the cells are intended for text or pictures (**fig. 41**).

'Item > Modify' changes table, cell and text formatting (**fig. 42**). Text can also be formatted using existing paragraph or character styles or in the Measurements window.

By selecting a table with the Item Tool, grid colours can be applied by going to 'Item > Modify > Grid' (**fig. 43**).

If you click on one edge of a table with the Content Tool, a colour can be applied to that edge alone, using the Colours window.

To combine cells in a row or a column, highlight them, by dragging with the Content Tool, and choose 'Item > Table > Combine Cells'. Tables can also be converted to tabbed text here, and tabbed text can be turned into a table by going to 'Item > Convert Text to Table'.

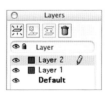
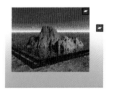

fig. 40 Using layers.

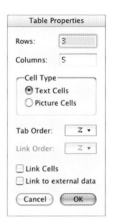

fig. 41 Creating a table.

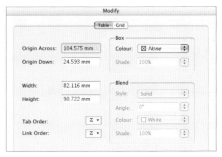

fig. 42 Modifying a table.

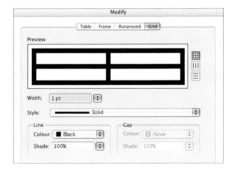

fig. 43 Modifying table cells.

Chapter 5

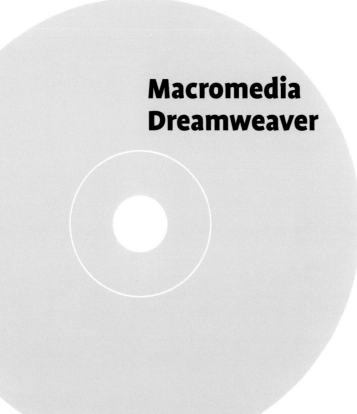

Macromedia Dreamweaver

The images in this chapter were generated using Macromedia Dreamweaver Studio 8.

A Macromedia creation (purchased by Adobe in 2005), Dreamweaver is the website software that finally put the tools of the 'techie' in the hands of the designer. Until its release, those among us who wished to design websites needed to learn how to write HTML code. While a working knowledge of HTML remains advantageous, it is no longer a prerequisite. Using Dreamweaver, it is possible to create a decent website without knowing a single line of HTML.

For the techie, Dreamweaver offers the option of accessing and adjusting the code. Whether simply to fix code bloat – unnecessary lines of code, often tabular data, that when deleted allows pages to load that little bit faster – or whether to delve deeply into adjusting behaviours and Javascript, Dreamweaver can help.

For most of us, however, this kind of specialized ability is a distant goal. What we need to be able to do right now is format text, import images and have them stay where we intend them to stay and add rollover events (buttons that change their appearance when the cursor moves over them and maybe again when they are clicked on). We want to be able to link to other pages within our site and also to outside URLs (website addresses). We may want to offer email links, allowing viewers to contact us by clicking on a button. All this is straightforward enough to do, without needing to know any code at all. It is constructive, however, to pick up at least a rough knowledge of code as you build a site – doing so will definitely make the process easier and the production time shorter.

1   The Dreamweaver Environment

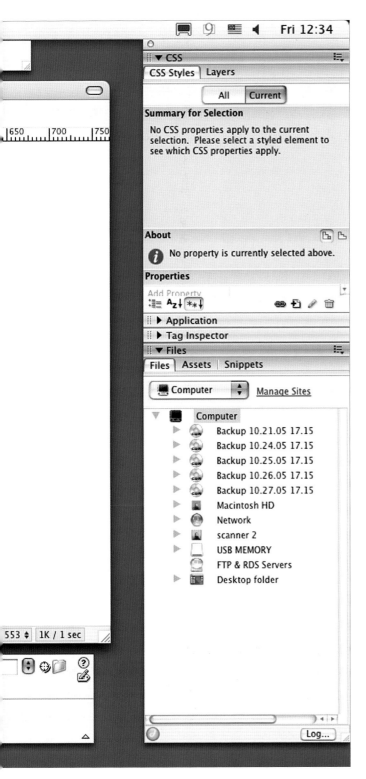

fig. 1 The Dreamweaver screen.

Dreamweaver is essentially a page-layout program, but, instead of building a page destined for print, it builds pages for websites. It allows you to position images, formatted text and interactive elements (such as Flash movies, 'rollover' buttons and image maps) in a 'WYSIWYG' environment, without having to know or understand the code behind it.

The evolution of the 'code behind it' is still very much an ongoing process, the downside of this being that, for many features, there is still no clearly agreed standard for viewing websites. So, while there are several popular browsers that support most site features, there are always some things that work in some browsers but not others. The upside is that, whereas only a very few years ago nobody had figured out how it would ever be possible to make money from the Web, it is now the most rapidly expanding marketplace in the world, and exciting new developments are regular events. Sites can now be 'static', i.e. with no server interaction, or 'dynamic', in which the server hosting the site interacts with the viewers' choices, or other input, to create new information which is then visible on-screen. Even a 'static' page can hold many different kinds of interactive elements.

Obviously, to make sure the widest possible audience sees a site in the intended way, grey areas regarding agreed standards should be avoided. If in doubt, and you are serious about website design, it may be in your interest to install several browsers on your system so that you can preview sites in all of them before uploading them for public use.

When you start Dreamweaver for the first time on a Mac, only a 'floating' format workspace layout is available. You can then easily customize the position of the various windows. In Windows, a box appears that offers a choice between a 'floating' and an 'integrated' layout, meaning that all the windows and panels are integrated into a single, large application window.

There are no zoom controls in Dreamweaver, and a vertical scroll bar only appears on the right side of the document if the page content makes it too tall to be fully displayed in the window. If a scroll bar appears beneath the document, a page element has been designated at more than 100% of the possible screen width. This is almost certainly a mistake, and should be avoided: visitors do not mind scrolling up or down a page, but they very quickly tire of scrolling from side to side.

1.1 A brief history of HTML

In the late 1980s, an application called Hypercard was developed for the Mac by Bill Atkinson. Hypercard enabled the user to construct digital filing cards that could be navigated by pressing on-screen buttons, which activated scripts that took the viewer to the next page. This was an ideal set-up for the generation of training courses in which the trainee could use the buttons to go forward or back within the 'pages' of a tutorial. The limitation was that it could only access the files available on a single computer.

However, the idea of an Internet had already been around for some time, and a new system for naming computers within it had been developed in the early 1980s. This used a simple series of letters separated by dots rather than the cumbersome numbers and unusual code symbols that had been common until then. A program called Distributed Name Service (DNS) was then used to map the domain names onto the IP addresses. As this system was so much easier than its predecessor, the use of internet addresses and email suddenly became accessible to the non-technical computer user.

The glue that bound the above together as a global digital communication system – what we now call the Web – was HTML.

The Web was invented by Tim Berners-Lee in 1989, in the European Laboratory for Particle Physics (CERN) in Geneva, Switzerland. He wanted to enable researchers all over the world to cross-reference between relevant documents by using links embedded within the text files themselves, and HTML was the coding language he developed to do it.

Originally, HTML was extremely simple. It had to be, because it needed to be understood by all the different kinds of computers that were connected to the Internet: PCs, Macs, Unix machines and more. Additionally, there were many different desktop publishing methods already in use, most of which were incompatible with all the others. The answer was to go back to an extremely basic level of formatting that broke text down into simple units, such as lists, headings and paragraphs. These were designated by the use of 'tags' – commands set between < and > symbols. One tag turned a command on, and it was turned off again with another tag that included the '/' character. For instance, to instruct a word in a line of type to be bold, a 'be bold' tag, , was inserted in front of it, and , the tag for 'stop being bold', was inserted directly following it.

Since then, HTML code has developed as a series of 'versions'. HTML 2.0, released in early 1994, added a large number of generally accepted new tag commands; HTML 3.0 contained the first steps towards what would eventually become Cascading Style Sheets and enable text to be formatted using custom text styles in much the same way as in page-layout programs; HTML 3.2, in 1995, included 'tables', layout grids that could be used to organize page content. **Fig. 2** shows an example of HTML code for a simple table.

A complete web page is included within HTML tags, <html> and </html>, which designate the whole thing (apart from certain kinds of advanced coding that can be outside the HTML tags) as being an HTML document. Nested within these tags are two sections: 'head' and 'body'. The main layout area of a web page is known as the body and contains all the elements that are visible on the page. The head section contains such elements as the title of the document and any script that governs the behaviour of rollover elements (see p. 163), and so forth.

In **fig. 2**, the body contains a table, which is opened by the <table width="250" border="1"> tag. This tag also describes the size of the

```
<body>

<table width="250" border="1">
  <tr>
    <td>Cell <strong>one</strong></td>
    <td>Cell <strong>two</strong></td>
    <td>Cell <strong>three</strong></td>
  </tr>
</table>

</body>
```

fig. 2 An example of HTML code.

table (250-pixels wide) and other elements, such as the thickness of any visible border (1 pixel).

On the next line is the tag that opens the first row in the table: <tr>. Within that row, the first cell is opened by <td>.

Immediately following this tag is the actual text that appears inside the cell. In this case, the word 'Cell' is not specified and therefore displays as the default style, but the word 'one' is contained within 'strong' tags, designating it as bold type. The sequence has to be closed in the same order as it was opened until the next cell is reached. So, after closing the bold designation (with </strong>), the cell is closed with </td>. This takes us back to cell level and we can open cell two.

(Incidentally, as time passes, some tags are depreciated, meaning that newer tags that do the same thing supersede them according to a general agreement among the programming community. For example, <strong> used to be <b>.)

At the end of the description of the third cell and its contents, the whole row has to be closed (</tr>), and, as this is also the end of the table, the table has to be closed (</table>).

As the table is the only thing on the page, it is the only body element and is, therefore, enclosed by the <body> and </body> tags.

In a Dreamweaver layout, the result looks like **fig. 3**.

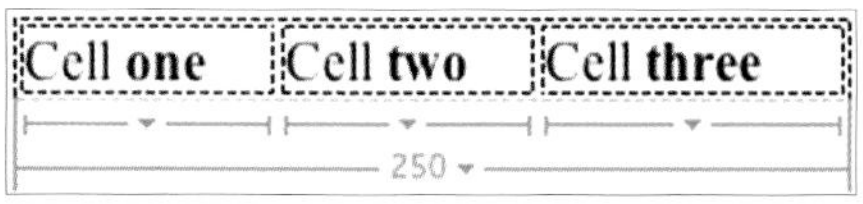

fig. 3 The code in fig. 2 as it appears in a layout.

The 'last' version of HTML, released in 1998, was called HTML 4.0, which introduced, among other things, highly evolved Cascading Style Sheets (CSS). Since then, its evolution has taken a turn as well as another step, combining the HTML features with those of XML, a similar but different code standard, and becoming (in 2000) XHTML.

XML is a language in which the syntax, if incorrect, makes the document invalid. The effect of this, when combined with HTML, is to separate data from presentation. In other words, the formatting of a document is no longer embedded within the data itself and relies instead on references to a separate file: a CSS.

This means that XML files can also be used in conjunction with page-layout programs such as Adobe InDesign. You can even create the tags yourself. Then, when the file is imported, each tag can be assigned to a paragraph style that has been created within InDesign rather than relying on anything present within the XML code, and it will then display on the page accordingly. **Fig. 4** shows an example of XML code.

The syntax of the tags is identical to basic HTML in that an instruction is turned on, and then turned off, either side of the material for which it is intended. Groups of instructions can be nested within larger tags, such as (in this case) <dogs> at the beginning and </dogs> at the end. However, as <dogs> is not a universally accepted tag, do not try to use it as part of the coding for a website!

As well as HTML, XML and XHTML, we now also have DHTML – dynamic HTML, which can be used to create pages with more interactivity than previous versions – and SHTML, a file extension that prompts the server to read it for such elements as 'Server-Side Include'

```
<dogs>

<dog>
<breed>Spaniel</breed>
<colour>Brown</colour>
<name>Suzy</name>
<favourite_toy>Tennis_ball</favourite_toy>
</dog>

<dog>
<breed>Labrador</breed>
<colour>black</colour>
<name>Arnold</name>
<favourite_toy>Cat</favourite_toy>
</dog>

</dogs>
```

fig. 4 An example of XML code.

(SSI) instructions (see p.175). This can be a reference to a separate file which, for example, contains the code for a series of links, and is 'included' in the on-screen display of another HTML document as if it were an integral part of that page. Then, when an edit is required, the 'SSI' file alone can be updated instead of every page within the site on which those links appear.

The really good news is that you do not *need* to know HTML code to create websites with Dreamweaver. However, a little knowledge of it will help you to refine things from time to time. It is easy enough to pick up a basic knowledge simply by keeping your eye on what is happening on screen while in 'split view' mode.

1.2 The Dreamweaver screen

On the Dreamweaver screen (**fig. 1**, see pp 144–45), there are seven main tool areas: the Menus, the Insert Bar, the Document Bar, the Document window, the Status Bar, the Properties window and the Panel Groups. Descriptions are given according to the integrated view and are, therefore, only approximate to the floating view display, in which they can be arranged to whatever works best.

Menus along the top include the Window Menu, which lists the various panel elements as 'on/off' toggles. Many panels contain more than one element; for instance, the 'files' panel contains two sub-panels: 'site' and 'assets'. These can be opened by clicking on the arrow on the 'files' panel or by selecting them under the Window Menu.

Some of the functions on the Insert Bar overlap with those on the Insert Menu; for instance, a table can be added to a document from either area. However, the bar is probably the easiest and quickest way to add many page components to your layout. Clicking on an item on the Insert Bar adds the appropriate HTML code to the document at the cursor insertion point (as does selecting the same item, if available, from the Insert Menu).

Running along the top of the Document window, the Document Bar allows you to toggle between 'code', 'design' and 'split' views of the page. It also lets you allocate a title to the page without having to scroll to the top of the code to insert it. The title is not the name under which the document is saved; it is the name that appears in a browser window.

Code view shows only the HTML code, while design view only displays the page layout. Split view divides the page into two horizontal sections: the upper half shows the HTML code and the lower half the page layout. If you select an object in the lower half, or highlight some code in the upper half, the corresponding element(s) are highlighted in the other section. This makes editing code much easier, as in this view, you can also see the code that relates to an object and its position on the page. It is, therefore, a very instructive tool. The Document window shows which of the three views has been selected.

On the left of the Status Bar are the tags – the nested code elements within the page – relating to a specific object selected in the layout.

On the right are the Document window dimensions, and an indicator of the document file size.

Beneath the Document window, the Properties window changes to display the options available for the selected page content. It is used, for example, to create links, format text, merge table cells and generate 'hotspots' in image maps.

Positioned to the right of the Document window, the Panel Groups contain the items listed under the Window Menu.

The windows and Panel Groups can be repositioned, either by dragging to a new position or by going to (Mac) the Dreamweaver menu and selecting 'Preferences > General > Change Workspace' or (PC) 'Edit > Preferences > General > Change Workspace'.

1.3 Static and dynamic page architecture

Static pages allow you to click on links to go to other pages or URLs. They may be enhanced by the inclusion of other interactive elements and, while they might look extremely dynamic to the viewer, they are nevertheless referred to as static pages.

Dynamic pages are edited according to how data changes. Examples are pages that give live football scores or pages that need forms filling in to buy products online, the completion of which determines how the next page appears. A site is made more complicated in terms of creation and design by the inclusion of dynamic elements. This is because their incorporation makes the design of a page crucial to its usability and requires ASP, PHP or Coldfusion coding – all advanced subjects outside the realm of HTML and not covered in this book.

1.4 Planning a site

Building a website is a bit like building a house. You have to plan ahead or problems will be encountered later. The more time devoted to the planning stage, the faster and easier the subsequent site creation is. For instance, it is much easier to enlarge a site if you plan *how* to do it before it actually *needs* to be done. Site planning should cover the hierarchy, deciding how many pages to create, what content appears on what page and how the pages are linked.

A typical site plan may begin with an introduction page, the first page a visitor sees, on which there would be links to the different areas of the site. For instance, my site, used to advertise consulting services and the graphics courses I teach, features a main intro page from which the viewer can link to a list of courses, a synopsis (on separate pages) of my books, a brief biography and a contact email link.

The list of courses, for example, links to the next layer of the hierarchy, which is a page detailing the subject matter covered on each course. It is a very basic website. There are no frills and no dynamic material, but...it works.

This leads to a very important consideration. Do not add animations, rollovers, Flash text or Flash movies unless they are needed to convey important information or to attract a particular audience who would expect that kind of content. Overdoing the design by adding too many animations and movies is a bit like telling the same joke over and over again: once is fine, twice a mistake, three times a disaster.

Using material from the accompanying CD, this chapter is based around planning and creating a simple site. Dreamweaver tends to move things around as versions develop, so occasionally you will see alternative locations for something (one for versions up to MX, another for MX 2004 and a third for Studio 8).

2   Getting Started

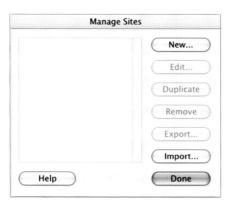

fig. 5 The Manage Sites window.

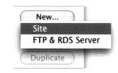

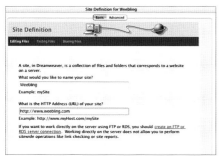

fig. 6 Naming a new site.

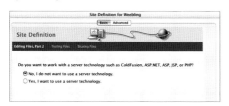

fig. 7 'Dynamic' site options.

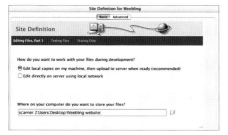

fig. 8 Determining the working method for a new site.

2.1 Defining a local site

Before defining a site in Dreamweaver, you should first create the necessary folder on your hard drive into which the various page elements will be saved. For a simple site, this process could be as straightforward as creating a root folder containing one folder called 'pages' for the HTML documents and another called 'images' for JPEGs, GIFs and Flash movies.

To see the relevant files and folders associated with a site, the site must be defined. This process tells Dreamweaver where the root folder is and what each folder contains. As pages and content are created and saved, they are added to the site definition.

Once a site is defined, the Files panel, which should already be visible on-screen, displays either a list of the files or a site map. If it is not visible, choose 'Window > Show Panels' ('F4'). You can toggle between files and map displays by choosing 'Site > Site Files' and 'Site > Site Map' or by clicking in the window on the right in the site section of the Files panel (MX). In MX 2004, go to the files section of the Files panel and choose 'Site Map' from the list on the right.

If you are working on several sites, the Files panel can store the sites in a list from which they can be selected as needed. Files from several different sites can be open at the same time, but this gets seriously confusing and is best avoided.

The tutorial site materials are on the CD. To use them, copy the entire folder named 'Sites' to your hard drive.

To define the new site, choose 'Site > Manage Sites', and the Manage Sites window opens (**fig. 5**). Click on 'new' and choose 'New Site'.

The Site Definition window appears (**fig. 6**). Click on the 'Basic' tab at the top.

Give the site a name and click 'Next'. (In Studio 8 you can also define a URL in this window.)

Choose (**fig. 7**) 'No, I do not want...' because this is going to be a static site. Click 'Next'.

Select 'Edit local copies on my machine...' (**fig. 8**), and scroll to the folder (created during the planning stage) on the hard drive where the site files will be stored – in this case, the folder to which you copied the CD folders. Then, press 'Next'.

In the resulting window (**fig. 9**), choose 'None' from the list, then click 'Next' to go to a summary (**fig. 10**), where you should click 'Done'. The new location appears in the 'Files' area (**fig. 11**), while any folders or documents already inside it feature in the list below it.

Anything left out during the above process can easily be added later. Double-click on the site name in the drop-down list at the top of the Site panel to re-open the Site Definition window.

To remove a site, choose 'Site' at the top of the drop-down list, then 'Edit Sites'. Select the site you wish to remove and click 'Remove'.

2.2 Creating pages

To create a new, blank page, go to 'File > New'. Click on the 'General' tab at the top of the window, select 'HTML' from the 'Basic Page' column, click 'Create' and the new document window appears.

Choose 'File > Save As' to save the new page. Browse to the 'New Site' folder (designated in the site definition process) and name the page. Click 'Save' and it appears in the list in the 'Site' window.

Tip   **Save the first page of a site as 'index.html', as this is the default page name browsers search for.**

2.3 Opening and saving pages

A page saved to a defined site is easily opened by either double-clicking on it in the 'Site' list or by dragging it into the document window. To save a page, choose 'File > Save As' and browse to the defined site folder (**fig. 12**).

Tip   **Technology continues to improve, but you may find yourself uploading pages to a server that does not understand upper-case letters or hyphens. Although rare, it is sensible to keep file names as simple as possible with no unusual characters or spaces.**

2.4 Adding structure to pages

Below the menus at the top of the screen, the Insert Bar (**fig. 13**) adds images, tables and forms to pages. Text can be typed in directly or copied and pasted from elsewhere, and then formatted using either the options in the Properties window or the cascading style sheets (see p. 180).

However, before adding content, the structure of the page needs to be determined. It is the structure that keeps things in place, rather than letting them re-flow due to the constraints of the viewing resolution.

There are several approaches to consider.

No structure

In this case, it is fine simply to click on the page and start typing. The text wraps when it fills the entire width of the screen, and it will re-wrap depending on the window size and resolution that each viewing system supports.

Try this for yourself: click and start typing. When you have a few lines of text on the page, choose 'File > Preview in Browser' ('F12', or 'alt + F12' in Studio 8). Resize the browser window and the text wraps as needed. The problem with this approach is that long lines of text are extremely difficult to read, so no one is likely to spend very long looking at the site.

Tables

To hold things in place more effectively, use a table. Everything in the page stays where placed and, as long as the viewing system can accommodate the table width, nothing reflows.

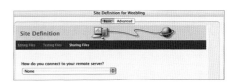
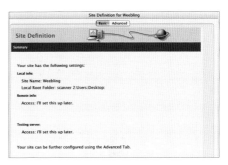

figs 9 and **10** Completing the new site definition.

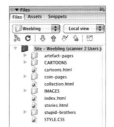

fig. 11 Once defined, the new site appears in the Files window.

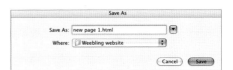

fig. 12 Saving a new page.

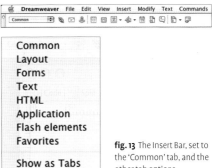

fig. 13 The Insert Bar, set to the 'Common' tab, and the other tab options.

fig. 14 The Table Tool icon.

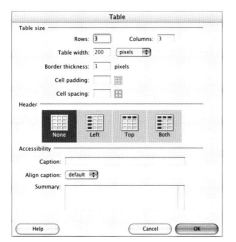

fig. 15 The Table window.

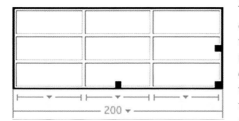

fig. 16 The resulting table in the layout.

fig. 17 The Image icon.

Note, however, that table width can be defined in two ways: as a fixed pixel width or as a percentage of the available window.

If reflow is not a major issue, percentages are fine to use. More often, though, a fixed width of 770 pixels is a better option. This format fits within a 600-x-800-pixel screen, a common resolution. On a higher resolution monitor, it does not fill as much of the available width. If having excess space on one or both sides of the web page were a source of dissatisfaction for the viewer, it would of course make no sense to use a fixed-width setting; instead, it would be better to use a percentage so that the table would stretch to better fill the screen. However, it has been proved that the additional space makes almost no difference to the viewer, who is much more involved with the page itself than the areas of unfilled screen. And, of course, the situation is helped enormously by inserting a page background colour (in the Properties window) that connects to the appearance of the site itself.

Tables range from the simple to the very complex. Do not make the mistake of thinking that a table is simply X-number of columns by X-number of rows; this is absolutely not the case.

To create a simple table, click first on the page to set an insertion point and then choose 'apple/control + alt + T' or click on the Table Tool icon (**fig. 14**) on the Insert Bar. This can be found in several places: on the 'Common' and 'Layout' tabs in MX 2004+ and MX and also on the 'Tables' tab in MX. In the Table window (**fig. 15**), enter the required number of rows and columns. The width can be set at this stage, either as a percentage or as a fixed number of pixels. A border thickness, cell padding (the buffer zone between the contents and the edge of a cell) and cell spacing (the buffer zone between cells) can also be entered.

Click 'OK' and the table appears (**fig. 16**).

Through the Properties window, table cells can be divided and merged, background colours can be applied to the entire table or to individual cells, background images can be added, the table can be aligned and the width and height can be changed.

To place an image in a table cell, either drag and drop it from the Files panel or use the Image icon on the Insert Bar (**fig. 17**).

Tables can be nested inside each other by clicking in a cell and then on one of the 'table' icons on the Insert Bar.

See the 'Basic Tables' movie on the CD and section 6 on p. 170.

Frames

Frames are composed of separate HTML documents that display together, each filling a pre-designated part of the screen, and an HTML file called a 'frameset', which defines the overall layout. In Dreamweaver, the pages can be viewed together as a frameset or individually.

Frames have been in and out of fashion over the last few years, seriously falling from grace when it was discovered that search engines could find individual pages but had much more difficulty finding the frameset that holds the site structure together (so there would be no means of navigating the found pages).

For more about frames, see p. 168.

2.5 Setting page properties

Page titles, background images and colours, text and link colours and margins are basic properties of every HTML document. All these can be applied through the Page Properties window ('Modify > Page Properties') (**fig. 18**).

MX versions show only one window, while MX 2004 onwards shows a list of items on the left of the window and the items' different options on the right. Among the most important features are:

Title This identifies and names the document and appears in the title bar of the Document window and most browser windows. Titles are important because search engines look for them.

Background image and background colour (fig. 19) A background image can appear as a single image or as a tiled background (meaning that the image repeats, seamlessly, to fill the entire page). Always bear in mind how distracting background detail can be to someone trying to read text placed on top of it. If in doubt about legibility, make the image lighter; as a rule of thumb, hold images back to no more than 20% of their original value. Otherwise, you are sending away people from the site.

A background colour does not hold detail and is much less likely to disturb the viewer. However, small, light text on a dark background is not easy to read. Also, be aware of line lengths and colour combinations before inflicting your choices on an unsuspecting public.

Text and links These control colours for text and links (and can also be accessed using Cascading Style Sheets, see p. 180). The colours help visitors to distinguish regular text from links and to see which links they have visited.

Left margin and top margin These settings are not recognized by all browsers. All values should be set at zero to avoid possible problems.

2.6 Using tracing images

A tracing image is a JPEG, GIF or PNG file that is only visible in Dreamweaver and not when you view the page in a browser. When placed in a document's background, it acts as a guide to help you to create a particular page design. A tracing image can be anything from a full-colour design view to a simple pencil sketch. You can hide the image, set its opacity and change its position.

To place a tracing image in the document window, go to either 'View > Tracing Image > Load' or 'Modify > Page Properties' and click the 'Browse' button next to the tracing image text box (**fig. 20**). Browse to the required image and select it. Drag the slider to specify the transparency and then click 'OK'.

To hide the image in the document window, choose 'View > Tracing Image > Hide'.

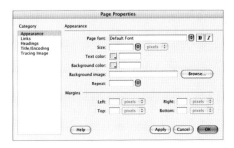

fig. 18 The Page Properties window.

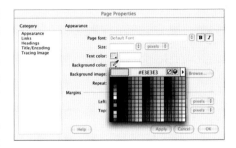

fig. 19 Assigning a background colour.

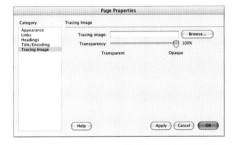

fig. 20 Assigning a tracing image.

To change the position of a tracing image, select 'View > Tracing Image > Adjust Position'. You can now do one of two things: enter coordinate values in the X and Y text boxes, or move the image around, one pixel at a time, with the keyboard arrow keys (to move it five pixels at a time, hold down the 'shift' key).

3   Adding Page Content

3.1 Previewing a site

It may seem odd to include this here – after all, as yet there is no site content – but you do not have to wait until a page is complete before previewing it in a browser window on your own system. You can, and should, regularly preview the pages you are working on. Choose 'File > Preview in Browser' ('F12' or 'alt + F12' in Studio 8). The browser opens to display the page as it will appear when uploaded. Any Flash elements will run, sounds will play and links will work...or not. It is, therefore, a very useful way to check exactly what your intended audience will experience.

3.2 Adding text

Website text can be problematic if the font used does not exist on the system viewing the site. If this is the case, it will default to a recognized font, which may be a long way from what you wanted people to see.

One way around this is to restrict yourself to fonts found on any computer the world over. The sans-serif (plain-cornered characters) fonts Arial, Helvetica, Verdana and Geneva are very similar, as are the serif (stylized cornered characters) fonts Times New Roman, Times and Georgia. Font lists were also created. By choosing the first available font from these lists, the web browser on the viewer's computer displays something that is at least very close to the original.

Cascading Style Sheets (CSS) allow a set of formatting commands to be applied with a single click, thus avoiding a lot of extra work. They are very similar to paragraph styles in page-layout programs. Edits to a CSS immediately apply themselves to all the text already formatted with it.

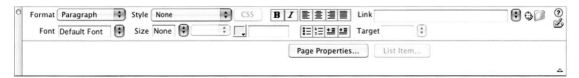

Highlight the relevant text and go to the Properties window below the document area (**fig. 21**) to introduce basic text formatting.

fig. 21 Text formatting options in the Properties window.

Use the 'Format' list to apply 'H tags', which are presets that range from 'Heading 1', the largest, to 'Heading 6', the smallest. Tag characteristics can be redefined using a CSS (see p. 180), and, again, any text already formatted with tags is updated.

To the right of the 'Format' area are buttons for styling highlighted text as bold and italic, applying alignment and indent options and accessing list options. List options style text as either an unordered (using bullet points) or an ordered (using numbers) list.

Highlighted text can be designated as a link, see 'Adding Links' on p. 161.

Basic font choices (serif or sans-serif groups) can be found under (MX) the 'A' list or (MX 2004+) the 'Font' list, and sizes can be applied (in all versions) in the 'Size' box.

Text is coloured by clicking on the small grey box to the right of the 'Size' area and selecting a colour in the window.

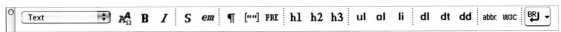

fig. 22 Text options on the Insert Bar.

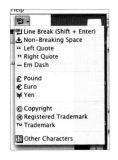

fig. 23 Useful text characters.

fig. 24 The Image icon.

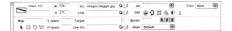

fig. 25 The Properties window shows information and options for the selected image.

In MX 2004+, you can access 'Page Properties' from the Properties window, whereas in previous versions you have to go to 'Modify > Page Properties'.

Regardless of how many times you press the spacebar, only one space appears within text. Additional spaces must be specified with a 'Non-Breaking Space' command. To do this, place the cursor insertion point where the additional spaces are to appear, choose (MX) the 'Characters' tab on the Insert Bar and click on the second icon from the left (if you hover over it with the cursor, the words 'Non-Breaking Space' appear). On the left of this icon is the 'Line Break' icon, which simply turns the line rather than creating a break of two lines, which is what happens if you press the 'enter' key. The keyboard shortcut is 'shift + enter'. In MX 2004+, the 'Non-Breaking Space' command (and others, including 'Line Break') is on the flyout menu under the last icon on the 'Text' section of the Insert Bar (**fig. 22** and **fig. 23**).

3.3 Adding images

Either choose the Image icon from the 'Common' set on the Insert Bar (**fig. 24**) or click and drag from the 'Site' list to add an image on the page. The image appears within text or a table cell, depending on where the cursor was positioned when the image was added. It is also possible to drag an image from the 'site' list and drop it directly into a table cell.

While an image is selected, its specifics are displayed in the Properties window (**fig. 25**). These include its size in pixels, and although the size can be changed here, it is best not to because you are not altering the size of the image, merely the size at which it displays.

Website images are always created at 72dpi for a very good reason: it is the resolution of Mac monitors. If the image display matches the resolution, everything appears as it should. If the display settings are slightly compressed or expanded, the image may appear jagged. Therefore, if you need to change the size of an image, by all means use the settings in the Properties window to do so, but only as a temporary measure. Later, re-create the image to that size and re-import it.

Alternatively, you can choose 'Preferences > File Types > Editors' and launch another image-editing application from within Dreamweaver. Dreamweaver automatically updates the image with any modification or changes saved in the application.

A very important detail, often overlooked, is image file size. Although broadband is now widespread, images that have not been optimized on site pages slow things down enormously. Always assume that your audience will pay attention to the site for only a few seconds before deciding that, as the page has not yet loaded, there must be something wrong and it is time to look elsewhere. To optimize images, see p. 46 of the Adobe Photoshop chapter, as it is not possible to do this in Dreamweaver.

Very often, images and text share space on a web page, so it is vital to know how to position an image within text and how to wrap text around an image. See the 'Adding Images' movie on the CD.

Open the page called 'Image-placement-1.html', which can be found in the 'adding images' folder in 'Sites' from the CD (**fig. 26**).

There is a simple 1-column-x-1-row table, containing a considerable amount of text. Click on the right edge of the table, thereby selecting it, and its properties display in the Properties window. A table is not particularly easy to select; if a solid border with 'handles' appears in the lower-right quadrant, the table is selected.

Scroll down the page until you come to several images placed within the text. Click on the first image – the medieval dagger blade – and the Properties window changes to display its attributes. In the upper half of the window, it gives not only the image name but also its location within the defined site. The '.../' in the location string indicates that the following folder ('Images') is a subfolder within the root folder ('Image Placement'). To the left of this area is the image width and height in pixels.

No settings are visible for the attributes in the lower half of the window.

Clearly, the current placement of the images seems to repel the text, but this is simply because these elements do not know how to relate to each other.

Now open 'Image Placement 2' and again scroll down the page.

This time, text and images work together to create a more balanced result (**fig. 27**).

Click on the 'dagger' image to see what has changed.

In the lower right of the Properties window, (**fig. 28**) the default setting has been changed to 'Left'. This tells the image how to align itself within the text, allowing the text to flow around it. To avoid the text being too close to the image, 'V space' (vertical) and 'H space' (horizontal) settings have also been entered at the left end of the window. By adding a value, in this case 5 pixels for each setting, text is held away from the edges of the image by those amounts.

Have a look at the settings on the other images and then try entering your own settings in 'Image Placement 1'.

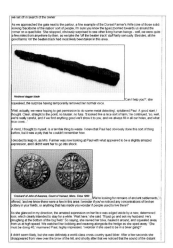

fig. 26 Text and images without image placement specified.

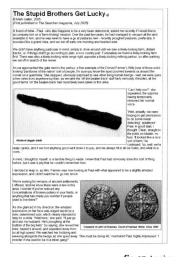

fig. 27 As above, but with image placement.

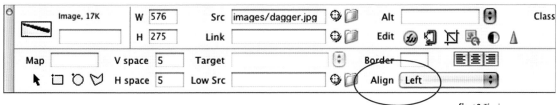

fig. 28 The image placement controls (circled) in the Properties window.

To move an image to a new location, click on it to select it, then press 'apple/control + X' to cut it, create a cursor insertion point in the new location and paste the image ('apple/control + V') there. The 'H' and 'V' space settings given to the image before it was cut still apply to the pasted version.

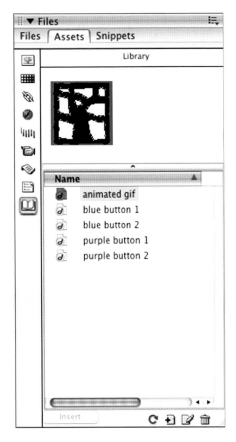

fig. 29 The Library window
in the Assets window.

If you delete an image, you can import it again by clicking and dragging its name from the list in the Sites window and onto the page. A cursor insertion point follows you as you drag it over the text. The image is added to the page wherever it is dropped.

Several other image types that also involve links are covered in the links section (opposite).

3.4 Libraries

Each site can have its own Library, a special Dreamweaver file that stores 'Assets' or commonly used items. For instance, if all the pages have the same headers and footers, they could be stored in the Library. Then, if the original item is updated, all copies will update, too.

A library item can be added to a page by clicking and dragging; however, Dreamweaver does not add the actual object, only a link to the library item. It is because of this that all 'instances' (copies) of the object can be updated simply by editing the appropriate item in the Library. This is particularly useful when elements of a site are still under development.

To add an object to a Library, either drag and drop it in the Library window or select the object on the page and click the 'New Library Item' button at the foot of the Library panel (**fig. 29**).

To add a library item to a page, click to produce a cursor insertion point at the right place on the page, select the item by clicking on it in the Library and then press the 'Insert' button at the foot of the Library window. Or, simply drag the object, by its name, onto the page, where a moving cursor follows it, indicating the placement position. Release the mouse button at the appropriate place.

Double-click on an item's name in the Library window to edit it. A new 'page' opens in which the item can be edited. When finished, choose 'File > Save' and all other copies of it update immediately.

If you do not want a copy to be updated, hold down the 'apple/control' key as you drag it onto a page. For such items as images, the Library only stores a reference to them. Therefore, for copies to work properly, the original item needs to remain where it was when the reference was created.

To re-name a library item, click once on the name, pause and then click again. You are then be able to type in the new name.

4   Adding Links

4.1 Linking to other pages on a site

In the 'Site' list you have defined using the CD files, click on the '+' sign next to 'Linking files' and double-click on 'Links-pg1.html'. There is a single line of text reading 'Link to page 2' (**fig. 30**).

Click and drag to highlight the text, then drag the 'Point to File' icon from the right end of the 'Link' field in the Properties window and drop it onto 'Links-pg2.html' in the 'Site' list. As you do this, the same name appears in the 'Properties 'Link' window.

Now, open 'Links-pg2.html' and repeat the above process, highlighting the words 'Link to page 1' and linking them to 'Links-pg1.html'.

Save both pages; then preview 'Links-pg1.html' in a browser and click on the link. There is a movie of this process – 'Adding Links' – on the CD.

With the exception of such objects as Flash elements, almost anything that can be selected can be designated as a link. As a default, text links are shown in a different colour from the rest of the text and are underlined. In Cascading Style Sheets, a different appearance for links can be assigned; for instance, in a customized colour and not underlined. A different appearance for visited links can be set up so that viewers can tell at a glance the areas of the site that they have already seen.

If an image is designated a link, it does not appear underlined or changed in any way in the browser window, i.e. it does not visibly stand out as a link. When planning a site, a primary objective should be to enable visitors to navigate it as easily as possible; image links, therefore, are unhelpful unless another more obvious link is also provided.

Targets determining how the link opens in the browser can be specified in the Properties window. If you want the browser window to be replaced by a new window, choose '_top'. If you prefer the linked page to open in a new window, select '_blank'. The other two choices offered refer more specifically to frame-based sites (see 'Flash text rollovers', p. 164).

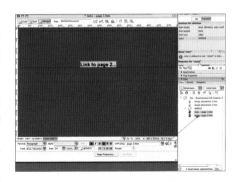

fig. 30 Using the Properties and Files windows to define a link by the 'drag and drop' method.

4.2 Linking to other websites

As you cannot define a site for something that does not exist on your system, you cannot use the 'drag and drop' method to link to it. Instead, highlight the text (or select the object on the page) that you wish to link *from* and type the address that you wish to link *to* in the link box in the Properties window (**fig. 31**). This must include the 'http://www.' section of the site address or else the link will not work.

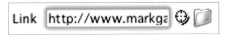

fig. 31 Links to other URLs must contain the 'http://www.' part of the address.

4.3 Linking to named anchors

To jump from the foot of a long document to the top, a special type of internal link called a 'named anchor' is used. This is a two-step process: first, the creation of a named anchor; second, the addition of a link to it from somewhere else in the document.

In the document window, place a cursor insertion point where you want to create the named anchor. Go to 'Insert > Named Anchor' or select the 'common' tab in the Insert Bar and click on the Named Anchor icon (**fig. 32**).

fig. 32 The Named Anchor icon.

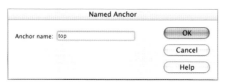

fig. 33 The Named Anchor window.

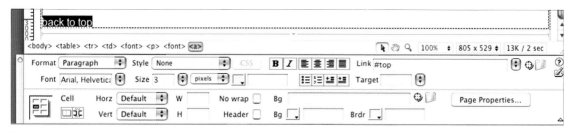

fig. 34 A named anchor destination point in a layout.

The Named Anchor window appears (**fig. 33**).

In the 'Anchor Name' field, type a name, for example, 'Top'. Click 'OK' and a small anchor icon appears at the designated point on the page (**fig. 34**). Input some text – for example, 'back to top' – at the foot of the page in the position you want the link back to the anchor to appear. Highlight the word 'top' and, in the 'Link' text box in the Property window, type a hash sign ('#') followed by the word 'top' (**fig. 35**).

Tip	The point at which the named anchor is placed appears at the top of the browser window when the link is used. Be careful not to place it too far down the page or else relevant heading material could remain hidden.

Multiple points in a document can link back to the same anchor.

To link to a named anchor on a different page that is saved in the same folder, create the anchor in the same way, but in the 'Link' text box, type, 'filename.html#top' ('filename' being a generic term to be replaced by the name of whatever HTML page you wish to link to).

fig. 35 Defining a link to a named anchor.

fig. 36 The Email Link icon.

4.4 Creating an email link

One or more email links can be created on a site to allow viewers to contact the site owners. When an email link is selected, the browser window opens a pre-addressed email in which the viewer can start typing. To add an email link to a document, click to create a cursor insertion point and then press the middle of the three Link icons on the left of the 'Common' Insert Bar (**fig. 36**).

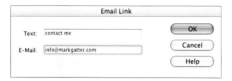

fig. 37 The Email Link window.

In the top text box in the resulting window, enter the text to appear as the link on the page. In the bottom box, enter the email address and click 'OK' (**fig. 37**). The link text immediately appears on the page, in the current 'Link' style.

4.5 Image maps

Another type of link associated with images is called an image map, in which an area within an image is designated as a link by creating a hotspot over it. A single image can contain many hotspots, each of which links to a different page or URL. As hotspots are invisible in a browser window, it must be made clear in some way – either through the nature of the image or in the accompanying text – that the image contains a link. See the 'Image Maps' movie on the CD.

For instance, to link to projects happening in different parts of the country, the inclusion of a map with those areas highlighted in some way might be enough to make it obvious that it holds links. However, as the golden rule is to make things easy for the viewer whenever possible, you may also want to include text or button links, or at least add information telling viewers what to do.

To create an image map, place an image on the page. Click on one of the light-blue shapes in the lower-left corner of the Properties window. For rectangular or circular shapes, click and drag on the image (**fig. 38**). To produce a polygon, click, move, click again, and so on until you have drawn the shape. Handles appear around the edges of all the shapes and can be used to customize (or, in the case of the circle, scale) the shape. If the shape is no longer selected, click on it to view the handles. Also, when selected, the whole shape can be moved by dragging it.

To define a hotspot link, select it and type the destination in the 'Link' field (**fig. 38**). Alternatively, drag and drop the 'Point to File' icon, as described above. For 'target' information, see the 'Flash text rollover' section on p. 164.

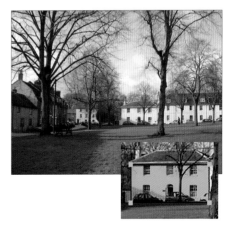

fig. 38 Above and below, defining a hotspot and its link.

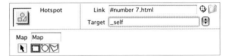

4.6 Rollover links

Links are very often assigned to buttons, which are commonly created as rollover images. That is to say, the button has an inactive appearance to begin with, but, when a cursor moves across it, it changes. Simple two-level rollovers can be created in Dreamweaver, but the images you wish to use must be generated in some other software.

See the 'Rollovers' movie and the sample rollover files on the CD.

Create a new page and save it to the 'Rollover' folder in the defined site. Open this folder in the 'Site' window and you will see that it contains several sets of rollover image JPEGs. Click on the page to place the cursor, and then go to (MX) 'Insert > Interactive Images > Rollover Image' or (MX 2004 onwards) 'Insert > Image Objects > Rollover Image'. You can also use the Insert Bar: for MX, click on the 'Common' tab, then on the 'Rollover Image' button (to the right of the red 'Flash' button); for MX 2004, select the 'Common' set from the drop-down list, click on the small arrow to the right of the 'Image' button and pick 'Rollover Image' from the list (**fig. 39**). The resulting window is the same in both versions of the software.

You can name the image, but it does not matter what it is called.

Click on the 'Browse' button to the right of the 'Original Image' area and select 'Number 1' on one of the button sets in the 'Rollover' folder. Then choose 'Number 2' of the same set to be the 'Rollover Image' area (**fig. 40**).

Make sure that 'Preload Rollover Image' is checked, as this means that the viewing browser will download the information it needs to display rollover images before they are actually required.

For text-only browsers, which are unable to display images, alternate text can be used to tell viewers what they are missing.

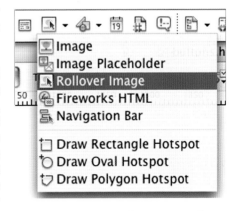

fig. 39 Inserting a rollover image.

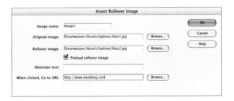

fig. 40 The Insert Rollover Image window.

The destination for the link should now be placed in the 'When Clicked' area. To link to an external URL (another website), type in the address because its name will not show up under the 'Browse' button.

Tip   **Always include the 'http://' prior to the 'www.' in the address or the site will not be found.**

To link to another page within the site, browse to the file name. When done, click 'OK' and test the page in a browser window.

4.7 Flash text rollovers

An alternative to using images for rollover buttons is to use Flash text. Despite its name, Flash itself is not required, and Flash text can be added to a site using Dreamweaver tools.

First, save the page. Then click on the page to define a cursor point.

In MX, choose the 'Media' tab on the Insert Bar and click on the 'Flash Text' button (third from the left). In MX 2004 onwards, click on the 'Media' button (to the right of the 'Image' button) and select 'Flash Text' from the list.

Another way to do this is to go to (MX) 'Insert > Interactive Images > Flash Text' or (MX 2004) 'Insert > Media > Flash Text'. Either way, the same window opens (**fig. 41**).

As the text within a Flash rollover button is displayed via the Flash (SWF) file, it can be created in any font installed on your system.

Type the button text and choose both an original and a rollover colour. Browse to or type in a link. Now select a target setting, which determines how and where the destination is displayed. There are four options:

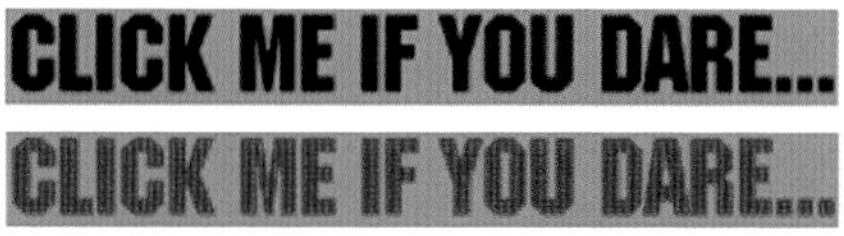

'_blank' opens the destination link in a new window and leaves the previous window open.

'_parent' loads the linked file by replacing the entire parent frameset in the browser window.

'_self' opens the link in the current frame, replacing the old frame completely. Only that particular frame is replaced, unless it is a non-frame-based site, when the entire window is replaced. This option is usually the default setting.

'_top' loads the linked file into the current window and replaces whatever was there previously (regardless of whether or not the site is frame based).

Tip   **If linking to an external URL, it is advisable to use either '_top' or '_blank', otherwise the destination may appear to be part of your site.**

If you would like the text to be enclosed within a coloured box, select a background colour.

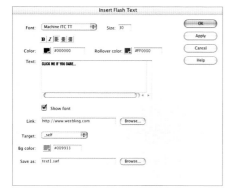

fig. 41 The Insert Flash Text window.

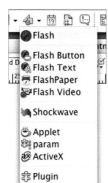

fig. 42 Examples of inactive and active Flash Text.

fig. 43 Inserting Flash Text or a Flash Button.

Lastly, if you do not want the SWF file to be saved in the same folder as the current page, browse to a suitable location. Then, click 'OK' and test the page in a browser window (**fig. 42**).

4.8 Flash button rollovers

These are similar to rollover links and Flash text rollovers and are a quick and easy alternative to creating a rollover image.

As before, click on the page to set a rollover location. Menu and Insert Bar locations for Flash buttons are adjacent to those for Flash text. Click on the Tool icon (**fig. 43**) and choose one of the button styles (**fig. 44**). If the style already contains the words 'button text', it is possible to type in the window and replace it with your own text; if the style does not, as with the 'control-play' button, it is an image-only button and text cannot be added.

Otherwise, the settings are identical to those for Flash text.

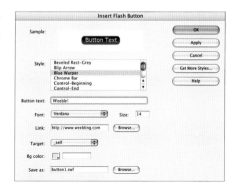

| Tip | To edit the settings for either a Flash button or Flash text, double-click on it and the dialogue window re-opens. |

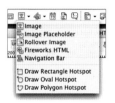

fig. 44 The Flash Button window (above), and the resulting button in the layout (left).

4.9 NAV bars

NAV (short for navigation) bars are blocks of rollover buttons arranged vertically or horizontally. You have to create the actual images for the buttons yourself. Each button should have four 'states': one for the inactive state; a second for the mouse-over event; a third for the mouse-click occurrence; and a fourth, the 'over-while-down', which produces a greyed-out appearance so the viewer knows the link has already been visited. There are some sample NAV bar images in the folder on the CD.

Create a cursor insertion point in the page and click on the 'Navigation Bar' button in the 'Common' Insert Bar icons (**fig. 45**) (this is on the flyout menu underneath the 'Image' button in MX 2004 onwards). The Insert Navigation Bar window appears (**fig. 46**).

To begin the production of the NAV bar, name the first 'element' (the first set of three or four buttons) and browse to the image files for each state.

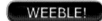

fig. 45 Inserting a NAV Bar.

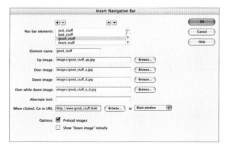

fig. 46 The Insert Navigation Bar window.

| Tip | The states for all the elements must be the same number of pixels wide and tall. |

Enter text (for text-only browsers) if desired and a URL link. Make sure the 'Preload Images' box is checked so that everything is loaded by the time the bar is used.

To add another element, click on the '+' button and repeat the above. To delete an element, click on its name in the 'NAV Bar Elements' area and click on the '-' button. To switch the order of elements, select them and click on the up or down arrows to change their hierarchy.

When finished, click 'OK' and the NAV bar appears in the window (**fig. 47**). To edit an existing NAV bar, choose 'Modify > Navigation Bar'.

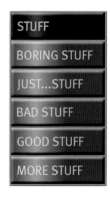

fig. 47 A NAV Bar, as it appears in a layout.

4.10 Setting up an e-newsletter

From time to time we all receive emails that look like a web page. They contain text, images and links, and may also, if the page is long enough, include internal named anchor links.

This kind of email is quite easy to produce and is a great way of keeping an audience in touch with new developments.

Tip   **The method described below only works for single pages: you cannot build a multi-page site and email it. Links to external URLs that appear in the newsletter will still work, but they will open the relevant page in the viewer's browser rather than as another email window.**

First, build your page in Dreamweaver. As many of us view email in a smaller-than-full-screen window, you may wish to enclose the page contents in a table to which a percentage, rather than fixed pixel width, has been assigned. Alternatively, if you do not want content to reflow, use a fixed table width of 580 pixels.

If the page is to be made up of text and images, then the text is actually part of the HTML page, i.e. not separate from it, the images are linked to the page and actually exist elsewhere – in an adjacent 'images' folder, for example.

If the page was part of a website, the HTML code for each image would include a reference to its location, enabling the viewer's browser to find it. For example, it may be a reference telling the browser that, at the URL location, there is a folder called 'images' in which there is a picture called 'hat.jpg'. Then, because you have already told your browser the 'root' address of the site, it can find the 'images' folder contained within it with no additional information.

However, when you are sending the page out as an email, the 'browser', which in this case is the viewer's email program and not a regular browser, is NOT being told to go and look for the file at a location on the Web. Instead, it is being handed the file in the form of email. So, the location of any images included in it remains unknown, and they are unable to display.

However, there is a way around this.

Once the HTML page is complete, copies of all the images included in it must be uploaded to a specific server location. For instance, 'http://www.weebling.com/ferrets/images'. For information about this process, see 'Uploading a site', p. 183.

Then, that exact address, *plus* the actual name of the specific image being referred to, must replace each image reference in the HTML code for the page. For example, if the image was called 'hat.jpg', and the current HTML code for it was '<img src="images/hat.jpg" width="504" height="255">', it would have to be changed to read '<img src="http://www.weebling.com/ferrets/images/hat.jpg"width="504" height="255">'.

Once all these changes have been made, Dreamweaver itself is no longer able to show the images when the page is opened, as the locations have been changed to something it no longer understands. Nevertheless, save the page.

Then, using Dreamweaver's 'Preview in Browser' ('F12'), open the page in your browser. Click on the page, hold down the 'apple/control' key and press 'A' to select everything. Choose 'apple/control + C' to copy it.

Open a new email document, click on the 'Format' menu and change the format of this email from 'Plain Text' to 'HTML'. The specific menu names may be slightly different, depending on your email program. Paste the page into the email document using 'apple/control + V'. It should then be ready to send.

It is always a good idea to test-send a file like this to someone else first to check that it all works properly.

Thus, when the email is received, and as long as the viewer is still online, the images will be found and will display.

5   Frames

Frames divide a browser window into multiple regions, each of which can display a different HTML document. A frame layout might consist of three documents: a tall, narrow frame on the left that contains a NAV bar; a frame that runs along the top, showing the logo and title of the website; and a large frame that takes up the rest of the window, displaying the main content. Each is a separate HTML document, held together by another, non-displaying HTML document called a frameset.

So, a site that appears in a browser as a single window comprising three frames actually consists of four HTML documents: the frameset file, plus the three documents containing the page content. When designing a page using framesets in Dreamweaver, each of the four files must be saved for the entire page to work properly in the browser.

To view a set of frames in a browser, the URL of the frameset file must be specified rather than one of the individual page names. This is one reason why frames are sometimes avoided. Frames are a useful format for displaying information, but search engines often locate pages according to the actual words used on them. If the engine finds one of the individual pages, rather than the frameset file, only that page shows in the browser window. The page, therefore, appears outside the context of its frameset and, as the frameset has not been loaded, the site does not function properly. A site's frameset file is often named 'index.html' and displays by default if a visitor does not specify a file name.

5.1 Creating framesets and frames

There are two ways of creating a frameset in Dreamweaver. You can design it yourself or select it from a range of presets (**fig. 48**). Choosing a preset sets up all the framesets and frames needed to create the layout and is by far the easiest way to produce a frame-based layout. They can be customized by first clicking in the frame you wish to divide and then clicking on the appropriate frame icon in the 'Layout' tab on the Insert menu. See the 'Frames' movies on the CD.

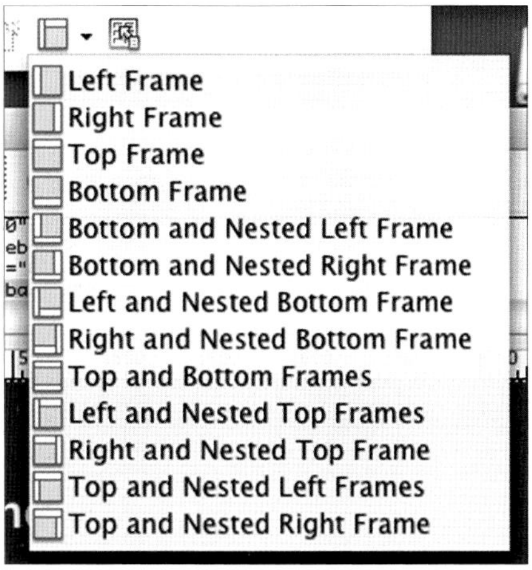

If you already have a document that you want to convert to the main window of a frame, open it and place the cursor insertion point anywhere within it. Then, (MX) click on a frameset style in the 'Frames' section of the Insert Bar, or (MX 2004+) choose from the 'Frames' flyout menu in the 'Layout' section of the Insert Bar. The document becomes the shaded section of the frameset icon on which you click.

To create a new frameset, open a new document and then select the frames style as described above. To split a frame into smaller frames, place the cursor in the frame and select 'splitting item' from 'Modify > Frameset'. To delete a frame, drag its border out to the edge of the document window area and release the mouse button.

fig. 48 The preset frames choices in the Insert Bar.

| Tip | If the frame borders are not visible in the Dreamweaver document window, go to 'View > Visual Aids > Frame Borders'. |

To select a frame, 'alt + click' inside the frame in the document window. But, as the content of each frame grows, it is easier to select individual frames in the Frames panel rather than in the document window. To view this panel, which provides a visual representation of the frames within the frameset, go to (MX) 'Window > Others > Frames' or (MX 2004+) 'Window > Frames' (**fig. 49**).

To open an existing document in a particular frame, click in the frame to create a cursor insertion point and choose 'File > Open in Frame'.

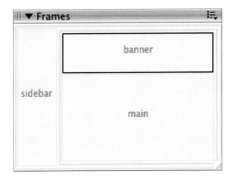

fig. 49 The Frames panel.

5.2 Saving frameset and frame files

Before you can preview a frameset in a browser, the frameset file and all the documents that are to display as the frames within it must be saved. They can be saved individually or all at once: to save a document that appears as one of the frames, click in the frame and choose 'File > Save Frame'; to save all the files associated with a set of frames, choose 'File > Save All'.

5.3 Controlling frame content with links

To use a link in one frame to open a document in another, a target must be defined. A link's target attribute specifies the frame (or window) in which the linked content opens. For example, if a NAV bar is placed in the left frame, but the linked material should load in the main frame on the right, the name of the main frame must be stated as the target for each of the NAV bar links.

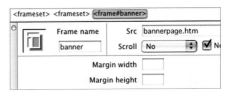

fig. 50 Renaming a frame in the Properties window.

To name the frames as something other than the defaults that appear in the Frames panel, first save the entire frameset. Click in the Frames panel to select a frame, and rename it in the window on the left of the Properties window (**fig. 50**). Click on the document window and the name is updated.

To see an example of a complete frameset, open the file 'frameset.html', which can be found in the 'frameset' folder from the CD. The tall narrow frame on the left is called 'sidebar', and contains links to different sections of the site. Across the top of the page is the 'banner', which might carry a company logo. Most of the window is taken up with the 'main' frame, in which all the content pages would appear.

Use the 'Target' menu in the Properties window to define the frame in which a linked-to file opens. Choices include replacing the displayed document in a particular frame, replacing the entire frameset or appearing in a completely new browser window, while leaving the original open.

First, define the link in the usual way: select either text or an object and click and drag the link target to the file name in the 'Sites' panel. The names that you specified for the various frames are listed in the 'Target' window, along with the default set of '_blank', '_parent', '_self' and '_top' (see 'Flash text rollovers', p. 164). In the 'Target' window, choose the name of the frame in which that file should open.

6   More about Tables

Until this point, only the construction and use of simple tables has been described. However, tables can be much more complex, and many web designers use them to define the placement of absolutely everything within a site. See the 'Complex Tables' movie on the CD.

There are two basic ways of viewing and manipulating pages containing tables: in Standard View, where tables are presented as a grid of rows and columns; and in Layout View, where you can draw, resize and move boxes on the page while still using tables for the underlying structure. Layout View is probably the easiest way to set up a page layout.

A table's appearance and structure can be modified in a number of ways after its creation: by adding content; by adding, deleting, splitting or merging rows and columns; by modifying table, row or cell properties to add colour and alignment; and by copying and pasting cells.

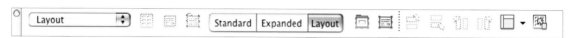

fig. 51 Layout options on the Insert Bar.

6.1 Layout and Standard views

To switch to Layout View, you must first be viewing the page in either 'design' or 'code and design' mode. Layout View cannot be enabled or disabled in code-only view.

In MX, choose the 'Layout' tab in the Insert Bar; in MX 2004+, choose 'Layout' from the drop-down list at the left of the Insert Bar. Then, click on (MX) 'Layout View', or (MX 2004+) 'Layout' (**fig. 51**).

Layout tables can be drawn on blank sections of the page or within existing layout tables. They cannot be drawn within layout cells. Layout cells can be drawn only within existing layout tables, and not in other layout cells.

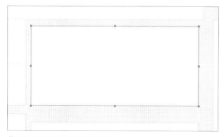

fig. 52 Drawing in Layout View.

Click and drag to create a table to suit your design. If you select either a layout table or cell (click on its edge and handles appear), it can be dragged to a new position, moved 1 pixel at a time with the arrow keys (hold down the 'shift' key to move it 10 pixels at a time) and resized using the handles. Content can be added to layout cells in this mode, but not to layout tables (**fig. 52**).

In the Properties window, specify such things as width, cell padding and spacing and background colour for the entire object or for individual cells or tables. In this mode, however, the parts of the whole that are not designated as layout tables and cells cannot be accessed to place content. To do that, return to Standard View by clicking on the 'Standard View' button. The combination of layout tables and cells created in 'Layout View' (**fig. 53**) are then converted into a single, complex table to which text and images can be added (**fig. 54**). Any cell into which content is placed displays as an active layout cell on the 'Layout View' and can be added to while in this mode. In MX 2004+, there is a third option: Expanded View, in which it is easier to manipulate the cell divisions. While it is possible to add text and images in this mode, it is not representative of how the result will look in a browser window.

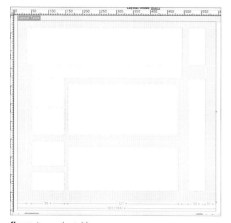

fig. 53 A complex table created in Layout View...

To align an entire table within the document window, select the table by clicking on its outer edge, go to Standard View and use the 'align' menu in the top half of the Properties window (**fig. 55**). Cell contents are aligned by selecting the cell or group of cells (by clicking and dragging through them) and choosing from the 'Vertical' and 'Horizontal' menus in the lower half of the Properties window (**fig. 56**).

To merge cells, go to Standard View, click and drag across those cells you wish to merge in either a column or a row. In the Properties window, click on the 'Merge' icon in the lower-left corner. If you want to split a cell, click on the 'Split' icon and select row or column from the window.

By toggling back and forth between Standard and Layout views, it is possible to create just about any table design you could ever want.

6.2 Importing tabular data
Tabular data can be imported into a document by first saving the files (such as Microsoft Excel files) as delimited text files. Delimiters are keystrokes within the text that indicate the end of a cell and the end of a row.

To do this, go to 'File > Import > Import Tabular Data', or choose (MX) 'Insert > Tabular Data' or (MX 2004+) 'Insert > Table Object > Import Tabular Data'. The Import Tabular Data window opens. Browse to the file you wish to import and select the 'delimiter(s)' used in the file – options include tab and comma. When finished, click 'OK' to import the text.

6.3 Using layers
Originally, with the exception of background colours and tracing images, it was not possible to make one element in a web document overlap another. Then layers arrived. They have enabled us to do just that, and have added a degree of flexibility very similar to that of regular page-layout documents. If, for example, you have an interactive button that needs to appear on top of an image, you no longer have to somehow create a composite of the two elements together before bringing it into your design. Now, it is simply a case of drawing a new layer over the top of the image and putting the button into it.

All newer browsers are able to see layers, but if your audience is likely to be using either Netscape or Internet Explorer versions earlier than 4, do not use layers.

To see a list of the layers in a document, open the Layers panel ('F2'). Each layer is assigned a name, which can be changed in the Properties window. Layer names can be made up of letters and numbers, but cannot begin with a number.

In the Layers panel, the stacking order – which controls which layer appears on top of another layer – can be adjusted by dragging a layer, by its name, to a different position in the list and then releasing the mouse button. Additionally, the panel can be used to control layer visibility. Click to the left of a layer name, in the column beneath the eye icon in the top left of the panel; the first time you click, a closed eye appears, and the

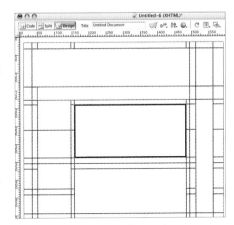

fig. 54 ...changes to a 'Standard' table in Standard View.

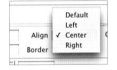

fig. 55 Aligning a table within a layout.

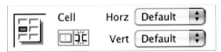

fig. 56 Aligning table cell contents.

layer becomes hidden. The second time you click, the eye icon opens, and the layer becomes visible again. The third time, the icon vanishes, returning the list entry to its original state, which is visible or the visibility state of its 'parent' layer, if appropriate. A 'parent/child' relationship is created when one layer is drawn inside another. The container layer is then called the parent and the contained layer the child.

To move a layer, select it by either clicking inside it or on its border. It can then be dragged by its border or its 'selection handle', which appears just above the top-left corner whenever it is selected.

If multiple layers are selected simultaneously ('shift-click' to select/ deselect additional layers) they can be moved together. If you use the keyboard arrow keys to move them, you can see the results as a live edit. If you use the mouse, only the layer on which you click and drag moves; the position of any other selected layer only updates when you release the mouse button.

When a layer is selected, the Properties window includes 'L' and 'T' information, as well as width and height. 'L' is the distance, in pixels, to the left edge of the document; 'T' is the distance to the top. These allow layers to be accurately placed on the page.

7   Templates

Created in much the same way as any other page, templates can be opened and edited in Dreamweaver. Also, areas within a template can be defined as editable regions, meaning that if a template is used as the basis of an HTML page, only the designated areas within it are editable and all other areas are protected. This prevents protected areas from being changed accidentally, thereby making it much safer to delegate work among a group of people involved in the production of a website.

When several pages of a site share the same basic layout, they can be created as a template on which all the pages are based. All the elements can then be updated simply by editing and re-saving the template.

To produce a template from scratch, choose 'File > New > (basic page) HTML Template' and proceed to create a page layout. Or, you can designate an existing page as a template. In either case, it is saved in template format by going to 'File > Save as Template'.

In the Save as Template window, you are prompted to choose the site to which this template belongs and to give it a name (**fig. 57**). Click 'Save' and a new folder called 'Template' is created in the defined site. If you do not see it immediately, click on the 'Refresh' button (**fig. 58**) at the top of the Site panel ('F5').

You can also click on the 'New Template' button at the foot of the Templates window, which is opened by clicking on the second button from the bottom on the left of the Assets window (**fig. 59**). When named, it can be double-clicked to open in the document window.

To designate editable regions on the page, highlight text, a table, cells within a table or some other part of the page content. Then choose 'Insert > Template Objects > Editable Region' (**fig. 60**, overleaf).

In the New Editable Region window (**fig. 61**, overleaf), give the area a name and click 'OK'. Then, save the page.

To generate pages based on a template, open a new, blank HTML page, save it and click and drag the template name from the Assets or Template panels onto the page.

Tip   An important point: do not drag the template from the 'Files' list, but always from the 'Assets' list.

If a template does not show up in the 'Assets' list, it may mean that the site location has been incorrectly defined. The template folder must be in the root folder you created when you defined the site. If it is further away in the folder hierarchy, Dreamweaver is unable to locate the template files.

Also, if you do not save the page as an HTML document prior to assigning a template to it, then every time you attempt to re-save the page, Dreamweaver prompts you to save it as a template and not as an HTML document.

Another way to generate pages based on a template is to, choose 'New' and then click on the 'Templates' tab. In the left column, 'Templates For', select the site name. The name of the template, and any

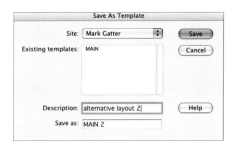

fig. 57 The Save As Template window.

fig. 58 The Refresh button.

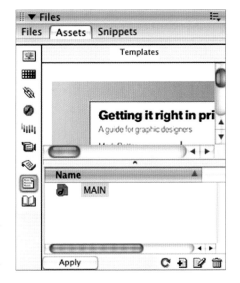

fig. 59 The Templates window in the Assets window.

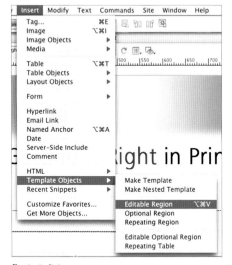

fig. 60 Defining a new editable region in a template.

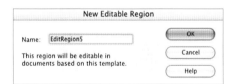

fig. 61 The New Editable Region window.

others you have created for that site, appear in the centre column, with a preview of the page on the right. Make sure that the 'Update page when template changes' box is checked and click 'Create'. The document page appears, but only the designated areas are editable in either design or code view.

If a page based on a template is open and you wish to edit the template to update the current page (and possibly others based on the same template), choose 'Modify > Template > Open Attached Template'. The template opens, and you can make changes to any part of it. Then, choose 'File > Save', select the document page(s) in the list that you wish to update and click 'Update'. You are then informed that the page has been updated successfully.

If a page based on a template is not open, you can simply open the template itself (double-click on its name in the 'Assets/Template window'), make changes to the non-editable regions and select 'File > Save'. Once again, you are presented with a list of the pages based on that template from which you can choose what to update. If the update does not happen, choose 'Modify > Template > Update Current Page' or 'Update Pages'.

8   Server-Side Includes (SSI)

Go to 'www.weebling.com', click on 'Collections' and you will see that at the top of the coin and artefact pages there is an array of links (**fig. 62**). These links are created by 'Server-Side Includes'.

A Server-Side Include is a completely separate document that is allowed to display as if it were part of another. The nature of your site determines whether or not such an element would be useful. In the case of weebling.com, my metal-detecting site, I have no idea what I will find the next time I am out, so I need a method that allows me to edit a single file and in so doing updates the links visible on all the pages in that section of the site. The alternative would be to have the code for the entire table of links embedded in each page, which would require me to update every single page individually.

The material for the links array was first created as a regular HTML page, on which there is a table (set to 770 pixels wide) that holds the links. Each one links to the relevant page in that folder – coins or artefacts. I saved that page and then opened it and switched to 'Code' view. I deleted everything, except for the table itself, and, of course, the text and link information it contained.

I then re-saved the page as 'artefacts-ssi.inc', in the same folder as all the other artefact pages. I could have used almost anything as an extension; the key thing was to enable Dreamweaver to identify which file to use. In fact, the file was a simple text file at that point, as all the code identifying it as an HTML page had gone. The only code remaining was that governing the layout of the table.

In split view, I opened each artefact page and placed the cursor at the top of the document, where I wanted the SSI element to appear. Seeing the page in split view allowed me to locate the *same* point within the code. Then, I copied and pasted a line of 'script' directly into the code before resaving the page: `<!--#include file="artefacts-ssi.inc" -->`

'Script' is a general term for an instruction, or a whole sequence of instructions, that are carried out by another program rather than by the computer processor. In the context of a website, scripts are carried out by the server. So, this script told the server to display the relevant file at that point in the page.

The browser I used was unable to show me the SSI in position when I previewed the page, because some interaction is required by the server to which the site is uploaded to make it visible, and, of course, it had not yet been uploaded. Dreamweaver, however, showed the SSI in exactly the right place in the document window. So, in this case, the Dreamweaver view should be regarded as the preview.

The only other thing that needed doing prior to uploading the pages to the site was to rename them in the Files panel. Instead of leaving them as HTML pages, I added an 'S' at the beginning. This is because many servers do not check documents for SSI objects unless they are prompted to do so by the 'SHTML' extension.

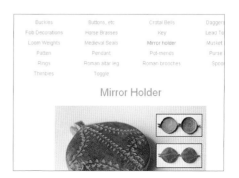

fig 62 A screenshot taken from 'weebling.com' showing the SSI – in this case an array of links – at the top of the page.

Now, when I dig up a new article worthy of inclusion in the artefacts section, all I have to do is add it to the SSI file as a new link in the array, upload it, and the entire section of the site is immediately updated.

This is made even easier because I kept the original array as a complete HTML page, as well as in its truncated 'SSI' format. Whereas opening the SSI file shows it as plain text (and not as an HTML table), the original shows the tabular format of the array as it will appear on-site. Then, after adding the new link, I can just delete the unwanted HTML code and resave it as my new SSI file.

There are several 'SSI' files in the 'www.weebling.com' folder on the CD to help you explore this area.

9   Adding Behaviours

Use behaviours with care. It is very easy to get carried away and load a site with them, but all that will do is deter visitors.

Usually added to images or text, behaviours can also be attached to entire documents (by clicking on the '<body>' tag in the 'Tag Selector' at the bottom left of the document window) and several other HTML elements. Not all browsers support all behaviours, so again, be sure of the audience before including a particular special effect.

More than one action can be specified for each event, and they occur in the order in which they are listed in the 'Actions' column in the Behaviours window.

Tip   **A behaviour cannot be attached to plain text.**

To attach a behaviour, select an element, such as an image, and go to 'Window > Behaviours' ('shift + F3') to open the Behaviours window (**fig. 63**). In MX, it opens in the Design panel; in MX 2004, it is in the Tag panel. Click the plus (+) button and choose an action from the list.

If certain objects do not exist in the document not all actions will be available; for example, if there are no timelines, 'Play Timeline' will not be available. Click on an action to select it and a window appears displaying the available options. Enter parameters for the action and click 'OK'.

The default event that triggers the action appears in the 'Events' column (**fig. 64**). If this is not the trigger event you want, choose another by clicking on (MX) the downward-pointing black arrow between the event name and the action name or (MX 2004+) the named event on the left. All available trigger events are then displayed.

If you attach a behaviour to an image, some events, such as 'onMouseOver', appear in parentheses, meaning that they are available only for links.

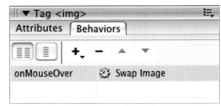

fig. 63 The Behaviours window.

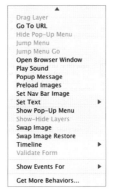

fig. 64 Behaviour options.

9.1 Adding behaviours to images

Any available behaviour can be applied to an image or an image hotspot. When applied to a hotspot, Dreamweaver inserts the HTML source code into the 'Area' tag. Three behaviours apply specifically to images: 'Preload Images', 'Swap Image' and 'Swap Image Restore'.

'Preload Images' refers to any images that do not appear on the page right away, such as inactivated states embedded in rollovers and NAV bars, or those that will be changed to in a 'Swap Image' behaviour (see p. 178). 'Preload Images' allow the images to be loaded in the background, so they are ready and waiting when the event is triggered.

'Swap Image' does exactly what it says: it swaps one image for another by changing the source (SRC) attribute of the 'img' tag in the HTML code. Use this action to create button rollovers and to swap more than one image at a time.

9.2 The 'Swap Image' behaviour

Place an image in the document. It is a good idea to name images, as they are placed, in the Properties window. Enter a name for the image in the box near the upper-left corner. The 'Swap Image' behaviour still works even if you have not named your images, as it automatically names previously unnamed images when it is attached to an object. However, it is easier to distinguish images in the 'Swap Image' window if they are all named beforehand.

Watch the 'Adding Behaviours' movie on the CD, which uses files you can find in the 'swap image' folder.

Insert some additional images into the document. Select one of them and open the Behaviours window.

Click the plus (+) button and choose 'Swap Image' from the 'Actions' list.

From the 'Images' list, select the same image that you chose in the document window. Click 'Browse' and select the new image file (**fig. 65**).

Repeat this process for any additional images you want to change. It is advisable to select all the images you wish to change at this stage; otherwise, the corresponding 'Swap Image Restore' behaviour will not apply to all of them.

The 'Preload Images' option should already be selected in the lower left of the window; if it is not, click to select it.

Then, click 'OK'. Check that the default event is the correct one and, if not, change it.

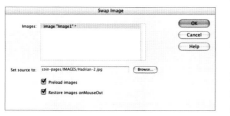

fig. 65 The Swap Image window.

The 'Swap Image' behaviour can be applied to other images, so that as the mouse moves over one image, several others change simultaneously.

To do this, place four images on a page, and choose another three images for the swaps. In all cases of 'Swap Image', if the images do not share the same dimensions, the results will be distorted.

Name the images using the Properties window.

Click on image one in the document window, and choose 'Swap Image' from the behaviours list. In the Swap Image window, select image two, then browse to the swap image. Do the same for image three, and again for image four. Click 'OK', and preview the file in a browser. Now, when the mouse passes over image one, and assuming that the default event chosen was '(onMouseOver)', the other three images change while image one remains the same.

9.3 Adding sound behaviours

To add a 'Play Sound' behaviour, select an object and open the Behaviours window. Click the plus (+) button and choose 'Play Sound' from the 'Actions' list. Browse to the sound file you wish to add and click 'OK'. Check that the default trigger event is the required one (if it is not, choose another from the list).

9.4 Changing a behaviour

After attaching a behaviour, you can change the event that triggers the action, add or remove actions and change the parameters for actions.

To do this, select an object with an attached behaviour. Go to 'Window > Behaviours' to open the Behaviours window, and choose from the following three options:

1) To edit an action's parameters, double-click the behaviour name (or select it and press 'enter'), then change the parameters in the dialogue box and click 'OK'.

2) To change the order of actions for a given event, select an action and click the up or down arrow button to move its position in the hierarchy.

3) To delete a behaviour, select it and click the minus (-) button (or press the 'delete' key).

10   Cascading Style Sheets (CSS)

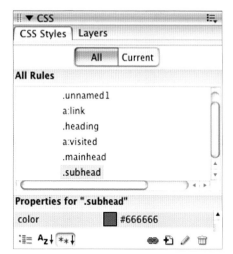

fig. 66 The CSS Styles window.

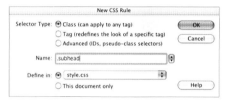

fig. 67 Choosing a style
type in the New CSS Rule
window.

Cascading Style Sheets are formatting rules that control the appearance of text in ways that HTML formatting cannot. They are similar to the ways in which paragraph and character styles are used in page-layout software.

The advantages of using CSS rather than HTML formatting are:

1) The appearance of the text is much more exciting and varied.

2) Multiple styles can be applied to the same web page. For example, you can create two styles – one to control the leading and another to control the colour – and apply both of them together.

3) The formatting of all the documents that use a particular style can be updated simply by updating the Cascading Style Sheet itself.

10.1 Creating new CSS styles

MX and MX 2004

To create a new CSS style, choose 'Text > CSS Styles > New CSS Style'. Alternatively, choose 'Window > CSS Styles' to open the CSS Styles window and click on the 'New Style' icon at its foot (**fig. 66**). In the New CSS Style window, you can choose between three kinds of style (**fig. 67**):

1) The top selection lets you create your own style.

2) The middle selection allows you to re-define HTML tags (the formatting styles available as 'Heading 1', 'Heading 2' and so on, in the Properties window).

3) The bottom selection allows you to specify styles for links; for instance, how they should appear in the browser window before, during and after they are clicked on.

Each state can be given a different appearance, so that it is clear which links have already been visited.

At the foot of the window, you can choose to create a set of formats, which can be saved as either a CSS file (allowing it to be used elsewhere) or as a set of instructions only for use within the current document.

Assuming you want to create styles for such elements as headings and body copy, use the top option, 'Make Custom Style (Class)'. Give the style a name, which must begin with a full stop and have no gaps or uppercase characters (for example, '.subhead'). Then click 'OK'.

If you chose to define these settings in a 'New Style Sheet File', you are prompted to save it. Pick a location within the defined site so that it is easy to use with all the pages. When you have saved the CSS file name, go to the CSS Style Definition window (**fig. 68**).

First, choose the attributes for the '.subhead' style. I usually define the type size in terms of pixels rather than points, but it is up to you. The 'Line Height' is the leading. It is also possible to pick a type colour on the right and to choose many other variables (background colour, list parameters) from the list on the left of the window. When you have finished, click 'OK'.

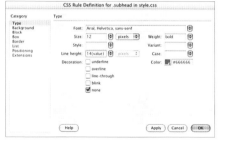

fig. 68 Defining the style.

To create a style for the body copy, choose 'Text > CSS Styles > New CSS Style', but this time enter '.body' as the style name. Once finished, click 'OK'.

Studio 8
To create new CSS rules in Studio 8, simply format text with options in the Properties window. When this has been done, click on the 'CSS' button to the right of the 'Style' field to open the CSS Rule window, in which each style created for that page is listed. To add other CSS attributes, double-click on 'Style' in the list to open the CSS Rule Definition window. Details regarding the three different types of style are given in the previous section.

As a default, the styles created and edited in this way are only available to the document currently open, but it is easy to turn them into an independent CSS style file that can be applied to other documents or even to entire sites. To do this, select the style in the list in the CSS Rule window and click on the 'New CSS Rule' icon at its foot. In this window, there are two checkboxes in the 'Define In' area. One allows this style only to be used in the active document. Instead, check the box to the left of the 'New Style Sheet' field, and click 'OK'. The style can then be saved as an external CSS file.

10.2 Applying CSS styles

Applying the new styles to the text on the page works slightly differently in MX and MX 2004.

MX
Use the CSS Styles window to apply styles ('Window > CSS Styles' or 'shift + F11').

At the top are two 'radio' buttons: 'Apply Styles' and 'Edit Styles'. Select the 'Apply Styles' button. The CSS styles you just created should be visible in the window ('subhead' and 'body'). Click and drag to select some of the text on your page, and click on one of the style names. The text appears with that formatting on the page. Click within a paragraph and then on the style name, and the entire paragraph changes format.

MX 2004 and Studio 8
When a CSS style has been created, it shows up in a list on the 'Style' menu in the Properties window (**fig. 69**). Either highlight the specific text to which you wish to apply the style, or click within a whole paragraph. Then, click on the style name.

You can create the two other kinds of style in exactly the same way. The middle option, 'Redefine HTML tags', relies on you having used the

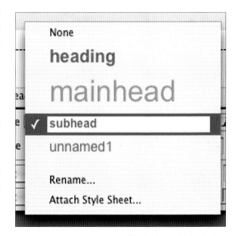

fig. 69 The styles list in the Properties window.

'Heading 1', 'Heading 2' styles, available in the Properties window, to format the text in the pages. Then, by redefining these, you can control their appearance more specifically. Similarly, use the 'CSS Selector Style' option to define the formatting for links.

Tip	**If you are having trouble linking an external (i.e. saved as a separate file) style sheet to your pages, click on the 'Attach Style Sheet' button at the foot of the CSS Styles window. Browse to your CSS file and choose either 'Link' or 'Import' (either should work). The styles are now available for the page on which you are working.**

11   Going 'Live'

Once your site is ready to upload, it is well worth doing a final check within Dreamweaver to make sure everything is going to behave as it should. Also, see the 'Checking Links' movie on the CD.

11.1 Checking links

To check links on a particular page, choose 'File > Check Page > Check Links' (**fig. 70**).

To check links in multiple documents, select the documents by holding down 'apple/control' and clicking on their names in the Site panel. Then go to 'File > Check Page > Check Links'.

To check links in an entire site, click on the site name in the Site panel, then click on the 'Site' button and choose 'Check Links Sitewide'.

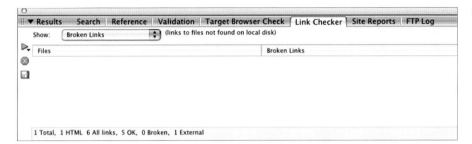

fig. 70 Checking links.

11.2 Uploading a site

Sites are most commonly uploaded using File Transfer Protocol (FTP) information, for which you will need to contact your Internet Service Provider (ISP). Typically, aside from a site name (which you can create yourself), three pieces of information are required: the URL address of the host site, a login name and a password. You can use FTP information to define the remote server site in Dreamweaver, to which you can then upload your files using the 'Put' button in the Files window (**fig. 71**).

To do this, select the site from which you are uploading pages, and choose (MX) 'Site > Edit Sites' to open the Edit Sites window or (MX 2004) 'Site > Manage Sites' to open the Manage Sites window. In either window, select the site name from the list and click 'Edit'.

In the Site Definition window (**fig. 72**), click on the 'Advanced' tab and choose 'Remote Info' from the list. In the 'Access' window, select 'FTP'. You then need to enter the information received from your ISP. When finished, click 'OK'.

Select the files in the Site panel that you wish to upload and click on the 'Put' button. A window opens, asking if you wish to transfer 'Dependent' files as well, i.e. images and so forth.

When the process is complete, the website is online. Do not worry if the site is not visible immediately as some ISPs take a day or more to process new files.

fig. 71 The 'Put' button in the Files window.

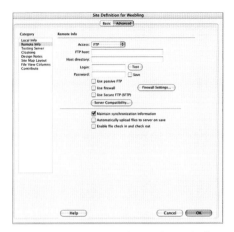

fig. 72 Defining uploading parameters in the Site Definition window.

Chapter 6

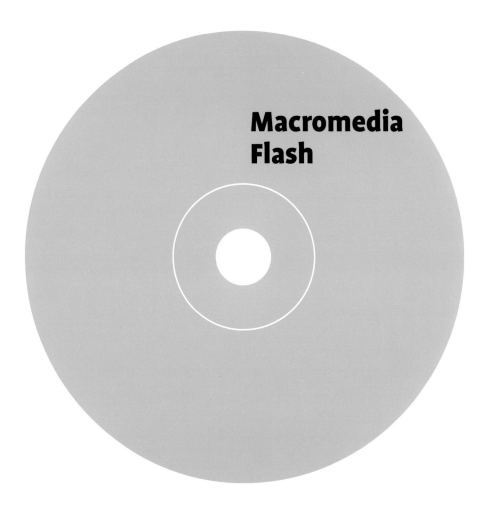

Another star of the Macromedia stable (purchased by Adobe in 2005), Flash has enabled the creation of many of the special features on contemporary websites with which we have become familiar – and in some cases, over familiar. Its over-use is almost legendary: most of us have experienced visiting a site for the first time and feeling completely overwhelmed by on-screen animations and special effects. However, a well-thought-out Flash addition to a website can add interest, information and interactivity – as well as sound and motion – to what might otherwise be just another page. Even beginners can work wonders with Flash, especially if they already have a background in vector drawing.

The images in this chapter were generated using Macromedia Flash Studio 8.

1   The Flash Environment

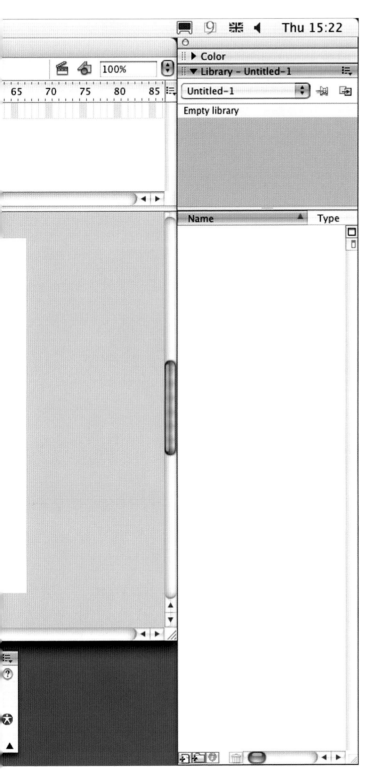

fig. 1 The Flash screen.

Most people use Flash to build animations (usually called movies) for websites, using a combination of objects, layers and timelines. Objects can be placed on layers and their movement plotted over a period of time. Flash has other uses, too – for example, to create games and presentations – but it is the movie aspect that this chapter explores.

Most Flash movies are produced using vector graphics because vector images are extremely small compared to bitmap images. Thus, even a dial-up modem connection is able to download information fast enough to display amazingly detailed animations. File size is extremely important. The larger something is, the longer it takes to download and the slower the page is to appear. We are incredibly impatient when waiting for websites to load, and in only a matter of seconds we are very likely to look elsewhere. So, anything that reduces file size to a minimum is hugely beneficial. This is particularly relevant for a dial-up modem connection, but large file sizes can slow down even a broadband connection to an unacceptable degree.

It is not only in terms of its use of vector graphics that Flash helps in this respect. Suppose several copies of a particular object are required for a movie; they could be copied and pasted to create duplicates, but each of them would be adding to the movie file size. As an alternative, Flash saves an object as a symbol in a library, from which it can be dragged onto the stage whenever needed. All appearances of the object are simply reflections (called 'instances') of the original in the library and the object's file size is only added to the movie once.

Vector objects can be drawn in Flash, or they can be imported from Adobe Illustrator or another vector-drawing package. If imported, some of the object formatting may be left behind, so it is best to avoid creating something complex and time-consuming only to find that it does not import properly.

Aside from creating movies, Flash also adds interactivity to a site by attaching behaviours (also known as actions) to objects. A behaviour simply means that something happens, usually in response to something done by the viewer, such as pressing a button in an animation. ActionScript, a code that is attached to the object, governs behaviours.

Writing ActionScript is advanced-level Flash and is not covered here. However, Flash contains many useful 'ready-to-go' actions, the basic uses of which are covered on p. 212.

1.1 The Flash screen

The most important part of the Flash screen (**fig. 1**, previous page) is the 'stage' area. This is where movies take shape and where they are previewed prior to publishing.

Above the stage area is the Timeline, with the object layers area to its left. The Timeline governs the temporal span of a movie in terms of frames. A movie can be set to run at any number of frames per second (f.p.s.), but the default (12 f.p.s.) usually works well.

The object layers separate the elements appearing in a movie so that they can be manipulated more easily. Objects on layers near the top of the stack, i.e. closer to the menus at the top of the screen, appear on top of objects placed on layers beneath them.

At the top of the screen are the menus.

On the left side of the screen is the Toolbox, although it can be moved by dragging on the bar at its top. This contains the drawing tools, the options available for each tool and options for outline and fill characteristics, among others.

At the foot of the screen, the Properties window displays options available for the selected object or tool.

On the right are the other window panels: the colour mixer, actions, and so on. These are opened and closed using the Window Menu at the top of the screen.

1.2 Getting around

Zoom in to the Flash stage by either holding down 'apple/control + spacebar' and clicking and dragging to indicate the area to zoom in on or by holding down 'apple/control' and pressing the '+' key repeatedly. To zoom out, hold down either 'apple/control + alt + spacebar' and click on the stage or 'apple/control' and press the '-' key repeatedly.

To scroll, press down the spacebar and click and drag on the screen. Alternatively, drag the sliders in the scrollbars, which are below and to the right of the stage area.

1.3 Getting started

To create a new Flash movie, first decide how large the stage needs to be. This specification can be changed later, but it avoids problems if its size is set accurately before starting. To do this, choose 'File > New' and open (if it is not already showing) the Properties window, 'Window > Properties' ('apple/control + F3') (**fig. 2**).

Click on the 'Size' button to open the Document Properties window (**fig. 3**).

Enter a stage size as a pixel width and height. Choose a background colour and a frame rate. The default frame rate (12 f.p.s.) does not produce movies as smooth as Disney animations, but it generally results in a reasonable balance between file size and playback quality. Click 'OK' and the new stage appears.

To see the rulers, above and to the left of the stage, choose 'View > Show Rulers'. Click on the rulers (not on their edges) and drag towards the stage to position horizontal or vertical guides. These act as either a visual guide or as an alignment aid by activating the snap setting under 'View > Snapping > Snap to Guides'. This means that they exert a slight 'magnetic' pull on objects that are near to them. Also, using the View Menu, guides can be locked into place or released. To delete guides, drag them back into the rulers or choose 'View > Guides > Clear Guides'.

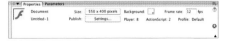

fig. 2 The Properties window.

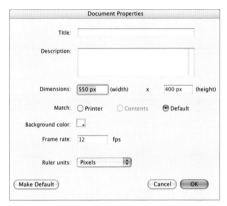

fig. 3 The Document Properties window.

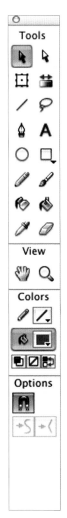

2

The Toolbox

fig. 4 The Toolbox.

The Flash tools (**fig. 4**) are quite easy to use: it is simply a matter of familiarization and confidence.

Tool options
When a tool is selected, options for its use appear in the 'Options' area at the foot of the Toolbox. These modify the tool itself and/or an object that has been created with one of them.

The sooner you figure out these tools, the sooner you will be able to create the shapes and effects you want. I strongly recommend trying them all out, with their various options, until you are familiar with them.

Fills and Strokes
Object fills and outline colours can be selected prior to drawing the shape or can be changed after drawing. Generally, it is better to make this decision first, because of the way in which Flash deals with objects that share the same layer (see 'Arranging and grouping', p. 196).

2.1 The Selection (or Arrow) Tool

Renamed the Selection Tool in MX 2004, this tool selects and moves objects and can be used for some shape editing.

To try it, select the Rectangle Tool on the Toolbox and click and drag on the stage to draw a rectangle. Choose the Selection Tool and hold the cursor near the edge of the shape outline, and a small, curved line appears below it. When this shows, the outline can be pushed or pulled to edit the shape. Hover near an anchor point and a small right-angle shape appears below the cursor and the point can be pulled to a new position. Hovering over an object adds a four-way arrow to the cursor, indicating that the position of the object can be moved.

2.2 The Subselection Tool

This tool edits the shape of an object by moving the anchor points on its outer edge. A selected anchor point appears as a solid point (it is hollow when unselected). Either 'shift-click' to select or deselect additional points or click and drag to draw a bounding box around the required points. Hold down the 'shift' key while clicking and dragging to select or deselect other anchor points.

Anchor points can also be 'nudged' when selected, using the keyboard arrow keys.

Selected anchor points on curved outlines have Bézier handles (**fig. 5**), which can be pulled to new positions with the Subselection Tool, thus changing the object's shape. Hold down the 'alt' key at the same time and the Bézier handles can be moved independently of each other, allowing the line to be something other than a smooth curve as it traverses the point. Anchor points can also be converted, see p. 191. See the 'Drawing and Editing – 1' movie on the CD.

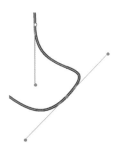

fig. 5 A selected anchor point showing Bézier handles.

2.3 The Line Tool

Click and drag with the Line Tool selected to draw straight lines. These can be turned into curved lines by 'pushing' them with the Selection Tool.

2.4 The Lasso Tool

Enclose, and thus select, objects or parts of objects with the Lasso Tool by clicking and dragging. Hold down the 'shift' key to add to the selection.

Although one of the Toolbox options offers polygon mode – to draw the selection area in straight line segments – it is easier to toggle into polygon mode, when the Lasso Tool is selected, by holding down the 'alt' key. When the outline is complete, simply let go of the 'alt' key and the mouse button. It is not necessary to join up the ends if all the objects you wish to select are already enclosed, because Flash does that for you by closing any gap with a straight line segment.

Tip   **There is an important difference between Flash and other vector-drawing software. In Illustrator, for example, it is not possible to select just one part of an object with the Selection Tool; the object is either selected, or it is not. In Flash, however, you can select parts of objects or complete objects. Click and drag to enclose part of an object, using the Selection or Lasso tools, and only the enclosed areas are selected. This takes some getting used to, so be careful.**

To see the uses of the Lasso Tool with imported bitmaps, see p. 209.

2.5 The Pen Tool

Flash's Pen Tool is very similar to those of InDesign and Illustrator. See the 'Drawing and Editing – 2' movie on the CD.

With the Pen Tool selected, you can click, move and click again to draw straight line segments; or click, move and click and drag to produce Bézier curves.

To create an enclosed shape, return to the starting point and click on it when a small 'o' appears next to the cursor. To see the anchor points, click on an open or closed path, in the same way as when using the Subselection Tool.

A drawn shape can be manipulated in several ways. To add anchor points, click on the outline with the Pen Tool. To delete curved or corner anchor points, click twice on the point. The first click on a curved line segment point converts it to a 'corner' (i.e. deleting any curves) point; the second click deletes it.

Anchor points can also be moved using the Subselection Tool. To convert a corner to a curve, hold down the 'alt' key and click and drag on the point with the Subselection Tool, not the Pen Tool.

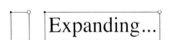

fig. 6 An expanding text frame.

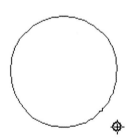

fig. 7 A fixed-width text frame.

2.6 The Text Tool

When the Text Tool is selected, the options in the Properties window display useful things like font, size, colour and alignment. It is a good idea, although not essential, to make these basic choices before proceeding. To set paragraph options, click on the 'Format' button.

There are two basic types of text frame that can be drawn on the stage: an expanding text frame and a fixed-width text frame. To produce an expanding text frame (**fig. 6**), click on the stage. The resulting box is very small with a circle in the upper-right corner to indicate that the frame expands to accommodate text as it is typed. To create a fixed-width frame, click and drag to draw a rectangular box that is one line deep. A small square appears in the top-right corner (**fig. 7**). This kind of frame causes the enclosed text to wrap to the next line as it fills the box's width.

Click inside the text with the Text Tool and drag on the small circle or square to resize either kind of frame. Double-click on a square handle, and the block reverts to a single line of text with a round handle.

To reformat all the text within a frame, select the frame with the Selection or Subselection tools and update the options in the Properties window. To change formatting on only part of the text in a frame, click and drag to select it with the Text Tool and then adjust the 'Properties' options.

Choose 'Flash > Preferences' ('Edit > Preferences' on a PC) for options allowing the creation of vertical, rather than horizontal, frames.

| Tip | Some fonts are not suitable for inclusion as static text in a movie. To check, choose 'View > Antialias Text'. If the text appears with a smooth outline, it can be exported; if it has a jagged outline, it cannot. |

The shape of individual characters can be changed, but the characters must first be converted from editable text into an editable shape (at which point they are no longer text). Select the text block with the Selection Tool and choose 'Modify > Break Apart' ('apple/control + B'). Do this once to break words into individual, but still editable, letters; do it a second time to convert characters from text to a shape. At this stage, the Selection, Pen and Subselection tools can edit the shape in exactly the same way as any other object.

2.7 The Shape Drawing tools

Ovals and rectangles

Clicking and dragging with the shape-drawing tools creates ovals, circles, rectangles and squares. To produce an oval, select the Oval Tool and click and drag non-diagonally. To create a circle, drag diagonally. The shape snaps to a perfect circle if the cursor is dragged close to a diagonal path (i.e. at 45° to the starting point) and a small circle appears beneath the cursor (**fig. 8**). The same is true when drawing squares as opposed to rectangles.

If you click on the Rectangle Tool, a window opens in which you can enter a radius value to produce a rectangle with rounded corners.

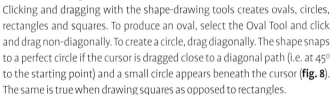

fig. 8 Constraining a shape to a circle.

PolyStar

The PolyStar Tool, new in MX 2004, is on a flyout menu and is accessed by clicking and holding on the Rectangle Tool and then sliding down to the PolyStar Tool and releasing the mouse. The number of sides can be adjusted by clicking on the 'Options' button in the Properties window. This opens the tool settings. To draw a star with inset points, choose 'Star' in the 'Style' box and enter a value between 1.00 and 0.00 in the 'Star Point Size' area. Values close to 1 create a fuller shape than those nearer to 0, which produce a sharper star (**fig. 9**).

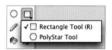

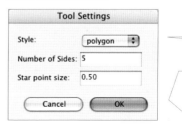

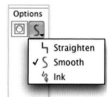

   For all of the above tools, a stroke style can be applied by clicking on the 'Custom' button in the Properties window. The preview area in the left of the Stroke Style window updates as choices are made, and the 'Type' box offers a variety of line appearances.

fig. 9 PolyStar Tool Settings window and resulting shapes.

2.8 The Pencil Tool

This tool has three options that appear at the foot of the Toolbox when the tool is selected (**fig. 10**): 'Straighten', 'Smooth' and 'Ink'. Choose one of these before drawing a line, as the options available after drawing may not allow you to create the shape you want.

   'Straighten' recognizes when such approximate simple shapes as triangles, squares and circles are drawn. When the mouse button is released, the shape snaps to whatever Flash considers to be the actual shape you are trying to draw.

fig. 10 Pencil Tool options.

   Mice are not especially suited to drawing operations, and jagged spots are likely to occur when using them. However, these can be smoothed out with the 'Smooth' function.

   'Ink' hardly reshapes the line you draw, although it does a very small amount of smoothing.

   Once a line has been drawn with the Pencil Tool, it can be selected and then straightened or smoothed using the options at the foot of the Toolbox.

2.9 The Brush Tool

'Painted' colour strokes – which are not actually strokes, rather 'strokeless fills' – are produced using the Brush Tool. When one is selected with the Subselection Tool, the anchor points clearly indicate that it is a filled object. The shape is manipulated in the same way as the outline of any other shape.

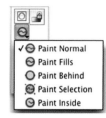

   Toolbox options (**fig. 11**) include size and style selection and also two modifiers that are only available to those using a graphics tablet rather than a mouse.

fig. 11 Brush Tool options.

   In the options area, there is also a small circle with a red line through it. This is a flyout menu, and it holds some very useful features that allow painting work to be fairly sloppy while still producing clean results:

   'Paint Normal' paints over anything on that layer.

   'Paint Fills' does not cover existing outlines but it does paint over everything else.

'Paint Behind' paints blank areas of the stage while leaving outlines and fills unaffected.

'Paint Selection' repaints only a selected fill area – at least, that is the idea. In fact, it often catches a small part of an object outline and deletes it.

'Paint Inside' paints either outside or inside an object but does not affect existing outlines. When painting inside an object, begin on an area of a different colour or else it will not work. Similarly, if the area to be painted is too small for the current brush size, this function will not work.

2.10 The Free Transform Tool

This tool resizes, skews, scales, distorts and rotates objects.

Select the tool and click on an object to enclose it within a frame that has handles on each corner and in the middle of each side.

The 'Rotate' button is not needed, as an object can be rotated by holding the cursor outside one of the corner handles and dragging when it changes into a 'Rotate' icon (**fig. 12**). The small white circle at the centre of the object is the point of rotation, which can be repositioned by clicking and dragging.

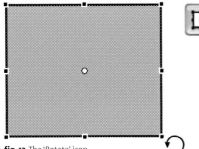

fig. 12 The 'Rotate' icon.

To skew an object, hold the cursor over part of the outline between a central and a corner handle. When the cursor changes into a 'Skew' icon (**fig. 13**), click and drag. The 'Scale' option button is also unnecessary, as dragging on a corner handle of an object scales it. To maintain proportions, hold down the 'shift' key while dragging. Toggle into 'Distort' by holding down the 'apple/control' key, and distort the object by dragging on one of the handles. Additionally, and not available as a Toolbox option, an object can be resized from the centre point by clicking and dragging on a handle while the 'alt' key is held down. When the 'Envelope' shaper is selected, the object is surrounded with handles that can be moved independently of one another to edit the shape.

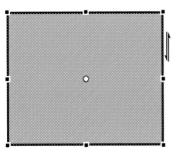

fig. 13 The 'Skew' icon.

Tip   **Objects can also be resized and moved using the Info window. To see this, choose (MX and Studio 8) 'Window > Info' or (MX 2004) 'Window > Design Panels > Info' ('apple/control + i'). Select either the centre or top-left handles of the small 'Element Model' box as the reference point for the object and enter new data in the windows.**

2.11 The Fill Transform Tool

This tool resizes, reshapes, moves and rotates fills. With the tool selected, click on a radial gradient fill to modify it. A circle appears with a central point, which indicates the centre of the fill itself. To move the fill in relation to its object, drag the central point. To change its shape, click and drag on the square icon on the perimeter. To resize, click and drag on the central circular icon, while to rotate, click and drag on the lower circular icon. A slightly different set of tools, allowing the fill to be scaled, moved and rotated, appears if a linear gradient fill is selected instead.

This tool can also skew, rotate and resize bitmap fills (see p. 209). If it is a tiled fill, all the elements are affected even though only one seems to be selected.

See the 'Applying colour' section on p. 197 for more about colour.

2.12 The Ink Bottle Tool

To add a stroke to a filled object or to edit an existing stroke, use the Ink Bottle Tool. Select the tool and then set the colour, thickness and style of the stroke in the Properties window. Click on the outside edge of a filled shape to apply it. Existing strokes can be modified using the same method.

2.13 The Paint Bucket Tool

Fill areas enclosed by outlines and change existing fills using the Paint Bucket Tool. Select a colour and click on a filled or enclosed area. The modifiers allow the tool to ignore small, medium or large gaps in the enclosing outline.

2.14 The Eyedropper Tool

This tool picks up colour information from an object and turns into a temporary paint or ink pot to apply those attributes elsewhere. For example, if you click on an object's solid fill with the Eyedropper, you can then click on another object to fill it with the same colour. If you click on the stroke instead, you can apply the stroke characteristics to another object in the same way.

Tip   **If you use this tool to pick up a gradient fill, the source and target objects are filled as if they were one object. Each can subsequently be moved independently. However, if they are on the same layer then, prior to being moved, their fills can be rotated, among other things, as if they were a single item, using the Fill Transform Tool. But, as soon as one of the objects is moved, this temporary link is broken.**

2.15 The Eraser Tool

To erase whole or parts of objects, use the Eraser Tool. Double-click on it to delete everything on the stage.

A size and style for the eraser 'brush' is chosen using the Toolbox options. To delete contiguous object fills or strokes, click on them with 'Faucet' selected; to use any of the other options, first deselect 'Faucet'.

'Normal' erases everything it is dragged across, while 'Erase Fills' only deletes fills and not strokes.

'Erase Lines' rubs out strokes but not fills, while 'Erase Selected Fills' erases the selected part of a fill.

'Erase Inside' only erases fills and only then if it begins on part of the fill itself. If it begins on an empty area, it does nothing.

3   Basic Techniques

3.1 Arranging and grouping

The tools in the Toolbox allow you to draw simple objects with particular characteristics. Parts of the objects can be selected and moved, leaving other parts behind. Also, if one object is drawn (or moved) on top of another *on the same layer* and then deselected, those parts of the object that it covers are deleted. See the 'Arrange and Group' movie on the CD.

Try this for yourself: draw two shapes in different parts of the stage. Then, change the fill colour of one of them, using the Paint Bucket Tool, as described in the previous section. Click and drag around this second object with the Selection Tool, thus selecting it, and drag to position it partly on top of the first object. Deselect it by clicking on a blank area of the stage. Then, select and move its fill by clicking on it and dragging. The parts of the first object that it covered have vanished.

Clearly, this could be a serious problem. But, fortunately, it is easy to overcome, simply by grouping each object and thereby changing its status. The object can then overlay another object without causing any part of it to be deleted.

Any object (or group of objects) can be designated as a 'group'. If it is a single object, it does not even have to be made up of more than one element (such as fill and stroke).

To create a group, select the object(s) and choose 'Modify > Group' ('apple/control + G'); to ungroup, select the grouped object and choose 'Modify > Ungroup' ('apple/control + shift + G').

To edit one or more of a group's objects, select the group on the stage and either double-click on it or go to 'Edit > Edit Selected'. Stroke and fill colours can then be changed or otherwise edited. To return to the grouped format, choose 'Edit > Edit All'.

To change the hierarchy, i.e. which object overlaps which, select an object and choose 'Modify > Arrange' and then either 'Bring to Front' or 'Send to Back' ('apple/control + shift + up [or down] arrow').

3.2 Copying and pasting objects

Select an object and choose 'apple/control + C' to copy it, followed by 'apple/control + V' to paste a duplicate elsewhere on the stage. To paste a copy exactly on top of the original, use 'apple/control + shift + V', which works even when copying from one layer and pasting to another.

3.3 Creating duplicate objects

Select an object and drag on it while holding down the 'alt' key. This works with single objects, grouped objects and symbol instances (see p. 200).

3.4 Aligning objects

A quick and easy way to align objects, regardless of the layer(s) on which they have been placed, is available using the Align panel. Choose 'Window > Design Panels > Align' ('apple/control + K'). Draw two objects on the stage in such a way that they do not line up, either vertically or horizontally. It does not matter whether they are on the same, or different, layers. Nor does it matter whether they are simple, drawn shapes, grouped objects or symbols.

Select them both by clicking and dragging a bounding box around them with the Selection Tool.

Then, click on one of the 'Align' options in the Align panel. The icons on the left in this area deal with horizontal alignment, while those on the right align objects vertically.

You can also use this panel to distribute objects evenly, so that the spaces between specified edges, or their centres, are equal.

Objects can be resized using the icons in the 'Match Size' area. Several objects can be made the same width or height (or both) as the largest of those selected. The icons in the 'Space' area can even out the space between objects.

If the 'To Stage' button on the right of the panel is clicked, all the adjustments refer to the stage rather than the objects themselves. Thus, they would be distributed across the entire width of the stage, rather than in the current spread of the objects themselves.

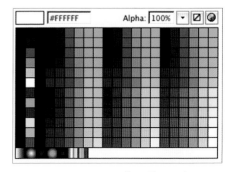

fig. 14 The swatches display, from the Properties window.

3.5 Applying colour

Select an object on the stage, click on the 'Stroke' and/or 'Fill' colour chips in the Properties window and pick a colour from the swatches display (**fig. 14**). If the required colour is not there or if you wish to create a gradient fill, click on the button in the top-right corner to open the Colours window (**fig. 15**). While the layout of this varies according to the version of Flash being used, the methods are virtually identical. See the 'Solid Colours' movie on the CD.

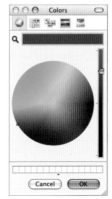

fig. 15 The Colours window.

Tip	Remember, this is different from the Colour Mixer window, see below.

In the Colours window, use the colour circle and the slider to its right to produce the required colour. To save it for future use, (pre-Studio 8) click on the 'Add to Custom Colours' button, or (Studio 8) drag from the bar at the top onto one of the empty squares at the foot of the window.

To create a custom gradient, select the fill of an object and open the Colour Mixer window (**fig. 16**) by choosing (MX and Studio 8) 'Window > Colour Mixer' or (MX 2004) 'Window > Design Panels > Colour Mixer' ('shift + F9'). See the 'Gradient Colours' movie on the CD.

Click on (pre-Studio 8) the window to the right of the solid colour chip and choose either 'Radial' or 'Linear' from the list, or (Studio 8) select from the 'Type' choices. A gradient bar appears. Click on one of the paint pots beneath it and create a new colour using the colour picker square and the slider to its right. Click under the bar to add more pots or drag the pots away from the bar to remove them. Each time the colour of a pot is edited, the object's colour updates.

Open the Swatches window (**fig. 17**) – (MX and Studio 8) 'Window > Colour Swatches' or (MX 2004) 'Window > Design Panels > Colour

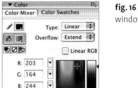

fig. 16 The Colour Mixer window.

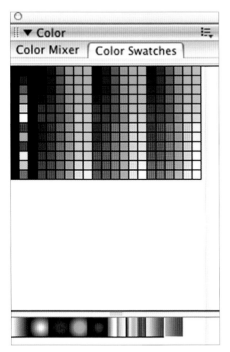

fig. 17 The Swatches window.

Swatches' ('apple/control + F9') – to save a new gradient by clicking in the lower section of this window, while the object's fill is selected. This adds it to the library.

3.6 Applying transparency

The transparency or 'alpha' settings of an object are changed in the Colour Mixer window (see p. 197).

In addition to colour chips for fill and stroke, there is a Colour Picker window. If an object's fill is selected, its colour can be changed here. To the right of the colour picker is a slider, which adds white or black to the colour in the larger square.

In the top right of this window are three fields, one each for R, G and B; below these is an alpha percentage area. This group also has sliders on the right side, with which adjustments can be made.

While selected, fill and stroke colours can be updated simply by choosing a different colour. However, to see the results of an alpha setting adjustment, you should double-click on a blank area of the stage after making a change.

See the 'Transparency' tutorial movie on the CD for details on applying transparency to drawn objects and imported bitmaps.

3.7 Revert

Flash encourages you to test your ideas, on the stage, by allowing you to revert to the last saved version of a file. This means that you do not have to close everything down and start again. Simply choose 'File > Revert', and carry on playing.

4   Animation

4.1 Frame-by-frame animation

In the days of Disney, every frame in an animation was hand-drawn. Points at which the action changed direction were known as 'keyframes', while the frames between them were called 'in-between' frames. Artists who created keyframes were paid considerably more than in-between artists.

To see how frame-by-frame animation works, draw an object on frame 1 of a new document. Create a series of additional keyframes by selecting frames 2–10, one at a time, and pressing the 'F6 'key for each one (**fig. 18**). The object drawn in frame 1 is duplicated on all the keyframes. Had the keyframes been created before anything had been drawn, they would have been blank.

Select frame 2 and move the object slightly to one side. Select frame 3 and move the object a bit further, and so on for all the frames. Return to frame 1 and press the 'enter' key (or choose 'Control > Test Movie') to create a temporary '.SWF' file that plays immediately.

The movement probably seems slightly uneven, as, even if considerable care is taken, it is hard to ensure that the object follows a smooth path.

Frame-by-frame animation is labour-intensive stuff and the solution is 'tweening'. This process defines the keyframes that dictate the direction of each change in action and performs the necessary adjustments in the object state between one keyframe and the next.

It is useful to first open the Controller window, 'Window > Toolbars > Controller', (**fig. 19**) when creating animations as it provides VCR-type buttons for playback and other actions. Alternatively, use 'enter' for play, 'apple/control + alt + R' for rewind and the full stop or comma keys to move the animation forward or backwards one frame at a time.

Changing the frame preview
There are several different viewing options available for the ways in which the frames in a Timeline are displayed. To see them, click on the small icon in the top-right corner of the frames area, directly above the vertical scroll bar.

4.2 Tweened animation

There are two kinds of tweening: shape and motion.

Tip	While shape and motion tweening share many characteristics, an essential difference between them remains. If the vector graphics involved in the tween need reshaping, you must use shape tweening. If the changes can be done through the Properties window, or another dialogue box or panel, motion tweening can be used.

Useful commands are 'F6', which creates a keyframe, and 'shift + F6', which removes a selected keyframe. 'F5' adds a normal frame, while 'shift + F5' deletes selected frames.

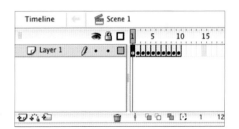

fig. 18 Frame-by-frame animation construction.

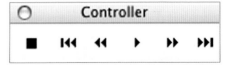

fig. 19 The Controller window.

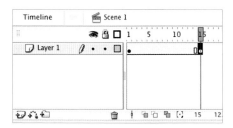

fig. 20 Setting up a shape tween.

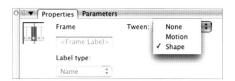

fig. 21 Choosing the tween type (above), and the result in the Timeline (below).

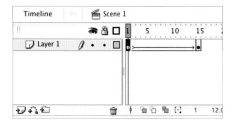

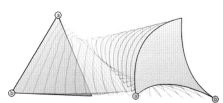

fig. 22 How shape hints work.

4.3 Shape tweening

Draw a shape in frame 1, which automatically becomes a keyframe. Create another keyframe ('F6') further along the Timeline (**fig. 20**) and either draw another shape on it or edit the current shape. Click on the first keyframe and, in the Properties window, choose 'Shape' as the tween variety. In the Timeline, a solid arrow (rather than a dotted arrow) appears across the range of the tween (**fig. 21**), stopping just short of the second keyframe. Test the animation by selecting the first frame and pressing the 'enter' key. See the 'Shape Tweens' movie on the CD.

More keyframes can be added within the original tween, and the shape and other properties of the object can be changed on each one. The animation can also be extended by creating a second tween that uses the end keyframe of the previous set as the beginning keyframe for the next set.

Flash is sometimes unable to create a smooth transition from one shape to another in a shape tween. To create a smoother movement, add 'Shape Hints', which are positioned on the outlines of the beginning and end shapes and tell Flash where individual components end up.

Position shape hints by selecting the initial keyframe of the tween, thereby selecting the object, and choosing 'Modify > Shape > Add Shape Hint' ('apple/control + shift + H'). Drag the hint to a section of the outline and add another hint. Repeat this until there are several hints in place.

Click on the final keyframe in which the hints appear. Sometimes, if Flash does not know where to place them, they are on top of each other in the centre of the object. If this is the case, drag them to the appropriate positions on the final outline and play the tween again (**fig. 22**).

4.4 Using symbols

Before looking at motion tweens, it is *extremely* important to understand symbols. One of the commonest mistakes made in the creation of Flash animations is not to use symbols. As a result, each time a copy of an object is required, the object is selected, then copied and pasted into its new location.

Consequently, every single copy is a separate object, and the filesize continues to grow each time a new copy is created. This can easily mean that the final animation is too big to load quickly enough to satisfy the audience. The golden rule is to never, ever over-estimate the length of your audience's attention span! It is *always* shorter than you think.

Instead of creating multiple copies of objects, just use one, which has been converted into a symbol. This way, even if several thousand of them are used in a movie, the object is only added to the filesize once.

Tip	Symbols are incredibly important. If you do not understand them, you will not be able to use Flash effectively.

Any object can be saved as a symbol. Then, whenever that object is required, the symbol is used instead. The result, on the Flash stage, is an object called a 'symbol instance', and all such objects are simply reflections – useable reflections – of the original object.

Flash stores symbols in a Library, from where they can be dragged onto the stage. To see the Library window, choose 'Window > Library' ('apple/control + L') **(fig. 23)**.

To save an object as a symbol, select it with the Selection Tool and drag it into the lower part of the Library window. Alternatively, after selecting it on the stage, press the 'F8' key to open the Convert to Symbol window. Choose a symbol 'Type' (use 'Graphic' for now, as the other types are dealt with later) and click 'OK' **(fig. 23)**.

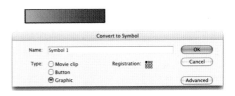

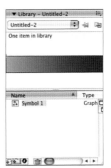

fig. 23 Converting a shape into a symbol and the Library window.

Editing a symbol

To change the appearance of *all* the existing instances of a symbol, do one of the following:

1) Double-click on the symbol's picture in the Library

2) Click on the symbol's name in the Library and press 'apple/control + E'

3) Select an instance of the symbol on-stage and press 'apple/control + E'.

Whichever method is chosen, the stage converts to 'Edit' mode and a small crosshair appears in its centre. It can then be selected, and the tools in the Toolbox can be used to edit it. Transparency can be adjusted using the 'Alpha' settings in the Colour Mixer panel. When you are done, either type 'apple/control + E' or click the 'back' arrow in the top left of the stage. All existing instances of the symbol update, although instances that have been individually edited using the Properties window will combine both sets of editing.

One symbol instance can be swapped for another by selecting one of the instances on the stage and clicking on the 'Swap' button in the Properties window or (MX) choosing 'Modify > Swap Symbol' or (MX 2004) 'Modify > Symbol > Swap Symbol'.

Copy an existing symbol by selecting it in the Library list and choosing 'Duplicate' from the options. This allows you to create variations without changing the original.

To change a symbol instance back into a simple graphic, select it on the stage and choose 'Modify > Break Apart' ('apple/control + B').

You can drag and drop symbols and instances between Flash movies as long as both movies are visible on-screen.

Editing a symbol instance

Edits made to a symbol instance only change the appearance of that one object. Other occurrences of the same symbol remain unaffected.

Create a 'Graphic' symbol, then drag an instance of it onto the stage and use the options in the Properties window to change its appearance.

Tip   **A symbol instance cannot be broken into its constituent parts, so this kind of edit applies to the entire object, fill and outline.**

'Brightness' adds white to the existing colours, but does not change the transparency of an object, although it appears to, unless it is placed over another coloured object.

'Tint' changes the colour. You can click on the colour chip and select from the Colour window or edit the individual RGB settings. Use the percentage slider to adjust the strength with which the new specification overlays the original colour.

'Alpha' alters the transparency of the instance, using the percentage slider (100% is opaque).

'Advanced' changes both the colour and the transparency. Each component colour (R, G and B) has its own slider and below them is an alpha setting.

Individually edited instances can then be added to the Library as new symbols.

Sharing symbols between files
Sharing symbols between Flash files is very easy. Open the file in which the symbols exist, and open its Library ('apple/control + L'). Then, open a new Flash file.

There are now two Libraries visible in the panel area. One has the same name as the original Flash file, and the other has the name 'untitled', as its file has not yet been saved. Symbols can then be dragged, by their names, into the lower section of the 'untitled' Library.

Symbols shared in this way are completely separate – symbols in one Library can be edited without affecting those in another.

4.5 Motion tweening

Draw an object in frame 1 of a new movie, which automatically converts frame 1 to a keyframe. Click on the frame to select it, and choose (MX) 'Insert > Create Motion Tween' or (MX 2004) 'Insert > Timeline > Motion Tween'. The object becomes a symbol instance (see p. 200).

Tip   **This conversion does not work if you use the Properties window to select 'Motion' as the tweening option.**

Click on a frame further along the Timeline to select it and press the 'F6' key to change it into a keyframe. A solid, rather than a dotted, arrow connects the two frames, indicating that a complete motion tween now exists between them (**fig. 24**). While the second keyframe is selected, drag the object to a new location on the stage with the Selection Tool.

Press 'enter' to play the animation and the object moves smoothly from its starting point to its position in the final frame. The tween is extended by creating additional keyframes and dragging the object to

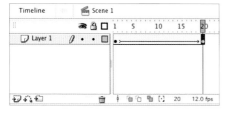

fig. 24 A motion tween.

different positions in each of them. To extend the Timeline between any two keyframes, select one of the in-between frames and press the 'F5' key to insert more frames. To shorten a tween segment, select a range of in-between frames (click on one, then 'shift-click' on another) and press 'shift + F5' to remove them.

When the keyframe is selected, the Properties window deals with things relating to that frame, such as the kind of tween, if any, that has been applied, or the events, if any, that are triggered at this particular point. However, when the object is selected, the Properties window focuses on the object's appearance: the kind of object it is, its size and where it appears on the stage. Also, in the 'Colour' area, such specific attributes as colour, brightness and alpha (transparency) can be adjusted.

To see an example of motion tweening, see the 'Motion Tweens' movie on the CD.

5   Working with Layers

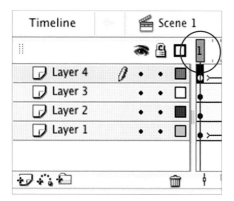

fig. 25 Multiple layers.

To the left of the timelines, which govern the movement of objects, are the layers, which hold the objects themselves (**fig. 25**). Layers can hold single or multiple objects. Each layer is allocated a name, which can be changed by double-clicking on it. When a layer is selected, it becomes shaded and shows a pencil icon to the right of its name, indicating that any object created while it is selected will exist on that layer.

To the right of the pencil icon are two dots, one beneath each of the 'Eye' and 'Padlock' icons at the top of the layers area. By clicking on the 'Eye' dot, a layer is temporarily turned off and made invisible. This is useful when, for example, a guide path has been attached to an object's movement (see 'Creating a motion guide path', p. 205), after which it is no longer required as a visible element. However, a guide path layer should not be deleted or else the guide path function would also be lost. Click on a layer's 'Padlock' dot and it turns into a padlock icon, preventing any of the objects on it from being edited or moved.

Tip	The ability to lock layers is an especially useful feature for new users of Flash, as one of the commonest mistakes is to work on the wrong layer. While this can always be undone, it invariably involves the loss of considerable time and effort. Therefore, it is a good habit to lock each layer whenever a particular task is complete, thus excluding it from those on which you can work.

Each layer has its own colour marker, which shows at the right end as a solid square. By clicking on this marker, all the objects on that layer display as outlines; by clicking on the square icon above these markers, all objects on all layers are set to display as outlines. While displayed in this way, animations can still be played and the objects and layers can still be edited or moved.

The three icons showing in the bottom-left corner of the layers area are:

'New Layer' – click here to create a new layer, which appears directly above the currently selected layer.

'Guide Path Layer' – governs the movement of the object on the layer directly beneath it (see 'Creating a motion guide path', p. 205).

'New Layer Folder' – too many layers are cumbersome and difficult to work with. To simplify things, layers can be stored in layer folders, which can be opened and closed when needed.

To store layers, click and drag them onto the layer folder. Click on the arrow to the left of a layer folder icon to open and close the folder; when open, the names of the included layers are slightly indented.

Tip	Layer folders are not layers and therefore have no timelines.

Tip   To preview just a portion of an animation, without having
to play through the whole thing, use 'Scrubbing'. Drag the
red block that indicates the frame currently visible on the
stage (it is just above the Timeline, in the frame numbers
area, and it is highlighted in fig. 25) through the frames
you want to see.

5.1 Creating a motion guide path

A motion guide path acts as an (invisible) guide along which a (visible)
object travels. See the 'Motion Guide Paths' movie on the CD.

Create a new layer and draw an object. As before, frame 1
automatically becomes a keyframe. Select it and choose (MX) 'Insert >
Motion Guide' or (MX 2004) 'Insert > Timeline > Motion Guide'. A new
guide layer appears above the layer just created (**fig. 26**). Click on its first
frame and, using one of the line-drawing tools (the Pen or Pencil tools
are usually best), draw a path for the object to follow. Again, the first
frame automatically becomes a keyframe.

Select the Selection Tool and then click on the keyframe in the object
layer. Check that the snap feature is on (the 'Magnet' icon in the 'Options'
area at the foot of the Toolbox should be highlighted), and go to (MX)
'Insert > Create Motion Tween' or (MX 2004) 'Insert > Timeline > Create
Motion Tween'. The object should snap onto the path at some point
(**fig. 27**). If it does not, use the Selection Tool to drag the object to the
starting point of the drawn guide path. If it is dragged from a point close
to its centre, a circular spot appears, which snaps onto the guide path.

Create a new keyframe for the object on frame 30 by selecting it
and pressing 'F6'. The motion tween appears across frames 1–30 in
the Timeline.

Now, select frame 30 in the motion guide layer and again press 'F6' to
insert a keyframe. The whole range is filled with a grey colour and the
path is now visible throughout the entire animation.

Choose the object's end keyframe (frame 30) and drag the object to
the other end of the guide path. It should not be possible, as the snap is
still operational, for the object to be positioned away from the path.

Then, play the movie.

The guide layer can be visually turned off (click on the dot beneath
the 'eye' icon for the guide layer), so the object seems to move
independently. The guide path is edited in the same way as any other
drawn line.

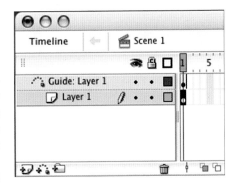

fig. 26 Adding a motion
guide layer.

fig. 27 Snapping an object
to a guide path.

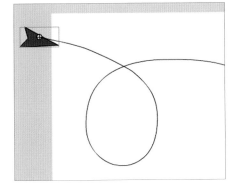

Tip   Layers containing guide paths and the objects attached to
them cannot be masked, see p. 207.

5.2 Orienting objects to a guide path

Should an object need to not only follow the path but also turn as it
follows it, then, after setting up the guide path and object motion

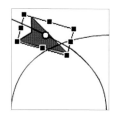

fig. 28 Orienting an object to a guide path using the Free Transform Tool.

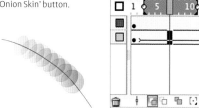

fig. 29 Checking orientation using the 'Onion Skin' button.

tween, select the object on frame 1 of the timeline and click in the 'Orient to Path' box at the foot of the Properties window.

Test the movie and look for any places where the object's orientation is not quite right.

Click anywhere on the object's Timeline and it moves to that point on the guide path, making it easy to locate the exact frame at which it starts to become unstable. Select that frame and turn it into a new keyframe ('F6'). Choose the Free Transform Tool, which creates a transform frame around the object when the keyframe is selected. Hold the cursor just outside one of the corners of the frame to turn it into a 'Rotate' icon, allowing the object to be rotated back to the correct path orientation (**fig. 28**).

The 'Onion Skin' button, at the bottom left of the Timeline window, also aids in determining where new keyframes should be added. It shows several 'ghost' images for the object (**fig. 29**); the currently selected frame is the darkest shape, while progressively lighter shapes show in the few frames to either side of it. This area makes visible any of the object's changes in orientation in that part of the path. The next button along displays only the object outlines for the same range of frames, which can be easier to work with in a complex drawing.

5.3 Accelerating and slowing down tweened movement

A bouncing ball does not move at the same speed throughout its bounce cycle, but slows towards the top of the curve and accelerates as it falls back to the ground. This kind of movement can be duplicated with the 'Ease' slider in the Properties window. To see how, open and play the 'bouncing ball' files in the 'Guide paths' folder on the CD.

First, play the movie to see the slowing down and speeding up of the ball's movement. Then, select keyframe 15 and look at the 'Ease' setting. Positive settings create acceleration at the beginning of a tweened section and a slower motion towards the end. Negative settings produce slower movement to start with, but acceleration towards the end. Also, look at the settings for keyframe 1.

Put both the 'Ease' settings back to zero and run the movie again. The overall length of the animation remains the same, as it still runs at 12 frames per second, and the number of frames does not change. However, the movement is now much less convincing.

Of course, you can add or delete frames to increase the effect, which changes the overall length of the animation.

In 'bouncing ball 2', some adjustments were made to the shape of the ball to simulate the compression caused by bouncing.

5.4 Mask layers

To create a mask layer, draw an object on a new layer (**fig. 30**). Create another new layer and draw a second object so that it overlaps the first (**fig. 31**). Then, (MAC) 'control-click' or (PC) 'right-click' on the second layer and choose 'Mask' from the list. Alternatively, choose 'Modify > Layer Properties > Mask'. The drawn object becomes a transparent window through which the layer immediately below it can be seen (**fig. 32**).

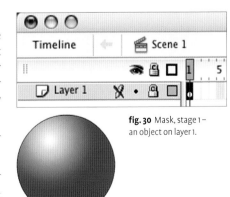

fig. 30 Mask, stage 1 – an object on layer 1.

Tip   **The mask object must have a solid or gradient fill, otherwise it may not be able to function as a mask.**

If there is already a frame sequence on the mask layer and if the mask needs to apply throughout the whole animation, the mask must be extended across the entire sequence. Click on the final frame of the animation in the mask layer, and press 'F5'. To link an additional layer to the mask, select it and choose 'Modify > Masked'. To function, the mask layer and any linked layers must be locked, by clicking on the 'Padlock' icons in their layers.

Mask layers are commonly used to create the appearance of scrolling text. To try this, open 'scrolling text.fla' in the 'Masks' folder on the CD.

As the text will vanish as soon as a new layer above it is designated as a mask, a motion tween governing its movement should be created first. However, the shape that will become a mask can be used as a guide for the movement of the text before this happens.

Create a new layer, and draw a rectangle (with a solid fill colour) on it just above the top line of the text. It should be about 5 lines deep and slightly wider than the text.

Click on frame one of the text layer, choose 'Insert > Timeline > Create Motion Tween'. Then, click on frame 60 of both layers, in turn, and create a second keyframe. These objects then exist for the duration of the animation.

Select frame 60 of the text layer, and drag the text frame vertically (constraining the direction of its movement by holding down the the the 'shift' key as you drag) until it is just above the rectangle on layer 2. Then, select layer 2 and turn it into a mask layer using the method described above. The text should vanish as you do this.

Play the movie. The text should become visible as it scrolls through the area of the rectangle on the mask layer. If it does not work properly, open 'Scrolling text 2' on the CD and check your work against it.

Tip   **Masks cannot be applied to guide layers or their objects.**

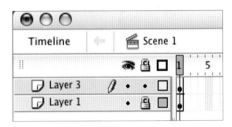

fig. 31 Mask, stage 2 – an object on layer 2 overlaps the object on layer 1.

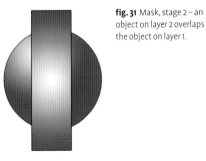

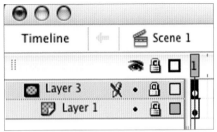

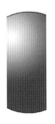

fig. 32 Mask, stage 3 – the object on layer 2 becomes a mask.

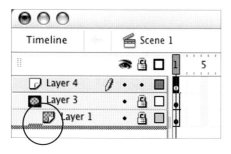

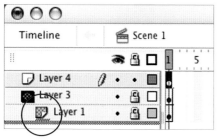

fig. 33 Adding another layer but not to the mask group (top) and adding another layer to a mask group (bottom).

5.5 Timeline effects

Flash contains several Timeline effects that are very easy to apply. However, do not forget that they are available to everyone else, too. If you want your efforts in Flash to look unique, you need to come up with your own!

Draw an object on the stage. Select the keyframe on frame 1 and choose 'Insert > Timeline Effects > Effects'. There are four to choose from, some of which may not be available depending on the selected object: blur, drop shadow, expand and explode.

If you choose 'drop shadow', for example, a window opens allowing you to change the appearance of the shadow, and then update the preview so that you can see how the result will look. Click 'OK', and the object on the stage is transformed from a simple object into a graphic symbol, and added to the Library.

Any application of a Timeline effect results in the creation of a new symbol.

To remove a Timeline effect from a symbol instance, choose 'Modify > Break Apart'.

Tip   Additional settings, such as motion tweens, can be added to objects to which Timeline effects have already been applied. However, doing so removes the ability to adjust the effect settings. So, if you create a 'blur' effect that lasts for 15 frames, but the motion tween then created lasts for 30 frames, the 'blur' takes place twice as the object moves through the tween.

You can also add a 'Transitional' effect to a symbol, to change the way it appears on or vanishes from the stage. Drag an instance from the Library to the stage, and choose 'Insert > Timeline Effects > Transform/Transition > Transition'. You can update the preview as you change the settings. Objects can be set to fade in or out, or to be 'wiped' in or out. More frames are added to the Timeline automatically, if needed.

5.6 Scenes

Just as a table of contents displays sections of a book in a fixed order that is easy to navigate, so a list of scenes can break a large movie into manageable chunks and, when published, the scenes play back in a designated order.

To view the Scene window (**fig. 34**), choose (MX) 'Window > Scene' or (MX 2004) 'Window > Design Panels > Scene' ('shift + F2').

To add a new scene, click on the '+' button at the foot of the window. To rename a scene, double-click on its title. Scene order is changed by dragging the names to alter the hierarchy in the Scene window.

To select a scene to edit, click on its name in the Scene window.

5.7 Using bitmaps

Aside from using vector shapes to create a Flash movie, images can also be imported. However, if you decide to do this, remember that images usually have a much larger filesize than a vector graphic that covers the same area on the stage. Therefore, their inclusion might make the resulting movie too big to be useful.

Issues such as size, resolution and optimization should be dealt with before an image is imported. Adobe Photoshop, or even Photoshop Elements, can help with these things. Make your image the correct size before bringing it into an animation. Set it to 72dpi and optimize it using the method described in the Photoshop chapter (see p. 46), so that the appropriate balance between lower filesize and higher quality can be achieved beforehand.

To import an image, select the first frame, keyframe 1, in a new movie and go to 'File > Import'. Browse to an image, which must be a GIF or a PNG or JPEG in RGB format.

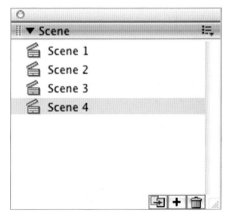

fig. 34 The Scene window.

| Tip | PNG and JPEG formats are similar in that they can support up to 16.7 million colours in RGB mode; PNG images, however, can be partially transparent. Both formats are suitable for 'continuous tone' (i.e. complex) images. GIF images also support transparency but can only hold a maximum of 256 colours and are, therefore, suitable for more simple images, such as maps, logos and type. |

If it is necessary, for the purpose of your movie, to change the size of an image once it is on the stage, the Free Transform Tool can be used. Remember to hold down the 'shift' key as you drag on a corner handle or the image will be distorted.

Images can be used within motion tweens, and they can have alpha settings applied to them, enabling them to be faded in and out of view. To see an example of the use of alpha settings with imported images, see the 'Using bitmaps' folder on the CD.

While an image and keyframe are selected, follow the procedure for creating a motion tween (see p. 202), which also transforms the image into a graphic symbol.

Reselect the first keyframe and click on the image on the stage. In the Properties window, choose 'Alpha' from the 'Colour' area and drag the slider to 0%. Choose the second keyframe, click on the object again and bring back the slider to 100%.

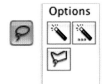

fig. 35 Lasso Tool options.

Now, play the movie and the image gradually fades into view.

By choosing 'Modify > Break Apart' when a bitmap is selected, the bitmap becomes editable with some of the tools. For example, it can be selected in the same way as a simple non-symbol object.

Select the Lasso Tool and click the 'Magic Wand Settings' modifier at the foot of the Toolbox (**fig. 35**). Enter a tolerance value of between 1 and 200: the higher the number, the greater the range of adjacent shades are selected. Click 'OK', select the Magic Wand modifier and click on the image. The area that falls within the tolerance value is selected. To add to the selection, hold down the 'shift' key and continue to click. Selected areas are deleted by pressing the 'delete' or 'backspace' keys.

A broken-apart bitmap can also be applied as a fill. Click on the image using the Eyedropper Tool. Then, any shape drawn on any layer will have that fill.

In the case of a simple image that is made up of blocks of colour, such as a diagram or map, it is better to convert it from being a single bitmap to being one or more vector shapes. This is known as 'tracing', and usually creates a far smaller filesize, while being visually indistinguishable from the original. Alternatively, it may make it possible to work with the appearance of the image in ways that would be impossible while it is in bitmap form, such as adding animation to just part of it.

To trace an image, select the image and choose 'Modify > Bitmap > Trace Bitmap'. In the Trace Bitmap window, the smaller the numbers in the 'Colour Threshold' and 'Minimum Area' fields, the more detail is preserved. 'Curve Fit' and 'Corner Threshold' can be set to create smoother or more detailed edges to the resulting vector paths.

6   Animated Graphics Symbols

A movie may contain many objects and layers and lots of animation. Despite such complexity, it can be turned into an animated graphics symbol, which holds the movie's contents and allows them to be placed into another movie on a single layer. However, if the original ran for 50 frames, the destination layer must also allow 50 frames for it to play completely. Animated graphics symbols cannot have a soundtrack and any interactivity in the original is lost in their creation. Movie-clip symbols, on the other hand, run in a continuous loop from just one frame on one layer in the movie in which they are placed; they can have a soundtrack and do not lose any interactivity.

6.1 Creating animated graphics symbols

Imagine an animation of a flame that is made up of three separate layers, each 20 frames long. On each layer is a single shape: one has the outer shape, one contains the middle of the flame and one holds the inner shape.

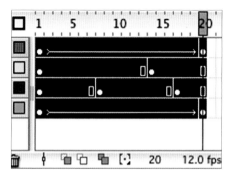

fig. 36 Highlighting multiple frames on multiple layers to copy and paste them.

An animated graphics symbol can include the entire animation. Click on frame 1 on layer one and then 'shift-click' on frame 20 of layer 3. All the frames on all the layers become selected (**fig. 36**).

Choose (MX) 'Edit > Copy Frames' or (MX 2004) 'Edit > Timeline > Copy Frames' ('apple/control + alt + V'). Go to 'Insert > New Symbol' ('apple/control + F8'), type a name, choose 'Graphic' as the behaviour type and click 'OK'.

Select the single frame that appears in the Timeline and paste the copied frames into it, using (MX) 'Edit > Paste Frames' or (MX 2004) 'Edit > Timeline > Paste Frames' ('apple/control + alt + V').

The animation can be adjusted at this point if necessary. Return to the movie by pressing 'apple/control + E'.

In the symbols Library, the new symbol appears with play button controls so that the animation can be tested.

To use an animated graphics symbol, create a keyframe on a blank layer, select it, and drag an instance of the symbol onto the stage.

Tip	Make sure that enough frames are created after that point to allow the entire animation to play.

6.2 Creating movie-clip symbols

This operation follows exactly the same sequence as when creating animated graphics symbols (see above), except that 'Movie Clip' should be chosen in place of 'Graphic' as the symbol type.

As before, all the selected frames should be pasted into the single keyframe in the Timeline. However, if an instance of an animated movie clip is dragged onto the stage in the same way as for the animated graphics symbol, the whole clip can be embedded in a single keyframe.

7   Actions and Behaviours

Actions and behaviours are quite similar in Flash. Both deal with an event or sequence of events that is triggered by something else. For example, when a button has a 'Get URL' *action* attached to it and the 'Event' or trigger *behaviour* is 'On Release', then, as the mouse is clicked and then released on the button, the action takes place. In this example, it would send the viewer to a new web page.

> **Tip**   **Actions do not affect the playback on the Flash stage unless 'Control > Enable Simple Frame Actions' is chosen first.**

There are two basic kinds of action 'scripts' in Flash: those attached to keyframes and those attached to a button or movie clip. Keyframe actions do not accept input from the viewer, whereas movie clip and button actions do.

> **Tip**   **If two or more actions are placed on different layers but share the same frame, only the action on the uppermost layer is acted upon.**

fig. 37 An action applied to frame 3.

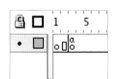

7.1 Keyframe actions

The most common keyframe actions are those telling the movie to stop, play or 'go to' a particular frame. For example, an action can instruct a keyframe on frame 3 of a movie to jump to frame 25 and stop there. To do this, create a keyframe at frame 3, select it and open the Actions window by choosing (MX and Studio 8) 'Window > Actions' or (MX 2004) 'Window > Development Panels > Actions' ('F9').

In MX, click on 'Actions > Movie Control' and double-click on 'Go To'. Enter '25' alongside 'Frame' and at the top select 'Go To and Stop'. In MX 2004 and Studio 8 versions, click on 'Global Functions > Timeline Control' and double-click on 'gotoAndStop'. Enter '25' in the parentheses at the end of the action statement.

Close the window. A lowercase 'a' appears on frame 3, indicating that an action is assigned at that point (**fig. 37**).

Now, test the movie. First, choose 'Control > Enable Simple Frame Actions' to allow the movie, including the action, to play on the stage just as it would in a browser window. Alternatively, choose 'Control > Test Movie' ('apple/control + enter') to see a temporary '.SWF' file play in full-screen mode.

To clear an action, select the keyframe and re-open the Actions window. Highlight the action by clicking on it and press delete.

7.2 Buttons

Buttons are a great way to add interesting interactive elements to a Flash movie. Take a look at the files in the 'Buttons + Links' folder on the CD.

Choose 'Insert > New Symbol' ('apple/control + F8') to show the Create New Symbol window. Type in a name for the button, select

'Button' as the behaviour and click 'OK' (**fig. 38**). The Timeline changes to reflect four potential button states (**fig. 39**):

'Up' – how the button appears on the stage when inactive.

'Over' – how the button changes when the cursor moves over it.

'Down' – how the button changes when it is clicked on.

'Hit' – this is not a visible image, but defines the area that responds to the mouse click. It is usually the same size and shape as the other three states.

Draw the button on the stage. The small circle in the 'Up' state frame becomes solid black, indicating that it is a filled keyframe. Click in the 'Over' frame to select it and press 'F6' to create a new keyframe. The button image immediately duplicates itself in the new frame and becomes selected. Change the colour of the fill for the 'Over' state. Repeat this for the 'Down' state. Enter a keyframe for 'Hit' but do not change the colour for this state (**fig. 40**).

When the four states are completed, return to the movie by doing one of three things: pressing 'apple/control + E'; clicking on the 'back' arrow to the top left of the stage (in MX 2004, the arrow is just under the name tab at the top of the movie screen); or by double-clicking elsewhere on the stage. To enable button actions on the Flash stage, choose 'Control > Enable Simple Buttons' ('apple/control + alt + B').

Click where it says 'Scene 1' near the top of the screen (in MX, it is at the top left of the stage window; in MX 2004, it is at the top of the movie window, just below the name tag).

Make sure the Library – containing the new button symbol – is open on-screen ('Window > Library') and click on the button's name. A copy of the button appears in the top window with a small play icon next to it. Click on the icon to see the button scroll through the states just created.

If an instance of the button symbol is dragged onto the screen, it does not work until 'Control > Enable Simple Buttons' is chosen. It then scrolls through the states as the cursor interacts with it. To work with it in any other way, the 'Enable' command must be turned off.

Alternatively, by choosing 'apple/control + enter', a temporary working version of the movie plays, in which the button functions.

The method employed to attach an action to the button – for instance, to direct the viewer to a specific URL – depends on the version of Flash used.

In MX versions, open the Actions window and choose 'Actions > Browser Network' to open a list. Double-click on 'Get URL'. It is important that the 'On Release' line appears too, otherwise the object has not been recognized as a button. Type in the full URL (including the 'http://') in the 'URL' area.

In MX 2004+, the process is easier. Open the Behaviours window, (MX 2004) 'Window > Development Panels > Behaviours' or (Studio 8) 'Window > Behaviours' ('shift + F3'), and click on the '+' sign to add a behaviour. From the 'Web' area, at the bottom of the list, choose 'Go To Web Page'. Type in the full URL (including the 'http://') and select an

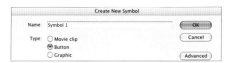

fig. 38 Creating a button.

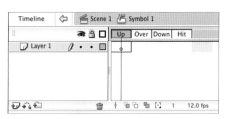

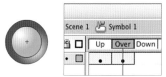

fig. 39 Defining the 'Up' (inactive) stage of the button.

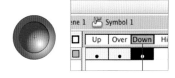

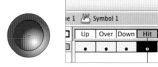

fig. 40 Defining the other three button states: 'Over', 'Down' and 'Hit'.

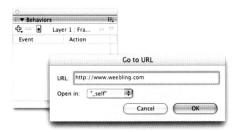

fig. 41 Attaching a 'Go to URL' command to a behaviour.

option from the 'Open In' area (for instance, '_self' replaces the current browser window with the new URL, whereas '_blank' opens the URL in a new window) (**fig. 41**).

Preview the movie and test the button. The button appears in its 'Up' (no interaction) state. Move over it with the cursor and it changes to the 'Over' state. As it is clicked on, the button toggles to the 'Down' state and, if the system is online, opens the specified URL.

7.3 Combining movie-clip symbols, buttons and behaviours

For those readers who do not yet see the advantages that movie-clip symbols and 'Go To and Stop' behaviours can bring to an animation, this section should make it much clearer.

First, open the file called 'buttons.swf' in the 'Buttons + Behaviours' section of the CD. Double-click on it, and move the cursor over the buttons. Click on them, and, as long as you are online, they will take you to the two sites mentioned.

This is by far the most advanced section of this chapter and is detailed and involved. So, if you are feeling bright-eyed, read on. Otherwise, skip to the next section!

The first thing to be done is to create the various states needed for a button to pulse as the cursor moves over it. It will be saved as a movie clip. Then, text will be added next to two instances of the button. The changes in the appearance of the text will be triggered by 'stop' commands, which are linked to the button states. Finally, a 'Go to Web Page' behaviour will be added, triggered by clicking on the button.

Creating the button

1) Choose 'Insert > New Symbol', give the item the name 'button fade', choose 'Movie Clip' as the 'Type' and click 'OK'. Then draw the button, exactly as you wish it to appear in its 'Up' state, on the stage.

2) Select frame 1, and choose 'Insert > Timeline > Create Motion Tween'. Then add two additional keyframes to the timeline, spaced evenly apart. The example on the CD adds one on frame 8 and the other on frame 15.

3) Select the keyframe on frame 8 and choose the Free Transform Tool. Grab the button by one of the corner handles, and pull diagonally away from it. Because a motion tween has been added to the object, it resizes from the centre. Expand it to the size you want, then choose 'Alpha' from the 'Colour' field in the Properties window, and give it a degree of transparency.

4) Test the action by pressing 'enter'. It should appear normal on frame 1, then grow and fade up to frame 8, and then return to normal by frame 15.

5) Reselect frame 1, and choose 'Edit > Copy'. This provides a 'Non-Active' copy of the button shape for the other button states, which will

be needed later. Then, click on the left-pointing arrow in the top-left corner above the Timeline to return to the stage.

Open the Library, and you will see the movie clip, as well as the graphic objects that were produced to create it.

Choose 'Insert > New Symbol' again, but this time pick 'Button' from the list. Name it and click 'OK'.

Of the four frames, the 'Up' state is already prepared. Choose 'Edit > Paste' to place the button image on the stage. Then, click on the frame for the 'Over' state, but instead of adding a keyframe – which would immediately copy into it the button showing in the 'Up' state – choose 'Insert > Timeline > Blank Keyframe'. Drag the movie clip for your pulsing button from the Library and onto the stage. Drag it to the same position as shown in the 'Up' state. You can toggle between the two views by clicking on the frames, and fine-tune the position of the objects using the keyboard arrow keys.

Now, click on the 'Down' frame, and once again choose 'Insert > Timeline > Blank Keyframe'. Choose 'Edit > Paste' to add another dormant button image. For the final frame, 'Hit', simply press 'F6' to add a copy of the 'Down' keyframe state. The 'Hit' state merely provides the active area of the button state, and does not actually display anything in the browser window.

Click on the left-pointing arrow to return to the stage.

Drag an instance of the button onto the stage from the Library and preview it in a browser (F12).

Adding text

In this example, the text next to each button is visible from the start, but not at full strength. As the cursor moves over the button next to it, the text grows to full strength. If the cursor moves away again, the text fades back to its original appearance. If the button is clicked on, the browser screen is replaced by the new URL window.

This interaction is provided with 'Stop' commands added to a second layer above the motion tween that governs the appearance of the text. Each 'Stop' is linked to a particular state of the button. So, initially, the text movie is stopped at frame 1, in which it appears slightly faded. When the cursor moves over the button, it not only triggers the button action, it also tells the text movie to go to frame 2 and play.

As the movie plays, the text grows to full strength. A second 'Stop' then halts the action at that point. If the cursor moves away from the button again, it triggers a second action that tells the text movie to go to the frame immediately after the second stop and play, causing it to fade again. A third stop command, placed on the final (key)frame of the text movie, tells it to halt.

If all the text labels are created first, and then brought onto the stage, it is very difficult to deal with them if they are the wrong size. Therefore, it is better to create the first text block on the stage itself, so that it can be scaled correctly. To do this, choose the Text Tool and click on the stage (rather than clicking and dragging) to create a text box that will expand to fit whatever is typed inside it. Type the word(s) you wish to appear next to the first button. Click and drag across it, then use the Properties window to format it with the font, size, colour, and so on.

When it looks OK, select it and choose 'Edit > Copy'. Then choose 'Insert > New Symbol', select 'Movie Clip' as the 'Type' and click 'OK'. Choose 'Edit > Paste' to place the text in the window.

The original text from which it was copied can be deleted later, when it is no longer required.

Select keyframe 1 and choose 'Insert > Timeline > Create Motion Tween'. Create two additional keyframes, one on frame 8 and another on frame 15, as before. Select keyframe 1, and click on the text object itself, using the Selection Tool. The information in the Properties window changes, and the 'Colour' field is now visible on the right. Choose 'Alpha' from the list, and, using the slider, fade the text back to 35% of full strength. Then do the same with the final keyframe (15). Leave the text under the middle keyframe (8) in its original state.

Create a new layer (its default name will be layer 2). It already has the same number of frames in its Timeline as the text layer beneath it (layer 1), and frame 1 is already designated as a keyframe. Create another keyframe on frame 2 by clicking on it and pressing 'F6', then another on frame 8, another on frame 9 and a final one on frame 15.

Now, open the Actions panel. In the list in the top left, click on 'Global Functions' and then on 'Timeline Control'. Scroll down until you see a command called 'Stop'. Select keyframe 1 on layer 2, and double-click on 'Stop' in the 'Actions' list. The phrase 'stop ( );' appears in the code frame in the Actions panel.

Do the same for frames 8 and 15. In each case, a lowercase 'a' appears within the keyframe, indicating that the action has been applied.

Then click on the left-pointing arrow to return to the stage.

Drag an instance of the text from the Library and onto the stage. Test everything again in a browser window. The button should behave as before, and the text should just sit there looking slightly faded. Now we will tie the button actions to the text actions.

Drag an instance of the text movie clip from the Library to the stage.

Although instances placed on the stage have already been named as library items, multiple examples of each one can be placed on the same stage. Therefore, to apply specific behaviour to a particular instance, it is necessary to name each one individually. To do this, select the text object and name it in the 'Instance Name' field, in the top left of the Properties window.

Each instance of the button (and each related text object instance) that is placed on the stage should be individually named in the same way.

Select the first button instance (I named mine '1') and open the Behaviours panel. This has similar properties to the Actions panel, but less knowledge of script code is required to use it. Click on the '+' sign, then on 'Movie Clip' on the list, and then on 'Go to and play at frame or label'.

In the window, select the text object that you wish to connect the button action with, and enter the number '2' in the frame window in the bottom left corner. Then, click 'OK'.

In the Behaviours panel, the action and a default 'Trigger' event is listed. Click on the event, which currently reads 'On Release', and then on the small downward-pointing arrow that appears at its right-hand end, and choose 'On Roll Over' from the list. This changes the event that triggers the text action.

Click on the '+' again, and choose 'Movie Clip'/ 'Go to and play at frame or label'. This time, enter '9' as the number, and click 'OK'. Click on the event label and choose 'On Roll Out'. Finally, click on the '+', but this time choose 'Web' from the list, and then 'Go to Web Page' as the event. Enter the *full* URL (i.e. including the 'http://') and pick a 'Target' from the 'Open In' list. For example, 'self' replaces the current browser window with the new address, whereas 'Blank' opens a second browser window with the new address. In this case, the default event, 'On Release', means that if the button is clicked on, the event is triggered as the mouse button is released.

Preview the results in a browser window.

To see the script that governs these events, select the button and look in the Actions panel. Each 'Trigger' event and its resulting action is listed, and can be edited here. The text shown in grey is not strictly necessary and would not be created if the script was being written, rather than encoded using the Behaviours and Actions panels.

7.4 Adding sounds

Sounds can be applied to movies in two ways: event or stream.

Event sounds, if longer than the movie itself, continue to play after the movie has finished. If the movie is set to loop, a separate event sound begins each time that keyframe is played and the result is a build up that could overload the sound system. Event sounds have to download completely before they can begin to play.

Streaming sounds are broken up into very small chunks of information and are streamed in, more or less as they are needed. Flash calculates how much of the sound needs to download for it to be able to start playing, while the rest of the sound continues to download in the background. This avoids the movie catching up with itself and creating a gap.

To add a sound, it must first be imported into the Library. Choose (MX) 'File > Import to Library' or (MX 2004+) 'File > Import > Import to Library') and browse to the sound. Select it, click 'Open' and it is added to the Library (**fig. 42**).

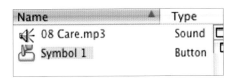

fig. 42 A sound file added to the Library.

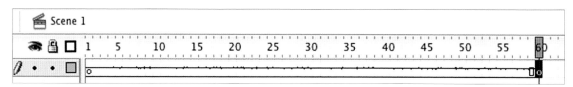

fig. 43 The sound, as it
appears in the Timeline.

To apply a sound to a document, it is best to assign it a separate layer. Create a new layer and, while it is selected, drag the sound from the Library onto the stage.

The first frame of the layer Timeline changes to show that a sound is present. If the sound should not begin to play at the very start of the movie, drag this frame to the right, along the timeline, and drop it on the appropriate frame (**fig. 43**).

A sound event can be set to repeat itself a specified number of times by (MX) setting a 'Loop' number in the Properties window. In MX 2004 onwards, set a 'Repeat' number, as 'Loop' would make it repeat endlessly.

Sounds can be made to stop on a particular frame. Create a keyframe at the required point, choose the sound file from the 'Sound' list in the Properties window and select 'Stop' from the 'Synch' list.

Tip   **This only works if, on the first frame in which the sound appears, it is set to 'Stream' in the 'Synch' list. If it is set to 'Event', the sound continues to play regardless of 'Stop' commands.**

Sound volume and stereo balance can be adjusted. To do this, place the cursor on one of the 'Sound' frames in the timeline and click on the 'Edit' button in the Properties window.

The two windows in the Edit Envelope window (**fig. 44**) represent the division of a sound into left and right channels. At the foot of the channels is a scroll bar, while the small square in the top-left corner of each channel is the volume. Click and drag the square down the window to reduce the sound of that channel at that point. Click on the horizontal line running from the right of the box, thus creating another box, which can be pulled to a new position, thereby changing the volume again. Pre-set effects can be applied using the 'Effects' list at the top. To begin playing the sound at a point other than its start, drag the small slider on the frame bar between the channel windows to cut off some of it.

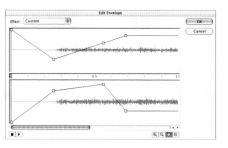

fig. 44 Editing a sound in
the Edit Envelope window.

In the lower left of the window are 'Stop' and 'Play' buttons, allowing changes to be previewed.

An example of the use of sound in a Flash animation can be found in the 'Using sound' folder on the CD.

8   Previewing and Saving

8.1 Previewing a movie

Pressing 'enter' plays the movie under construction on the Flash stage at any time. To see a preview in a browser window, press (MX and Studio 8) 'apple/control + F12' or (MX 2004) 'F12'.

8.2 Checking movie download settings

To see how quickly a movie loads in a browser window, go to 'Control > Test Movie' ('apple/control + enter') and then choose 'View > Bandwidth Profiler' ('apple/control + B') (**fig. 45**). The preview window shows how much data exists in each frame of the movie and whether or not it might create a pause either at the beginning or at some point during playback.

Use the 'Debug' menu to check download times at different modem settings. These values are in fact reduced to better simulate how fast data actually downloads in the real world. Custom settings can be entered to simulate broadband or other bandwidths. The View Menu also shows the 'Streaming' rate, according to the modem speeds selected, and a frame-by-frame breakdown of movie data content.

8.3 Checking publishing settings

Publishing settings determine how the Flash movie is created from all of its components. The Publish Settings window (**fig. 46**) is seen by choosing 'File > Publish Settings' or by clicking on the 'Settings' button in the Properties window. At the top of the window are three tabs: 'Format', 'Flash' and 'HTML'. While generally fine, there are some settings worth checking:

'Format' – make sure that Flash and HTML are both checked. Normally, these are all that are needed.

'Flash'– compatibility with previous versions of the Flash player can be chosen here, but, be careful, as doing so may incapacitate elements specific to MX or MX 2004 versions. The 'Load Order' determines the point from which the movie is downloaded: from the bottom of the stack of layers (the default, 'Bottom Up', which is commonly the order in which they were created) or from the top. The JPEG quality setting affects the filesize of the movie. The 'Protect from Import' checkbox prevents others from downloading the '.SWF' file and converting it back into a Flash movie. This area can be made selective by entering a password in the 'Password' field. Anyone entering the correct password can import the '.SWF' file.

'HTML' – to control the playback of the movie, click on the HTML tab and check 'Loop' to play the movie repeatedly. Uncheck 'Loop' if you want the movie to run once and then stop.

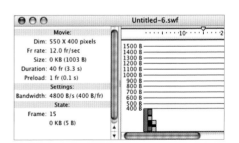

fig. 45 Checking the movie download settings.

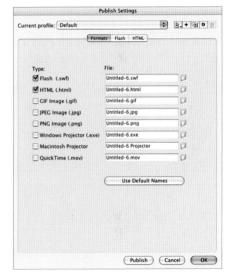

fig. 46 The Publish Settings window.

Chapter 7

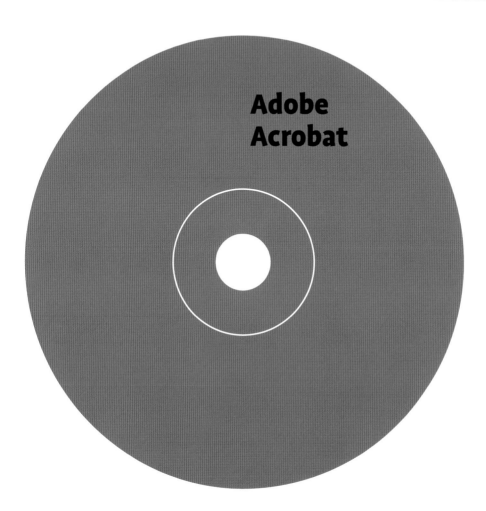

As more and more printers worldwide ask for jobs to be submitted to them in Adobe Acrobat rather than in native file formats, a working knowledge of this program is becoming essential.

A 'virtual' printer, it is able to produce anything from a low-resolution file suitable only for on-screen viewing to a high-resolution file suitable for full-colour offset printing. While editing PDF files is difficult, and sometimes impossible, each new version of the software increases the ease with which some editing can be achieved. Nevertheless, it is always best to ensure that the graphics file being converted is completely ready beforehand.

The images in this chapter were generated using Adobe Acrobat v.7.

| 7 | The Acrobat Environment |

As the reader will see, this chapter is rather different from those encountered so far.

Portable Document Format (PDF) files have been around for a while now, and yet their creation still seems to fill people with dread. Essentially, it is a wonderful idea: Adobe Acrobat allows the user to create something on-screen that looks identical to the original native file, such as Quark or InDesign. It does not stop there: the file can be produced with varying degrees of resolution and in different colour formats. There are three types of PDFs: ones suitable purely for screen viewing; those good enough for on-screen viewing and also for printing to desktop equipment; and those in CMYK colour at a high enough resolution to be printed on commercial offset presses.

PDF documents retain embedded hyperlink information, making them ideal solutions for on-screen manuals. All you need do is click on the link, whether it is a chapter listing or some other reference, and you immediately go straight to that part of the document.

So, what are the problems?

Historically, PDF documents have been impossible or very difficult to edit. This means that whatever mistakes the graphic designer has built into a PDF document end up staying there throughout the print process. If the fault is fairly easy to detect, such as previously black type suddenly becoming a blend of all four CMYK colours, the printer is likely to call a halt before the job goes on press. Unfortunately, other problems – unforeseen colour changes, a lack of trapping, RGB images – are much more difficult to spot and, therefore, often slip through the net.

There is a growing tendency among printers worldwide to ask for PDF files rather than native format. There are several benefits for them in doing this: they no longer have to maintain in-house expertise in a wide range of software programs; they do not need to buy each new version of a program to keep up with their customers; fonts are embedded in PDF documents, so there is no need to buy them either; and, because of the difficulties in editing PDFs, any embedded mistakes are the client's responsibility and not something the printer is supposed to fix. It is clear from this that the problems of the graphic designer are not going to disappear and need to be resolved. The best way to do this is with a clear understanding of the various Acrobat settings involved and the needs of the offset printing process.

In most cases, PDF documents are created from page-layout programs; therefore, this chapter deals with PDF generation from QuarkXPress and InDesign. For those of you who wish to produce a PDF from another program, rest assured that it is a very similar process. Acrobat is a virtual printer and appears within the list of any installed printers as 'Adobe PDF' or 'Acrobat Distiller'. The difference between the two is that the resulting Adobe PDF document is created directly from the native file, while the Acrobat Distiller document is produced from a PostScript (PS) file that is then 'distilled' into PDF format. The latter can be a more complex affair, as the initial PS file may have been created using a different PostScript printer, which would require an understanding of those settings as well. There are so many options that it is not possible to cover them all in a single chapter, so here the focus is on using 'Adobe PDF'.

The three most common levels of resolution for PDF files are 72dpi, 150dpi and 300dpi.

72dpi is the resolution of many Mac screens (PC screens are 96dpi, but 72 also works for them) and is perfect for documents that are only required for on-screen viewing. All colours are rendered in RGB rather than CMYK.

150dpi is the resolution needed for desktop printers (laser and inkjet printers), and it is also the required resolution for work going out to commercial digital printers, although many people who work in commercial digital printing are unaware of this fact.

I put this to the test a couple of years ago when a digital print shop asked me to supply 300dpi images for a job. I placed 4 copies of an image on an A4 page, three of them saved at 300dpi and the fourth at 150dpi. After they had printed a single copy, I asked them which one was the 150dpi version. They had to admit that they could not see any difference between them.

The printing and graphics industries continue to hold on to such misconceptions for no apparent reason. Normally it is not a problem, but in the above case it would have taken me a great deal of extra time to reproduce the work at 300dpi, so I took it a little further.

For desktop printers, colours should be rendered as RGB, because only PostScript colour machines are capable of translating CMYK colour despite the fact that all colour desktop printers use CMYK inks or toners to print. Commercial digital print shops can request CMYK or RGB colours, so it is best to ask before preparing a job.

300dpi is the required resolution for offset printing using a '150-line screen' – a grid made up of vertical and horizontal rows of round dots for each colour involved. Each linear inch of image that has 150 rows of dots is referred to as a '150-line screen'. It is not possible for a 150-line screen to hold more detail than 300 pixels to the linear inch. A lower number of pixels, on the other hand, would provide less detail than a 150-line screen is capable of displaying.

A 150-line screen is the most common screen value for work printed on coated paper. A slightly lower line screen of 133lpi (lines per inch) is often used for uncoated paper, but as long as the original image is 300dpi at the actual size (i.e. centimetres wide and tall) at which it is required to print, both screens can be accommodated.

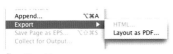

fig. 1 Exporting a
document in PDF format.

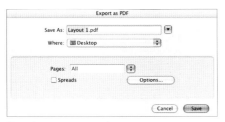

fig. 2 The Export as PDF window.

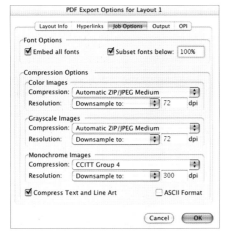

fig. 3 The PDF Export Options
window when generating a
72dpi PDF from Quark.

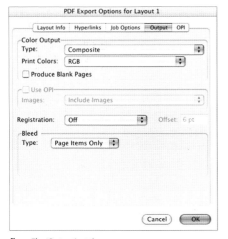

fig. 4 The 'Output' settings
when generating a 72dpi
PDF document from Quark.

Generating PDF Documents from QuarkXPress

This method assumes that Adobe Acrobat is installed on the system.

From v.5, in addition to the usual print settings, Quark has offered the option of exporting a document in PDF format. This is a much easier and less complicated way of creating a PDF file than the alternative 'File > Print' method.

Choose 'File > Export > Layout as PDF' (**fig. 1**) to open the Export as PDF window (**fig. 2**). Name the PDF file and choose a location. Then click on 'Options' to open the PDF Export Options window.

While the changes made to these default options cannot be saved, whatever settings were last used to generate a PDF are remembered, but only for that document. As far as any other project is concerned, everything reverts to the defaults.

Generating a 72dpi PDF document

(for on-screen viewing)

In the PDF Export Options window, nothing in the 'Layout Info' or 'Hyperlinks' areas needs to be changed. In the 'Job Options' area (**fig. 3**), check 'Embed all Fonts' and 'Compress Text and Line Art'. Enter a value of '100%' in the 'Subset Fonts Below' field. In the 'Compression' area, choose 'Automatic ZIP/JPEG Medium' for both colour and greyscale images. Choose a resolution option (also for both) of 'Downsample To' and enter '72' as the dpi value.

For monochrome images, choose 'CCITT Group 4' for 'Compression' and enter a resolution value of 300dpi.

In the 'Output' area (**fig. 4**), choose 'Composite' as the 'Type' and 'RGB' as the 'Print Colours'. Normally, on-screen documents do not require bleed or registration marks, but should you wish to include them, use the options given in 'Generating a 300dpi PDF document', below.

Click 'OK' to generate the PDF.

Generating a 150dpi PDF document

(for laser and inkjet machines, and commercial digital printing)

Follow the previous method, but, in the 'Job Options' area, choose 'None' for 'Compression' for colour and greyscale images (**fig. 5**, opposite). For the resolution option, choose 'Downsample To' and enter a value of 150dpi. For monochrome images, choose 'CCITT Group 4' for the 'Compression' method and enter a value of 600dpi.

In the 'Output' area, choose 'Composite' as the 'Type' and either 'RGB' or 'CMYK' as the 'Print Colours'. This choice depends on information received from your printer. If the printer requires registration marks and bleeds, choose 'Centred' and 'Page Items Only', respectively.

As before, click 'OK' to generate the PDF.

Generating a 300dpi PDF document

(for commercial offset printing)

Follow the method for generating a 150dpi PDF file, but enter '300dpi' as the 'Downsample To' value for colour and greyscale images and '1200dpi' for monochrome images (**fig. 6**).

In the 'Output' area, choose 'CMYK' as the 'Print Colours' (**fig. 7**). Click 'OK' to generate the PDF.

Generating PDF Documents from Adobe InDesign

It is quite easy to produce PDF documents from an Adobe source such as InDesign, as, with each version of its software, Adobe strives for better integration and compatibility. This means, for example, that there is no need to worry about custom page sizes, because Acrobat simply uses whatever size it finds in the specified InDesign document.

The method for generating the PDF file is identical in all cases and is based on the PDF preset that is selected.

Generating a 72dpi PDF preset

(for on-screen viewing)

Go to 'File > Adobe PDF Presets > Define', choose 'Smallest File Size' from the list and click on 'New' (**fig. 8**).

At the top of the New PDF Export Preset window, give the preset a new, unique name and adjust the compatibility setting as necessary.

In the first window, 'General', make sure that the 'Optimize for Fast Web View' box is checked. If the document contains bookmarks or hyperlinks, check those boxes as well.

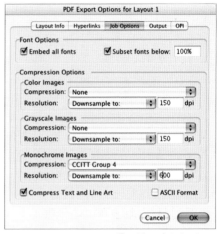

fig. 5 The 'Job Options' settings when generating a 150dpi PDF document from Quark.

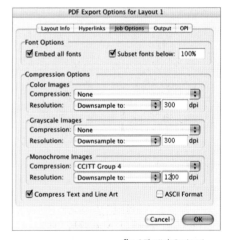

fig. 6 The 'Job Options' settings when generating a 300dpi PDF document from Quark.

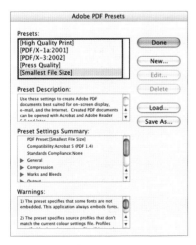

fig. 8 (left) Defining a 72dpi PDF document preset from InDesign.

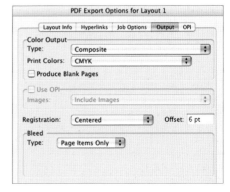

fig. 7 (right) The 'Output' settings when generating a 300dpi PDF document from Quark.

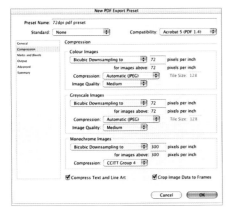

fig. 9 'Compression'
settings when generating
a 72dpi PDF document
from InDesign.

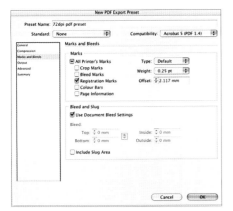

fig. 10 'Marks and Bleeds'
settings when generating
a 72dpi PDF document
from InDesign.

Click on 'Compression' in the list on the left of the window (**fig. 9**). For 'Colour Images', enter a resolution of '72' in both windows and choose 'Medium' as the 'Image Quality' setting. If the resulting file size is too large, two other settings can reduce the size further: 'Low' and 'Minimum'.

Enter the same values for 'Greyscale Images'. For 'Monochrome Images', set both resolution windows to '300'. The default 'Compression' setting, 'CCITT Group 4', is fine. Lastly, check the boxes for 'Compress Text and Line Art' and 'Crop Image Data to Frames'.

Now, click on 'Marks and Bleeds' in the list on the left (**fig. 10**). If the resulting document needs to show some, or all, of the available printer's marks, check the relevant boxes. If the PDF paper size should be enlarged to hold bleed elements, either check the 'Use Document Bleed Settings' box or enter specific values. The industry standard for a bleed margin is 3mm, but it is not usually applied on the inside edge of a facing-page document, as this is the binding (spine) edge. However, it should be included on all sides of a single-page document where bleeds occur.

Click on 'Output', on the left (**fig. 11**), and choose 'Convert to Destination' for the 'Colour Conversion' setting and 'Working RGB' as the 'Destination'. Everything in the document is converted to RGB, which is the most suitable mode for screen viewing.

Click on 'Advanced' in the list on the left (**fig. 12**) and ensure that a value of '100%' is entered in the 'Subset Fonts...' area. Click 'OK' to return to the Adobe PDF Presets window and then click 'Done'.

Generating a 150dpi PDF preset

(for laser and inkjet printers and commercial digital printing)
Go to 'File > Adobe PDF Presets > Define', choose 'High Quality Print' from the list and click on 'New'. At the top of the New PDF Export Preset window, give the preset a new and unique name and adjust the compatibility setting as necessary. In this first window, 'General' (**fig. 13**, opposite), uncheck 'Optimize for Fast Web View'.

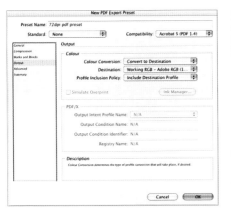

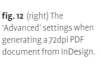

fig. 11 (left) The 'Output' settings when generating a 72dpi PDF document from InDesign.

fig. 12 (right) The 'Advanced' settings when generating a 72dpi PDF document from InDesign.

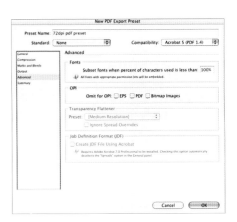

Now, click on 'Compression' in the list on the left (**fig. 14**). For 'Colour Images', enter a resolution of '150' in both windows and choose 'High' or 'Maximum' as the 'Image Quality' setting to give progressively better image quality.

Enter the same values for 'Greyscale Images'. For 'Monochrome Images', set both resolution windows to '600'. The default 'Compression' setting, 'CCITT Group 4', is fine. Check the boxes for 'Compress Text and Line Art' and 'Crop Image Data to Frames'.

Click on 'Marks and Bleeds' in the list on the left (**fig. 15**). Check the relevant boxes for any required printer's marks. Either check the 'Use Document Bleed Settings' box or enter a value of '3mm' for each side on which bleeds are required. Bleed margins are not applied on the inside edge of a facing-page document, as this is the binding (spine) edge, but should be included on all sides of a single-page document where bleeds occur.

Click on 'Output', on the left (**fig. 16**). If the document is destined for commercial digital printing, check with the printer to see if the PDF needs to be in RGB or CMYK format. If it should be CMYK, choose 'Convert to Destination' as the 'Colour Conversion' setting and 'Working CMYK' as the 'Destination'. If RGB colour is required, select 'Working RGB' as the destination.

Click on 'Advanced' in the list on the left and ensure that a value of '100%' is entered in the 'Subset Fonts...' area.

Click 'OK' to return to the Adobe PDF Presets window and then click 'Done'.

Generating a 300dpi PDF preset
(for commercial offset printing)
Go to 'File > Adobe PDF Presets > Define', choose 'High Quality Print' from the list and click on 'New'.

At the top of the New PDF Export Preset window, give the preset a new and unique name and adjust the 'Compatibility' setting as necessary.

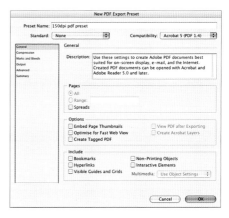

fig. 13 The 'General' settings when generating a 150dpi PDF document from InDesign.

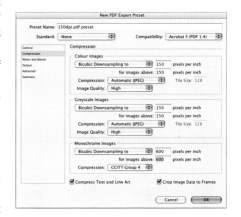

fig. 14 The 'Compression' settings when generating a 150dpi PDF document from InDesign.

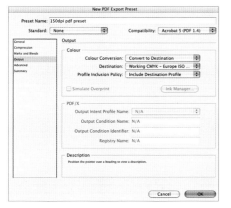

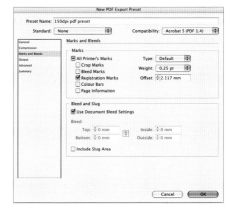

fig. 16 (left) The 'Output' settings when generating a 150dpi PDF document from InDesign.

fig. 15 (right) The 'Marks and Bleeds' settings when generating a 150dpi PDF document from InDesign.

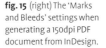

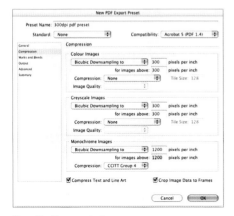

fig. 17 The 'Compression' settings when generating a 300dpi PDF document from InDesign.

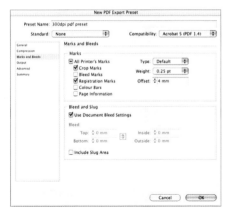

fig. 18 (above) The 'Marks and Bleeds' settings when generating a 300dpi PDF document from InDesign.   **fig. 19** (below) The 'Output' settings when generating a 300dpi PDF document from InDesign.

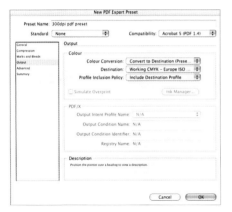

In this first window, 'General', uncheck 'Optimize for Fast Web View'.

Now, click on 'Compression' in the list on the left (**fig. 17**). For 'Colour Images', enter a resolution of '300' in both areas and choose 'None' for the 'Image Quality' setting to ensure the best possible image quality.

Enter the same values for 'Greyscale Images'. For 'Monochrome Images', set both resolution areas to '1200'. The default 'Compression' setting, 'CCITT Group 4', is fine. Check the boxes for 'Compress Text and Line Art' and 'Crop Image Data to Frames'.

The above settings for colour and greyscale images result in larger files than the defaults, which allow for a degree of JPEG compression. However, if you want the best possible image quality, JPEG compression is not wanted.

Click on 'Marks and Bleeds' in the list on the left (**fig. 18**). Check the relevant boxes for any required printer's marks. Some printers prefer to add some of these elements themselves, but, at the least, you should include crop marks. After checking that box, enter '4mm' as their 'Offset' value to set them that distance from the corners of the document page. This helps printers who find the default offset setting a bit too close for comfort.

Either check the 'Use Document Bleed Settings' box or enter values of '3mm' for each side on which bleeds are required. Bleed margins are not needed on the inside edge of a facing-page document, as this is the binding (spine) edge, but should be included on all sides of a single-page document where bleeds occur.

Click on 'Output', on the left (**fig. 19**). As this document is destined for commercial offset printing, everything needs to be rendered in CMYK colours. So, choose 'Convert to Destination (Preserve Numbers)' as the 'Colour Conversion' setting and 'Working CMYK' as the 'Destination'. The name of the current working CMYK CMS setting appears, following the words 'Working CMYK' in that window, depending on what has been selected. For additional information on this, see 'CMS settings' on p. 229.

Click on 'Advanced' in the list on the left (**fig. 20, opposite**) and ensure that a value of '100%' is entered in the 'Subset Fonts...' area.

Click 'OK' to return to the Adobe PDF Presets window and then click 'Done'.

Creating a PDF document from a PDF preset

Once the appropriate PDF preset has been created, open the document to be converted to PDF format and choose 'File > Export'. Navigate to a location for the PDF file, name it and click on 'Save'.

| Tip | If the Text Tool is active within any type when this process begins, the 'Save as Type' setting in the Export window shows as 'Adobe InDesign Tagged Text'. Select 'Adobe PDF' from the list, instead. |

In the Export Adobe PDF window, choose the preset from the list at the top of the window and click 'Export'.

Colour Management Settings (CMS)

The methods for creating high-resolution PDF documents mention the use of Colour Management Systems (CMS), which are probably the most obscure and least well understood area of graphic design. The idea behind them is great: the tagging of documents with a set of instructions to maintain consistent appearance, particularly for images, from design right through to print. A CMS can be applied in Quark and Adobe software, and, from Adobe CS2 onwards, the CMS can be synchronized across all the (Adobe) software used in the production process. However, whereas the default CMS in Photoshop used to be for sheet-fed printing machines operating in the USA, they are now set for 'SWOP', i.e. 'Standard Web Offset Printing', settings. Sheet-fed and web machines are completely different in terms of appropriate CMS. If you use a USA web setting for a job that will be printed on a sheet-fed press in Europe, the settings will not be correct...unless, of course, the printer is used to receiving files to which the default SWOP settings have been applied, and has figured out how to adjust the printing settings in response.

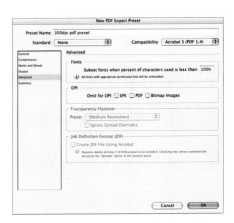

fig. 20 The 'Advanced' settings when generating a 300dpi PDF document from InDesign.

Tip	When you attempt to open an image in Photoshop, and instead a window opens giving you an embedded colour profile warning, you need to choose whether or not to leave the applied profile in place, or change it to match the current program settings. If it is an image you want to use, then you should first set up a useful CMS and then tell the opening image to convert to it.

Printers may also decide to remove the tags altogether. A colleague – who works in one of the larger printing companies in the UK – recently told me that this was now their standard policy. In his view, CMS settings are a classic example of putting the tools of genius into the hands of idiots. 'Anyone can create their own CMS,' he complained, 'the problem is, almost nobody knows how to do it properly.'

So, the first thing to do is ask your printer if they recommend using the default settings or not. However, it is also quite possible that the printer will not have ventured into this territory – or at least, not very far.

An additional complication is thrown into the mix by the complexity of the Imagesetters (highly sophisticated 'printing' machines that produce the film or plates used by the printer) that are now found in many CTP (Computer To Plate) print shops. I was recently asked to help figure out why an apparently perfect PDF document printed all the colour images very well, but the greyscale images had picked up an unacceptable amount of contrast. In response to my enquiry, the printer (in Singapore) assured me that, no, they had made no adjustments *at all* to the PDF file they had been sent. They had simply run it through the 'normalizer' and....At this point, I stopped him. Upon investigation, it appeared that the function of the 'normalizer' was to completely strip away some, but not all, of the CMS settings that had been applied, a process of which the printer was completely unaware.

However, when the same job was run by a film-based shop in Delhi, who were still using an earlier generation of Imagesetter, it printed perfectly. Their machinery was too primitive to adjust the CMS settings, which were allowed to accompany the work right through the press – just as they should.

As you can see, anything is possible.

The CS2 package has gone further than other software in its ability to not only apply but also synchronize CMS settings between Photoshop, InDesign and Illustrator. If you live in the USA, you probably do not need to adjust the default settings. However, if you live in Europe, you might want to try the following – assuming, of course, that your printer agrees:

In all three programs, choose 'Colour Settings' from the program menu (i.e. in Photoshop, it is under the Photoshop Menu; on a PC, these are under the Edit Menu). In the Colour Settings window, in the 'Settings' field, choose 'Europe Prepress 2'. Click 'OK'.

To do this in QuarkXPress, open the Preferences window (under the Quark Menu on a Mac or the Edit Menu on a PC) and choose 'Quark CMS' in the 'Default Print Layout' section. Check the 'Colour Management Active' box at the top left and select 'Euroscale Coated v2' or, if available, 'Europe ISO Coated FOGRA27' for the 'Composite Output' and 'Separation Output' settings in the 'Destination Profiles' area. Click on the CMYK tab in 'Default Source Profiles' and pick the same option for 'Solid Colours – Profiles' and 'Images – Profiles'. Check the 'Colour Manage CMYK Sources to CMYK Destinations' box.

That should be all you need to do. This gives you a much better standard for the printing conventions usually found in European print shops, and, unless your printer is doing something strange to incoming work, it should produce good results.

However, the lack of common standards for the treatment of CMS profiles within the printing industry as a whole leads me to suspect that this will be a problem area for many years to come. Good luck!

Glossary

action A sequence of operations that is saved as a macro, meaning that the entire sequence can be activated with a single command.

algorithm A mathematically generated pattern that determines the level of complexity in the 8 x 8 pixel cells comprising a JPEG image.

anchor point A point that connects two adjacent line segments within a vector path. Usually one of three types (symmetrical, smooth and corner), the anchor point defines the shape of the vector object.

anti-aliased When a bitmap shape (such as text) is anti-aliased it acquires a slight falling-off of tone around the edges. This enables it to blend in visually with another image.

artboard Adobe Illustrator does not generate a page on which to work, rather an artboard.

artifacting When a JPEG algorithm is set too low, areas that should appear as flat colour in one part of an 8 x 8 pixel cell can be distorted by the detail in another.

behaviour A particular event, usually interactive, that takes place on a web page. For example, swapping one image for another as the cursor rolls over a predefined spot.

Bézier Named after the French mathematician Pierre Bézier. Vector lines are made up of straight line segments and/or Bézier curves. Anchor points governing the position of straight line segments have no Bézier handles attached, whereas anchor points connecting to curved line segments do. At the end of each handle is a 'control point', and it is the position of the control points, together with the anchor points, that determines the shape of the curve of that line segment.

bit Image complexity, or depth, is described in terms of bits. It is a single unit of binary information, which can be either 'on' or 'off'. A '1 bit deep' image is made up of two colours.

bitmap Any image that is made up of pixels is technically a bitmap, regardless of the actual format. TIFF, JPEG and GIF images are bitmaps.

bleed To enable a printer to generate a page on which the image runs right to the edge of the paper, the image is set to run beyond the page boundaries in the page-layout software. The amount by which it runs beyond the page, usually 3mm, is the 'bleed'.

blend A mix of colours within a single graphic object or image, often created by the Gradient Tool. Blends can be of several types, such as linear and radial.

body copy Text within a particular document may be defined as headings, sub headings, body copy, captions, and so on. Body copy usually defines most of the text visible on the page.

Book Quark and InDesign allow large projects to be broken up into smaller sections and connected in an overall format known as a Book.

bounding box Clicking and dragging with the Item (Quark) or Selection (InDesign, Illustrator) Tool on a page layout (or artboard) draws a rectangular shape that selects any object either contained within or touched by it.

buffer zone Also known as outset or cell padding, depending on the program, this is a defined gap between text and the edge of the text box or frame into which it has been placed. It is also the amount by which text is pushed away from an image to which a text wrap (or runaround) has been applied.

calibration A method that adjusts highlights, shadows and mid-tones to determine the overall appearance of an image when printed by a particular method. It can also refer to adjusting the colour settings on a monitor to produce a more accurate screen image.

Cascading Style Sheets Very similar to paragraph styles in page-layout programs, CSS have evolved beyond merely enabling the formatting of text and can now affect the appearance of websites in many ways.

cell Tables are composed of cells, which are commonly arranged in rows and columns.

channel One of the colour components of an image. For example, an RGB image contains three channels, one to hold the red information, another the green and another the blue.

clipping path A vector outline that acts as a mask, blocking out any areas of the image that fall outside it.

CMYK Cyan, magenta, yellow and black ('key'): the components of the four-colour-process printing method.

colour cast When a colour image has an appearance of too much of a particular colour it is said to have a 'colour cast' of that hue.

Colour Management Systems CMS are tags attached to images and layouts designed to enable digital graphics to have more consistency of appearance throughout their entire workflow, from their screen appearance to their final printed version.

compound path A shape or combination of shapes, which act as a single entity; for example, the letter 'e' is a compound of two paths, one governing the external outline of the letter and another governing the hole in its upper half. Typically, when components of a compound overlap, that area becomes 'negative' rather than 'positive', i.e. a hole in the shape through which other graphics or backgrounds can be seen.

compression A method of making a file occupy less disk space, compression can either be 'lossy', i.e. there is some loss of data (such as in a JPEG), or 'non-lossy', such as in the LZW compression of a TIFF file.

computer to plate CTP is a printing method that avoids the need for film by generating the image directly onto the plate.

cromalin A type of high-quality colour proof made by fusing extremely thin sheets of film, each printed with a toner of the appropriate colour, onto a bright white background.

crop Cutting an image down to a smaller size, either by reducing the frame in which it appears (such as in a page layout) or by cutting sections off it (such as in Photoshop).

CRT A cathode ray tube generates an on-screen image by combining red, green and blue light.

document A file saved in Adobe Illustrator or InDesign that typically contains text and graphics is known as a document. Quark now refers to documents as those parts of a 'project' that are designated for printing purposes rather than the Web.

dot gain When a halftone image is physically (rather than digitally) transferred from one medium to another, the dots tend to change size. Technically, the change undergone by the 50% dot is called 'dot gain', although the term has come to refer more to changes across the entire tonal range.

DPI Dots per inch, the dots actually being square pixels. This is the accepted measurement defining the resolution of an image made up of pixels.

drop cap When the first character appearing in a paragraph has been formatted to appear in a larger size, so that it 'drops' onto a baseline further down in that paragraph, it is known as a 'drop cap'.

dynamic page A web page that is formulated by the hosting server to appear on the user's screen with customized content based on user input, such as a search request.

effect In Photoshop, filters are used to produce an effect that changes the appearance of an image. However, in Illustrator filters and effects are separate. Filters, which can only be applied to images, change their actual structure. Effects change the appearance and not the structure itself, and can be applied to graphic objects as well as to images.

EM dash A dash positioned at the same level as a hyphen. It is the same length, in points, as the point size of the type in which it appears.

EN dash Similar to an EM dash, but only half its length.

EPS Encapsulated PostScript: an image format capable of holding both vector and bitmap information.

fill As well as having a stroke, or outline, that can be coloured, vector paths also act as containers that can be filled with a colour.

film A transparent acetate sheet coated with an opaque photosensitive emulsion on one side.

filter *see* 'effect'.

flyout menu In several graphics programs, tool buttons in the Toolbox contain a small arrow as well as the tool icon. The arrow indicates the presence of a flyout menu, which can be seen if the arrow is held down for a couple of seconds. The required tool can then be selected by sliding the cursor along the flyout to the appropriate icon, and releasing the mouse.

forced (alignment) An alignment specification that causes an otherwise short line of text to be spread across the full column width.

frame A frame-based website is made up of several separate pages that interact so that they each occupy a specified area within the screen image. For example, a banner across the top, a sidebar down the left side and a main frame in which the page content is displayed is a common 'frame' format.

FTP File Transfer Protocol: a method by which finished pages can be uploaded onto a server.

GIF Graphics Interchange Format: an image made up of a restricted (indexed) palette of 256 colours, one of which can be designated as transparent. This makes GIF images ideal for websites where they can be used for irregular shapes such as logos that can then be 'floated' over coloured backgrounds. GIF images are not suitable for inclusion in a job destined for offset printing.

glyph A specific form of character, such as a small cap alternative to the regular form.

gradient A blend between two or more colours that is used to fill a single object or an area of an image.

greyscale An image usually made up of 256 shades of grey pixels, printed using black ink.

guides Temporary, non-printing rules that can be pulled onto the working area to act as design aids by clicking and dragging from the horizontal and vertical rulers. They can usually be assigned a 'snap' setting, similar to a slight magnetic attraction, thus enabling objects to be easily positioned against them.

gutter The space between columns defined within the margins of a page or within an individual text box.

H&Js Hyphenation and Justification specifications in Quark are defined by H&J styles.

halftone An image made up of solid dots of one or more colours. Originally, halftones were created by projecting an image onto film through a sheet of glass etched with a grid of vertical and horizontal lines. It was thought that only half the information was able to get through.

handle *see* Bézier.

histogram A visual representation, similar to a detailed bar graph, of the tone contained within an image.

HTML HyperText Markup Language: one of the main codes used for website layouts.

instance In Flash, an instance is a copy of a graphic symbol. Any number of instances can be created from a symbol, which is then only added to the filesize of the movie once.

invisibles Typographic commands contained within text but which are normally unseen, such as tab or hard return keystrokes.

JPEG or JPG Joint Photographic Experts Group: an image format supporting greyscale, RGB and CMYK colour but which uses a lossy compression method. However, at high-quality levels, the loss is almost impossible to detect, while the file size is much smaller than the same image saved as a TIFF. Nevertheless, JPEGs should not be included in a job destined for offset printing.

justified (alignment) A block of text in which all but the final line of each paragraph spreads to fill the entire width of the specified column.

kerning The space between individual character pairs.

keyframe A frame within a Flash timeline that anchors the action (at that point) of the objects on that layer.

landscape An image in which width is greater than height.

layer In all graphics programs, layers are like clear sheets of film, laid over the page, stage or artboard on which other objects can be placed. This allows a degree of individual control over those objects without affecting objects on other layers.

leading The space between baselines in a block of text. So called because, in the days of metal type, lines of text were separated by shims of lead of a known thickness.

Library A file that can hold graphics, images, text and colour styles. These can then be dragged from the Library onto the working area of other documents in the same program. In the case of images, library items refer back to the source image at its original location on the hard drive at the time it was added to the Library. If this changes, the link between them is broken and only a screen representation will then be available for other documents.

link An image placed in a page layout is usually linked to the document, and not embedded. This means that while a representation of it appears, the document refers back to the original for operations such as printing. This avoids having to embed the entire image within the document, which can quickly result in huge files that are very slow to work with. Linked images have to be available to the printer as separate items, unless the whole document has been output in PDF format.

lossless An image-compression method that does not result in any data or quality loss.

lossy An image compression system that results in a degree of data, and therefore quality, loss.

LPI Lines Per Inch: the standard measurement of halftone resolution. It refers to the number of rows of halftone dots there are per inch.

macro A series of commands that can be saved and activated as a single command, such as an action in Photoshop.

margin The space between a page edge and its 'margin guide', i.e. a guide positioned a specified distance from that edge.

master page A page that, while not being counted within the document pages of a book, can be applied to those pages. Then, any objects (such as headers and footers) that have been placed on the master pages will appear on those document pages to which it has been applied.

mask In Illustrator and Flash, mask objects are themselves invisible, while their outline hides all portions of masked objects that fall outside the mask. In Photoshop, 'layer' masks are image layers that create degrees of transparency, while 'quick' masks create degrees of filter effects within an image.

menu The main headings across the top of the screen in graphics programs.

moiré pattern An interference pattern caused by the halftone grids ('screens') of two or more colours in an image being set at incorrect angles. This causes the dots to collide unevenly.

motion guide path An invisible path along which the attached objects in a Flash movie can move.

named anchor A type of link in Dreamweaver allowing the user to move around within a document without needing to use the scroll bars.

NAV bar A graphic that displays several buttons, each of which can have rollover behaviour and link instructions applied.

offset litho A printing method in which the image on a plate is transferred ('offset') to an intermediate roller prior to final transfer to the paper.

optimization Cutting down on image file size while trying to maintain the quality of the image's appearance.

orientation The designation of an image or page as being either portrait or landscape format.

orphan When the first line of a paragraph is left by itself at the foot of a column or page, it is known as an orphan.

outline see 'stroke'.

palette A range of saved colours, or a floating window.

Pantone The Pantone Corporation produces many aids for designers and printers, such as the Pantone Process Guide (for selecting CMYK tints) and the Pantone Matching System, which allows a wide range of non-CMYK colours to be accurately mixed by formula.

PDF Portable Document Format: a form of PostScript developed by Adobe that enables a printable document to be generated as anything from a low-resolution screen image to a high-resolution file suitable for offset printing.

pixel The building blocks of digital images, pixels are small squares of colour. The resolution of an image is determined by how many pixels there are per linear inch. The colour range of the pixels is determined by the bit depth of the image.

pixelated An image in which the pixels are large enough to be visible.

placeholder text 'Fake' text that can be used, temporarily, to help design a layout if the actual text is not yet available.

plate A sheet, usually either aluminium or zinc, coated with a photosensitive emulsion. When developed, either the remaining emulsion or the exposed background attracts ink.

PNG An image format suitable for websites that has the 'continuous tone' appearance of a JPEG and the ability to support transparency.

portrait An image in which the height is greater than the width.

posterize This is the method by which a restriction is placed on the number of colours within an image.

preview In Photoshop, a preview is a window in which the effect of a filter can be seen before it is actually applied to an image. In Dreamweaver, it is a way of checking the appearance and functionality of a web page in a browser prior to it actually being uploaded as part of a site.

process colour The colours used in the 4-colour process method of printing, i.e. cyan, magenta, yellow and black.

RAM Random Access Memory. As an analogy, a computer can be compared to a working office environment. The hard drive is like the filing cabinet – it is big, but it takes a little while to get things out and put them back. The speed of the chip is the strength of today's coffee and how many cups have already been consumed. The available RAM defines the size of the desk on which projects are displayed and worked on. Therefore, the more RAM a system has, the more programs can be open simultaneously.

rasterize This is the method by which a bitmap made up of pixels (which are square and have no space between them) is turned into a halftone made up of round dots arranged on a horizontal and vertical grid.

registration When a multicolour image is printed, it is essential that each colour is laid down in exactly the right place. If not, the result is said to be 'out of register'.

resolution Defined by the number of pixels to the linear inch, the resolution of an image is the main factor defining the level of detail that it is able to display.

RGB A colour space comprising combinations of red, green and blue light.

rollover Usually applied to a button, a rollover image changes its appearance as the cursor 'rolls over' it, and may change its appearance again as it is clicked on, prior to activating a link.

runaround Also known as 'text wrap', a runaround can be applied to images (and other graphics) so that text runs around them in a defined way, rather than right across them.

sans serif Without serifs, which are ornate corners on the letter shapes.

saturation Colour density. A saturated blue, for example, appears more colourful than a less saturated example. A desaturated image is one in which the colour values have taken on the appearance of greyscale.

scene Lengthy Flash movies are sometimes made up of shorter movies that are then strung together as 'scenes'.

scrolling Moving the visible area of a page or layout around by using the scrollbars or other techniques.

section Quark and InDesign allow any page in a multipage document to be designated as the beginning of a new section, introducing a different page numbering sequence at that point.

segment The portion of a vector line between two anchor points.

serif Ornate corners on letter shapes.

set off The unwanted transfer of part of a printed image from one sheet to another. This usually occurs within a stack of freshly printed sheets due to a lack of offset spray, or from too much ink (or both).

slug A definable area around an InDesign document, in addition to the 'bleed' area, in which notes for the printer, among others, can be placed.

smart quotes Also known as typographer's quotes, these appear as filled-in 6s and 9s (" and ") rather than as inch marks (").

spot colour A specific non-CMYK ink colour.

stage The working area in Flash on which the visual elements of movies are placed.

static page A page that contains no server interaction to be able to run.

story A contiguous piece of text that displays in one or more linked text boxes or frames.

streaming sound (or video) A file, either linked to a website or a Flash movie, that does not have to download fully before it begins to play.

stroke The outline of a vector object, which can be assigned a weight or thickness and a colour.

swatch A colour sample.

SWF The extension given to a Flash Player file, i.e. a 'published' Flash movie.

symbol The means by which multiple copies of a graphic object can be used in a Flash movie without adding to its filesize. Such objects are first saved as 'symbols', from which 'instances' (copies) are then created.

tab A keystroke that designates the start of a new column in text within a table, i.e. set in columns and rows.

template Template format exists in many programs. In page layouts it is a way of keeping a sample of the basic design layout safe from accidental editing. In Dreamweaver it is a basic design layout on which only certain areas can be edited.

text wrap see 'runaround'.

TIFF An uncompressed bitmap format that supports a variety of colour modes including greyscale, RGB and CMYK.

tiling Filling an area with copies of an image, rather than expanding the image to fill the space.

tint A percentage of full colour strength.

toggle An action that switches on and then off.

tolerance values Several tools in Photoshop (and some other programs) act within a defined tolerance related to their purpose. For instance, the Magic Wand Tool selects not only whichever pixel is clicked on, but all those adjacent to it that fall within the tolerance range. So, if the tolerance is set to 32, then all adjacent pixels that are up to 32 shades lighter or darker are also be selected.

Toolbox A floating window that contains most of the tool buttons for a particular program.

tracing image An image of a web page design that is placed on the page, and over which the actual design is then created.

tracking Tracking values define the overall spacing between words and characters within a block of type.

trapping The enlargement of a light-coloured area so that it slightly overlaps into an adjacent darker colour, thereby compensating for slight imperfections of registration on the press, which might otherwise cause a gap between the two.

tweening Derived from 'in-betweening', tweening is automatically created movement between two defined points (keyframes) in the action in a Flash movie.

vector A mathematically defined outline to which colour and thickness can be assigned. This is the native object format for elements drawn using Adobe Illustrator, CorelDraw and Macromedia Freehand.

widow When the last line of a paragraph appears at the top of the next page or column, it is known as a widow. This term can also be applied when the last line in a paragraph is a single, short word on its own line.

zero point The top-left corner of the document window in which the vertical and horizontal rulers intersect is called the 'zero point', because it can be dragged to another position on the screen to reposition the zeros in both rulers. Double-clicking in it then returns the zeros to their original default position, usually the top-left corner of the page area.

Index